Decoding the Tao Te Ching

《道德经》
玄妙解

Decoding the Tao Te Ching

SIM Pooh Ho
Edited and translated by **Tekson TEO**

World Scientific

NEW JERSEY · LONDON · SINGAPORE · BEIJING · SHANGHAI · HONG KONG · TAIPEI · CHENNAI · TOKYO

Published by

World Scientific Publishing Co. Pte. Ltd.
5 Toh Tuck Link, Singapore 596224
USA office: 27 Warren Street, Suite 401-402, Hackensack, NJ 07601
UK office: 57 Shelton Street, Covent Garden, London WC2H 9HE

Library of Congress Cataloging-in-Publication Data
Names: Sim, Pooh Ho, author. | Teo, Tekson, translator.
Title: Decoding the Tao te ching / Sim Pooh Ho ; translated by Tekson Teo.
Other titles: Xuánmiào jiě. English.
Description: New Jersey : World Scientific, [2021]
Identifiers: LCCN 2020051835 | ISBN 9789811232862 (hardcover) |
   ISBN 9789811231278 (paperback) | ISBN 9789811231285 (ebook for institutions) |
   ISBN 9789811231292 (ebook for individuals)
Subjects: LCSH: Laozi. Dao de jing. | Tai chi.
Classification: LCC BL1900.L35 S46813 2021 | DDC 299.5/1482--dc23
LC record available at https://lccn.loc.gov/2020051835

British Library Cataloguing-in-Publication Data
A catalogue record for this book is available from the British Library.

Copyright © 2021 by SIM Pooh Ho and Tekson TEO

All rights reserved. This book, or parts thereof, may not be reproduced in any form or by any means, electronic or mechanical, including photocopying, recording or any information storage and retrieval system now known or to be invented, without written permission from the publisher.

For photocopying of material in this volume, please pay a copying fee through the Copyright Clearance Center, Inc., 222 Rosewood Drive, Danvers, MA 01923, USA. In this case permission to photocopy is not required from the publisher.

For any available supplementary material, please visit
https://www.worldscientific.com/worldscibooks/10.1142/12133#t=suppl

Desk Editor: Dong Lixi

Typeset by Stallion Press
Email: enquiries@stallionpress.com

Contents

Foreword — ix
How It All Began — xi
Editor/Translator's Notes — xiii
Acknowledgments — xvii

Chapter 1	Taiji of the Universe (Tao Core, Tao Use) 易有太极 (道体，道用)	1
Chapter 2	Yin Yang of Taiji 是生两仪 (阴阳)	11
Chapter 3	Inspire the People, Lead the World 安民治世	21
Chapter 4	Fusion of Yin Yang 道冲	29
Chapter 5	Keep to the Center 守中	37
Chapter 6	Mysterious Feminine 玄牝	43
Chapter 7	Cling Not to Self 无私	47
Chapter 8	The Highest Good is Like Water 上善若水	51
Chapter 9	Step Back When the Job is Done 功成身退	57
Chapter 10	Mysterious Te 玄德	61
Chapter 11	The Non-Being that We Use 虚中	69
Chapter 12	Focus on the "Belly" 为腹	73
Chapter 13	Greet Praises and Insults with Alarm 宠辱若惊	77
Chapter 14	Discipline of Tao 道纪	81
Chapter 15	Seek Not to be Filled to the Brim 不盈	87

Chapter 16	Fulfillment of Destiny 復命	93
Chapter 17	The Supreme 太上	99
Chapter 18	When Great Tao is Lost 大道废	103
Chapter 19	Bring Down the Ego, Desire Little 少私寡欲	107
Chapter 20	The Mother of Wisdom 食母	111
Chapter 21	Now We See It and Now We Don't 恍惚窈冥	121
Chapter 22	Embrace Oneness 抱一	125
Chapter 23	What Is! 自然	131
Chapter 24	What People of Tao Avoid 道者不处	135
Chapter 25	Naming Tao 曰道	139
Chapter 26	Calm and Rooted 静重	145
Chapter 27	Inheriting the Light 袭明	149
Chapter 28	Great Governance Never Disintegrates 大制不割	155
Chapter 29	Give Up Control 不为不执	161
Chapter 30	Against Tao 不道	165
Chapter 31	Honor the Left 尚左	171
Chapter 32	Know When to Stop 知止	177
Chapter 33	Die but not Perish 死而不亡	181
Chapter 34	Achieve Greatness 成大	185
Chapter 35	Hold Fast to Tao 执大象	189
Chapter 36	Subtle Insight 微明	193
Chapter 37	The World Finds its Peace 天下自定	197
Chapter 38	Stay with the Thick and Solid 处厚处实	201
Chapter 39	One with Tao 得一	207
Chapter 40	Being and Non-being 有无	215
Chapter 41	Hear of Tao 闻道	219
Chapter 42	Blending Yin Yang 冲和	229
Chapter 43	The Soft Overcomes the Hard 柔克刚 (至柔)	233
Chapter 44	Knowing Enough and When to Stop 知足知止	237

Chapter 45	Stay Serene and the World is in Peace 清静为天下正	241
Chapter 46	Always Have Enough 常足	247
Chapter 47	Wander Not and Yet They Know 知见	251
Chapter 48	Let Go and Let Go 损之又损	255
Chapter 49	Goodness of Te 德善	259
Chapter 50	Where Death Cannot Enter 无死地	263
Chapter 51	Revere Tao and Value Te 道尊德贵	267
Chapter 52	Inheriting Constancy 袭常	273
Chapter 53	Easy Path of Tao 道夷	279
Chapter 54	Firmly Rooted and Embraced 善建善抱	283
Chapter 55	Steeped in Te 含德之厚	289
Chapter 56	Mysterious Union 玄同	295
Chapter 57	Govern a Country 治国	299
Chapter 58	Happiness and Misery 祸福	305
Chapter 59	Longevity and Continuity 长生（啬）	311
Chapter 60	Rule the World with Tao 道莅天下	317
Chapter 61	Positioning Low 为下	321
Chapter 62	The Mysterious Secret of Tao 道奥	325
Chapter 63	Nothing is Difficult 无难	331
Chapter 64	Force Not 不敢为	337
Chapter 65	The Great Path of Flow 大顺	345
Chapter 66	Staying Low 善下	349
Chapter 67	Three Treasures 三宝	353
Chapter 68	Use the Strengths of People 用人之力	361
Chapter 69	The Military Maxim 用兵有言	365
Chapter 70	Find Gems in Rough Clothes 被褐怀玉	371
Chapter 71	Sick the Sickness 不病	377
Chapter 72	Fear of Menace 畏威	381

Chapter 73	Net of Heaven 天网	385
Chapter 74	Mess with the Blades of a Master Carpenter 代大匠	391
Chapter 75	Live Wisely 贤于贵生	395
Chapter 76	Father of Maxims 教父	399
Chapter 77	Tao of Heaven 天之道	405
Chapter 78	Te of Water 水德	409
Chapter 79	Hold the Left Deed 执左契	413
Chapter 80	A Small Country with Few People 小国寡民	417
Chapter 81	Do and Contend Not 为而不争	423

Apply the Wisdom to Taijiquan	429
About the Author	449
About the Editor/Translator	451
The Tao Te Ching in Chinese	453

Foreword

Tekson Teo's translation of Master Sim Pooh Ho's book on the *Tao Te Ching* is masterly. To be precise, Teo's translation is an interpretation of Master Sim's book. Even the translation of 玄妙解 in the title as "decoding" calls for a judgment of what Master Sim intends to convey. It is certainly not Google's translation.

    Teo is a longstanding disciple of Master Sim and has a deep understanding of Master Sim's thinking. However, Master Sim's thinking is multi-layered and a disciple's grasp of his master's knowledge is never complete. I am reminded of what Master Sim said of his master, Wu Tunan. Master Sim once asked Grand Master Wu when he would complete his learning from him. Grand Master Wu did not reply the first time. When asked again later, he stroked his white beard and remarked wrily that he himself was still learning. Grand Master Wu's point which Master Sim keeps reiterating to us, his disciples, is that we ourselves should never stop learning.

    The deep sources of Taijigong are the *Tao Te Ching* and *I Ching*. Master Sim's understanding of the *Tao Te Ching* is a result of many years of patient study and deep reflection, including what he learned from Grand Master Wu. His book is profound and precious, and deserves to be read and re-read. As the disciple grows in knowledge and wisdom, he discovers or uncovers a new layer. Master Sim himself takes an interest in quantum mechanics and dark matter and stresses the need to update our understanding in the light of new scientific discoveries.

It is Master Sim's lifelong wish that the benefits of Taijigong should be made available to all people and not just to Chinese people. Having his book translated into English, or interpreted in English, is therefore an important task which he entrusted to Teo. Teo took this on not as a task but as a mission into which he has invested much time and effort. Indeed, he told me that this mission has become an all-consuming passion. As he wrestles with alternative interpretations, and clarifies them with Master Sim, he feels himself transformed.

In this process of interpreting Master Sm, Teo came to be dissatisfied with existing English translations of the *Tao Te Ching*, of which there are many, and has therefore decided to do his own translation which hews closer to Master's interpretation of the book. The result is an English translation of the *Tao Te Ching* as "decoded" by Master Sim.

Master Sim wrote his book principally for the benefit of his disciples. He asked Teo to do a translation principally for those disciples who do not understand Chinese. Like a seed that grows once it is planted, Master Sim's book has reached a wider readership. Teo's English translation will spread it further. Taijigong is a living tree that bears rich fruits.

George Yeo
Former Foreign Minister of Singapore

How It All Began

For centuries, Laozi's *Tao Te Ching* has fascinated people from every discipline of study, be it history, culture, military, politics, or management. My focus of this book is on its application to self-cultivation and Taijiquan.

Legend has it that Laozi revealed to the spiritually accomplished border guard Yin Xi the wisdom of Tao while penning the *Tao Te Ching* for posterity. The book sheds light on the origin of Tao. An excellent guide for self-cultivation, it explains the role of humankind in the universe and the importance of returning to the Source. Although it is concise and consists of only slightly more than five thousand Chinese characters, it is no less influential than scriptures many times its volume. Unfortunately, the gem of wisdom has been submerged in the sea of annotations for millennia.

The *Tao Te Ching* is about Oneness. It is penetrating, unembellished, and meant to be a guide for self-cultivation. Many people, unfortunately, miss the forest for the tree and fail to appreciate its essence. A similar fate befell the Chan (Zen) Buddhism, which was developed by Bodhidharma during his nine years of isolation. The essence of its wisdom was overshadowed by the Shaolin kungfu it was associated with. This explains why I feel compelled to share with my disciples what I have learned from the *Tao Te Ching*. The embedded messages I have discovered during decades of immersion in the teachings, verified through my Taiji practices, are profound. Through the methodology of Taijigong, which consists of the levels of *Shi, Jin, Qi,* and *Hua* (or Form, Inner energy, Qi, and Transcendence, respectively), I progressively demonstrate to the disciples what the wonders are in the book of wisdom.

Some readers are curious about the title of the book, *Decoding the Tao Te Ching*. It is meant to fill a gap. Most people rely on the dictionary definitions to interpret the *Tao Te Ching* and overlook the book's credentials in self-cultivation and eternal Tao. Their interpretations are usually directed with a temporal focus. We cannot rely on the dictionary definitions to attain Tao. It is, nevertheless, a necessary step. What is important is that we don't stop there. We have to probe below the surface to uncover the underlying messages. I hope the sharing can lead to a deeper appreciation of the teachings so that more people can bring back their innocence, gain new ground, and overcome obstacles along the way. It is with these in mind that I name the book as *Decoding the Tao Te Ching*.

Editor/Translator's Notes

Lauded as one of the greatest books of wisdom ever written in human history, the *Tao Te Ching* was written by Laozi, a Chinese Sage of some 2,500 years ago. Since then, the philosophy of life and a spiritual pursuit based on it, known as Taoism, has flourished, not only in China but also around the world. The *Tao Te Ching* has become one of the most sought-after books of wisdom and is said to be the most-translated work after the Bible.

Despite the tremendous influence it commands, the *Tao Te Ching* is surprisingly tiny. It is hard to imagine. The book of such renowned wisdom comprises only slightly more than 5,000 Chinese characters and can be printed on a few pieces of standard letter paper. However, we must never underestimate its profundity. The wisdom it embodies provides a glimpse into the dynamics of the colossal universe, inspirations for a meaningful and profound life, and freedom of the mind that helps readers to go beyond their confines.

Decoding the Tao Te Ching is Master Sim's interpretation of the ancient book of wisdom. Honestly, although I was honored when asked to translate the book, there was also a lot of hesitation. It is a tall order. The *Tao Te Ching* of Laozi is not at all easy to read. Embedded in each of its 5,000 Chinese characters are highly profound messages. At the same time, Master Sim's interpretations are full of references to Taijiquan, religious texts, and folklore, which are a feast to the mind but take patience to chew and digest. To grasp either of the books is intimidating, not to mention rewording them in English. Fortunately, I overcame the initial doubts, and boldly took up the challenge. Delightfully, the project turned out to be a refreshing and rewarding experience. Trudging through rigorous terrain is grueling. But it is also where the thrills are. I am humbled and inspired.

Master Sim's approach to the subject is anything but academic. It is both spiritual and experiential. The Taiji lineage he inherited from Grand Master Wu Tunan is a milieu for immersion in the wisdom, and the system of Taijigong the lineage inculcates is an exciting playing field to see the teachings in action. Taiji practices such as Transcendence with Heaven connects him to the core of the universe and enables his frequent "dialogues" with the Sage. His unique approach to the ancient book makes the interpretations penetrating, inspiring, and a class of its own.

The Chinese version of the book is a culmination of a series of lectures conducted in 2016. Upon requests from several of his senior disciples, the classes were given in Master Sim's abode located on a scenic mountain in China surrounded by acres of pine trees. It was a rare treat, and I was privileged to be in the audience, and subsequently, also in the editorial panel that put the book together.

I adhered to the original texts as far as possible when doing the first drafts of the translation, until it hit a snag. Many of Master Sim's references are culturally specific and can be bewildering for people without a similar background. His elaborations on Taijiquan are technical and not easy for non-practitioners to follow. Bearing the international readers in mind, I, with the permission of the author, adapted parts of the book. Several passages on Taiji, which were originally in different parts of the book, were also taken out to form a chapter.

While *pinyin* is the mainstay now for the notation of Chinese words, it is a relatively recent phenomenon. The key terms for the *Tao Te Ching*, however, are so entrenched in the Wade-Giles format. In order to avoid confusion, I have chosen to retain them. So, the *Tao Te Ching* is Dao De Jing, Tao is Dao, and Te is De. As for the rest, I use *pinyin* as far as I can. Therefore, Tai Chi is written as Taiji, Tai Chi Quan as Taijiquan, and the *I Ching* as the *Yijing*.

In addition, several terms are unique to the book, and I would like to highlight some of them.

The author uses a few unique terms to describe Tao, including Tao Core (道体) and Tao Zero (道零); and Tao Use (道用) and Tao One (道一). Tao Core and Tao Zero refer to the formless Tao. Tao Use and Tao One or One, on the other hand, refer to its manifestations, which may also be described as Te (德). The key difference between them is that the former is formless, while the latter is its manifestations that impact the myriads of things directly. Besides, the author uses the phrase "Now in the emptiness, now in the present" (即空即有) frequently. It happens when he refers to the oscillation between the formless Tao and its manifestations, or non-being (无) and being (有).

Another recurring term in the book is the *taihe* qi energy (太和之炁). Scientists today use terms like protons, atoms, neutrons, molecules, ions, quantum, or dark matter to describe tiny matter of the universe. Laozi calls them collectively as "something nebulous" (有物混成), and within it is the primordial qi energy. The *taihe* qi predates Heaven and Earth, but is still present and it underlies every existence, and keeps the entire universe in order. It is ultimately Tao and, in Taijigong, forms a conduit for us to connect to Tao Core.

In the time of Laozi, writing a book was laborious because every word had to be knife-engraved on the bamboo slips. It was time-consuming, so writers chose words with immense care. This explains why the words usually comprise multiple meanings and thus are hard to understand. It poses a major challenge for translation. 有 and 无, for example, can be literally translated as "have" and "have not", but they encapsulate a mammoth amount of information beyond what any dictionary definition can possibly contain. There is a lot of compromise when expressing many of the words in English, not to mention finding equivalents.

In addition to understanding the meanings of the words, it is important not to read the book as just another book. Reading of the *Tao Te Ching* is meant to be experiential, not just academic. It requires constant reflections and regular revisits to the book for its insight. This is what *Decoding the Tao Te Ching* does.

The author recalled what his Master told him, "If you want to really learn from me, turn the one thing you learn into three; then thirty, three hundred or three thousand!". We absorb and expand from what we have learned. From one simple idea, we generate another three, three hundred and three thousand. This is the approach the author uses in his decoding of the *Tao Te Ching*. I would think that it is one we should take, too.

Acknowledgments

The completion of this translation is impossible without the support from many people.

Chief among them is the sponsor for the project, who has chosen to remain anonymous. No words can express our appreciation of his generosity and support.

I would like to thank the author Master Sim Pooh Ho, for his trust in me and the continuous guidance in both the practice of Taijigong and cultivation of Tao.

I am grateful to Mr George Yeo for his encouragement and guidance, which are inspirational and motivating.

Thanks also to Mr Zach Jensen. His critique and comments from a native English speaker's perspective provide me with valuable insight that helped me to fine-tune my approach to addressing the international readers, especially those from the West.

Many of the fellow disciples are extremely supportive and helpful. Special mention goes to Mr Sim Pern Yiau for his many suggestions. I enjoy every discussion with him, be it about the use of words or the applications of the teachings in Taijigong.

Many thanks to others, including the many fellow disciples, who have helped me in one way or another. It is a regret I cannot mention every one of them here. The list is simply too long.

Chapter 1

Taiji of the Universe (Tao Core, Tao Use)
易有太极（道体，道用）

*The Tao that can be mentioned
Is not the eternal Tao.
The name that can be named
Is not the eternal name.
Non-being, the beginning of Heaven and Earth.
Being, Mother of all things.
Thus in the constant non-being,
There is a desire to view its mystery.
In the constant being,
There is a desire to view its boundary.
These two, share a common origin,
Yet come forth with
a different name.
Both are called a mystery.
One mystery after another,
The gate to all wonders.*

In the vein of the *Yijing*, one of the oldest books in the history of humanity, Laozi begins the *Tao Te Ching* by introducing Tao (道, *dao*4) as the origin of the universe. It is the One Source that generates the myriads of things and where they eventually return to. It is the root of all existence.

The Tao that can be mentioned is not the eternal Tao

No one, however, is able to tell us what Tao exactly is. As Laozi says in this chapter, it cannot be described by words. Even if it "can be mentioned" (可道, *ke3dao4*), analyzed, and discussed, something is bound to be lost in the process, and what we can conclude is never "the eternal Tao" (常道, *chang2dao4*).

A key reason why Tao cannot be explained is that it is "non-being" (无, *wu2*), with neither form nor shape. How do we describe something without form?

Tao, however, is too important not to be mentioned. Out of necessity, Laozi coined the word "Tao". This is, however, just a name, and it behooves us to be open to compromise — to talk about it within this constraint. That is what Laozi does anyway. In the 81 chapters of the book, he painstakingly explains Tao, in words, as best he could, so that others may better understand it.

The name that can be named is not the eternal name

Unlike Tao, naming (名, *ming2*) is perceptible, and it is never eternal. Naming is best interpreted in both the worldly and spiritual perspectives. First, the worldly perspective. Let's imagine the times we name things. We often do it out of convenience in order to know what we are talking about. There are many ways to name a thing. We can base it on the thing's behavior or appearance. However, whatever a name is, it isn't permanent; it changes when circumstances change.

For example, we name water as "water", when it is in liquid form, but we call it "ice" when it is solidified. When ice melts, we call it "water" again. A gust of wind turns water into a "wave", and a rise in temperature turns it into "steam". In this way, the names of water change as its behavior changes. Because circumstances don't remain constant, a name is always subject to change. It is not "the eternal name" (常名, *chang2ming2*).

Now, a spiritual interpretation. As we have established, a name is given to a thing with a set of conditions in mind. If we can be in control of the conditions, we can turn water into ice, steam, and waves at will. By the same token, as long as we are in control of the determining factors, we can optimize any situation that we are in, rather than allowing the situation to control us. If we aspire to be a sage, for example, we must learn the set of factors that condition a sage and allow the factors to arise. When the factors are present, and the condition is ready, we become what we aspire to be … naturally.

Non-being, the beginning of Heaven and Earth. Being, Mother of all things

Laozi next presents us with another pair of concepts: Being and non-being. These concepts are so fundamental that they are the two primary pillars of the book.

"Non-being" is a translation of 无 (*wu2*), which literally means "nothing". Being, on the other hand, is a translation of 有 (*you3*), which means "something".

How can "nothing" and "something" be so important? Even more perplexing is that Laozi describes "nothing" or non-being as the beginning of Heaven and Earth, and he adds that "being", or "something" is "Mother of all things" (万物之母, *wan4wu-4zhi1mu3*). But, when we break it apart, we find the reason for this is not confusing or complicated at all.

To understand what the Sage means, we have to go back to the very origin of Tao.

We may call the Tao origin as Tao Core (道体, *dao4ti3*). Tao is formless, and so is Tao Core. Although it is elusive, it is omnipresent and has been around since the beginning of time. Before the emergence of Heaven and Earth, Tao Core was in a nebulous state that Taoists describe as *wuji* (无极, *wu2ji2*). It means "infinity", where there was no awareness, no shape, no form; only a mass of qi (pronounced like "*chee*") energy known as *taihe* qi (太和之炁, *tai4he2zhi1qi4*) that revolved relentlessly in a state of chaos.

Then came the magical moment, something like the Big Bang explosion. At that moment, *taihe* qi converged with *Yuanyang* (元阳), or the Primordial Yang Energy. The convergence sparked off a beam of light that traveled thousands and thousands of miles. In a flash, Heaven was born. Soon, Earth came into being. All of a sudden, Tao became perceptible. While in itself still formless, it was now manifested in the newly born Heaven and Earth. With Heaven and Earth, Yin and Yang energies permeated the universe. Since *Yuanyang*, the Primordial Yang Energy, was life-giving, Yin Yang energies worked in harmony to generate life, and the myriads of things mushroomed. "Tao generates one, one generates two, two generates three, and three generates the myriads of things," exclaims Laozi in Chapter 42 of the *Tao Te Ching*.

This is how, from the One Source, the myriads of things were born. Because Heaven and Earth were generated by *wuji* or non-being, Laozi, therefore, says, "Non-being, the beginning of Heaven and Earth."

A common Western philosophical dilemma is: "Which came first? The chicken or the egg?" In Taoism, however, we go one step further and ask: "What existed before everything, that made everything possible?" As mentioned earlier, Tao is the One Source that everything comes from. It was originally "nothing", and all of a sudden, Heaven and Earth emerged from the nebula, and the myriads of things came into being.

Thus in the constant non-being, there is a desire to view its mystery

Non-being is the beginning of Heaven and Earth and being is the Mother of all things. In order to know the universe, we need a good understanding of both non-being and being.

Non-being is "constant" (常, *chang*2). It is always around us, brimming with possibilities of things waiting to be born into existence. While it is older than Heaven and Earth, it has not vanished and will outlive them. Even if Heaven and Earth someday disappear for whatever reason, non-being shall remain. It is, therefore, eternal.

When we align ourselves with the constant non-being, we can see the unseen and the wonders within it. For example, in the deep stillness of meditation or the practice of Taijiquan, we experience the serenity within non-being.

In Taijigong, the school of Taiji that I teach, we immerse ourselves in the *taihe* qi energy that takes us back to the constant non-being. In this state of marvels, there are neither forms nor divides. It allows us to behold the wonders of Tao Core, i.e., the origin of Tao.

In the "constant non-being" (常无, *chang*2*wu*2), "there is a *desire* to *view* its *mystery*". To witness the wonders three things, as mentioned in the clause, are essential: Desire (欲, *yu*4), view (观, *guan*1), and mystery (妙, *miao*4).

First, let's talk about "desire". There are two types of desires; one is instinctive, and the other is spiritual. The desire to eat when we are hungry and put on warm clothes in cold weather are instinctive. In contrast, spiritual desire is of a higher order. We admire the sages and want to learn what they do. This is also a desire, and it is this desire Laozi mentions in this chapter.

"View" means "to see". But, the kind of sight Laozi talks about is not visual. Here, "to see" refers to a reflective technique that prompts us to look inward and conduct dialogues with our inner self. It is common in spiritual practices, including Taoism and Buddhism.

The pictogram of "mystery" is 妙, which means "wonders". It consists of two sub-characters: 女 and 少. 女 means "female". It is about being feminine and mild-mannered, so it carries the connotation of modesty, humility, and tolerance. 少 means "small in quantity" and implies that the wonders are in having less. It may sound absurd because we are accustomed to always wanting more. Here, the word "mystery" implies that, if we are going to witness wonders of the universe, we will have to begin by staying both humble and frugal. At the same time, we must also be ready to work with the "non-being", a behavior known as non-doing, or "*wuwei*" (无为, *wu2wei2*).

Putting the three things together, the "desire to view its mystery" provokes us to look inward to see the mysteries surrounding non-being, and it answers questions like who we are, where we are from, and where we are heading. This desire leads to a deeper appreciation of life and helps us uncloak many of its mysteries.

In the constant being, there is a desire to view its boundary

Now, let us look at the "constant being" (常有, *chang2you3*). Being and non-being correspond to each other. Non-being is about the non-being, i.e., formlessness, of Tao, while being is about the present and the material world in which we live.

The word "boundary" perplexes many people. It is a translation of 徼 (*jiao4*), which means "boundary" or "border". Let's begin by looking at the structure of the pictogram. Radical 彳 implies "do and reflect", and carries a connotation of observation and reflection. It is reminiscent of what we mentioned earlier: In between being and non-being, we find the wonders of the universe. So, the "boundary" is the border between being and non-being. There is a desire to see it because it is a delicate thin line and can be difficult to detect. On one side of the line is being, and on the other side is non-being. We can witness wonders of the universe only if we are aware of the line.

The boundary is delicate because while being and non-being appear to be different, they are one. We see being in non-being and non-being in being. Being refers to things that we can see and touch, like a person or a house. The beings, nevertheless, are essentially non-being. They are illusory. Yes, a person standing in front of us is alive and kicking, so they are a being. We can feel their breath, talk to them, and pat them on the back. But are they just a being? Where will this person be one hundred years from now? They will likely have passed on. By then, they will have returned to non-being because they are no longer living in this world. As such, the person is both a being and a non-being. While a person has a lifetime of "being" for a hundred years or so, not all creatures are that lucky. Houseflies, mosquitoes, and germs have only days or hours.

Of course, being and non-being are not just about life and death. We don't return to non-being *only* upon death. We return to it now and then. Non-being is our root, it is with us all the time, and we cannot live without it. It is just that, more often than not, our attention is on being, so we are oblivious to the presence of non-being.

Living in a world of constant being, we are faced with all kinds of challenges it poses, and it is no wonder it consumes all our attention. To earn a living, not only do we have to work hard, but we must also learn new things and continue to hone our skills. As an academic, we cannot stop reading and conducting research. As business professionals, we must manage our people and ensure that the business is profitable. As a medical doctor, we must stay on top of new advances in medicine while taking care of our patients.

The *Tao Te Ching* is down to earth. It is not against us doing what we need to make a living. That doesn't mean, however, that we can forget the constant non-being. We need both, and it is important to maintain a delicate balance between them.

How do we keep a balance? The simplest thing to do is to observe the presence of non-being when we go about whatever we do for being. If we are in business, the constant being requires us to make a profit. Without profit, the business isn't sustainable. It, nevertheless, doesn't mean that we can upset the constant non-being within us: our perpetual self.

We must not use the challenges of being as an excuse for misconduct. For example, we must not try "making a killing" by running a casino or a brothel. It is shortsighted to ruin the eternal for the temporal: To tarnish our perpetual self for the sake of worldly indulgence. The consequence isn't worth it. By viewing its boundary, we are regularly reminded to reflect on what we do and guard against unwittingly straying from Tao. "If we conform to

Tao, the power of Tao flows through us," says Laozi in Chapter 23. By constantly viewing the boundary, Tao is with us, and we are blessed.

These two, share a common origin, yet come forth with a different name, both are called a mystery

"These two" refers to the constant non-being and the constant being. They are different. One is formless; the other is form. However, they share a "common origin" (同, *tong*2). As if two sides of a coin, they coexist and are mutually dependent. They "come forth" (出, *chu*1) with a "different name" (异名, *yi4ming*2). Tao is non-being. Te (德, *de*2) is being. Te is a manifestation of Tao, so it is ultimately Tao, but given a different name.

How the "come forth" takes place is mystical. It transforms Tao from the constant non-being to the constant being, leading to a change of name but not the essence. For example, we often refer to Shakyamuni — founder of Buddhism — as the Buddha. This is what we know him to be when he is out and about in the constant being, as a person teaching and helping people. When he is in deep stillness, however, he is in the constant non-being known as Tathagata. The two names refer to the same person but in different states.

In "Both are called a mystery" (同谓之玄, *tong2wei4zhi1xuan2*), Laozi uses the word "mystery" to describe the enigmatic connections between the being and the non-being. A question that puzzles everybody is what we had been before we were born. Using the terminology of Tao that we have just learned, we used to be non-being. But how different is the non-being to our current being, i.e., what we are now? Similarly, when we pass on, we are back to the non-being. Does the non-being that we become carry any characteristics of our current being? How is it going to be different from the non-being we used to be? How did all these come about? Nobody knows. Like Laozi says, "Both are called a mystery." Are they not mysterious? They are, indeed.

One mystery after another, the gate to all wonders

We find mysteries in the ways things operate and change and the manners in which Tao is pursued. It is said that before attaining complete enlightenment, the Buddha went through 500 rebirths; each was built on the attainment he had accumulated over previous lives. When he finally arrived, there was a radiance of light that traversed millions of miles and brightened up the entire universe. Things continue to change with "one mystery after another".

"The gate to all wonders" (众妙之门, *zhong4miao4zhi1men2*) is the source from which all mysteries are generated. To find the gate, we must observe not only the wonders but also the boundary where being and non-being intersect. Enter the gate, and we return to the constant non-being. Exit the gate, and we see the constant being. By going in and out of the gate, we see the mysteries of the universe unfold.

Chapter 2

Yin Yang of Taiji
是生两仪 (阴阳)

We all know beauty as beauty
Because of ugliness.
The good as good
Because of the not-so-good.
Being and non-being engender each other.
Difficult and easy complement each other.
Long and short define each other.
High and low play off each other.
Sound and voice harmonize each other.
Front and back follow each other.
Thus the Sage does by non-doing,
Teaches by not saying a word.
Things are left to live by their nature,
And the Sage rejects none.
They create but possess not.
Do but seek no glory.
Accomplish but claim no credit.
Alas! As they claim no credit,
Tao leaves them not.

Having introduced being and non-being in Chapter 1, in this chapter, Laozi talks about another pair of fundamental concepts: Yin and Yang. They accompanied the emergence of Heaven and Earth and brought with them what is commonly known as "divides"; a state of divisiveness that is opposed to oneness.

We all know beauty as beauty because of ugliness

"Beauty" (美, *mei*3) here refers not only to pleasant appearance, but also things like prestige, wealth, glory, domination, and power. We know beauty because there is ugliness (恶, *e*4). Beauty is coveted. Everyone wants to be beautiful, and some even resort to unscrupulous means to be so. This is why the corrupted, sly, and hypocritical slip into the cloak of beauty to fool others, and corrupt leaders menace the world in the name of justice to plunder and kill.

The true beauty, however, must not be tainted with an ulterior motive. When there are divides, selfishness, and intrigue, a thing is no longer beautiful but ugly. Beauty is a reward of the good seeds we planted earlier, sometimes as far back as our previous lives. The surest way to have beauty is, therefore, the cultivation of true virtues.

The good as good because of the not-so-good

It is interesting to note that while Laozi compares beauty to ugliness, he compares "good" (善, *shan*4) with "not-so-good" (不善, *bu*4*shan*4). Why is there such a change in tone? The reason is simple: A good deed is, after all, a good deed, even if it is less-than-perfect. There is no need to be harsh about it.

The word "good" here is a translation of 善, which carries a connotation unique to the *Tao Te Ching*. It means not just "good", but the "highest good"; almost as good as Tao. Those who are "good", in this sense, are non-discriminatory. They treat everything as equal and harbor no prejudices. In the *Tao Te Ching*, the virtue is also described as the highest "Te" (德). "A person of the highest Te does not think of Te but lives naturally with Te," says Laozi in Chapter 38. They don't even think of doing good when they are doing good.

In contrast, those who are "not-so-good" are discriminatory. They have divides and are self-centered. Not only do they harbor likes and dislikes when doing good, but they also cannot wait to announce to the world the good deeds they have performed. Even then, they are doing good! Laozi, therefore, is less critical when describing them. From this, we can see how meticulous the Sage is in his choice of words. Each one of the 5,000 characters of the *Tao Te Ching* is carefully picked.

When there are divides, there is a difference between you and me and the good and bad. Laozi thus says, "Being and non-being engender each other. Difficult and easy complement each other. Long and short define each other. High and low play off each other. Sound and noise harmonize each other. Front and back follow each other." Let's see how a person of Tao should handle such differences in the things they do.

Being and non-being engender each other

When we see differences in things, we must observe the underlying forces and discern whether the forces are mutually enhancing (相生, *xiang1sheng1*) or defeating (相克, *xiang1ke4*). An engineer and someone in marketing may have conflicting views in a product design, but their differences are meant to make the product stronger. Such relationship is mutually enhancing. On the other hand, when a competitor launches a campaign to smear a product, it is meant to harm the standing of the product, so the relationship is defeating. When handling differences, a person of Tao goes for the enhancing and avoid the defeating. By doing so, they thrive with Tao.

The interplay between being and non-being is mutually enhancing and they help each other. As a person of Tao, we must go with the mutually enhancing flow.

Beings are things that can be perceived. Underlying every being, however, as pointed out in Chapter 1, is non-being, which is formless. In fact, in the final analysis it is engendered by non-being. A pot, for example, is envisioned in the mind of the artist before it is created as an object. Although a being is tangible, it is temporal, not permanent. It is essentially illusory and will eventually return to non-being. When there is birth, there is death. When there is tide, there is ebb. "Being and non-being engender (相生, *xiang1sheng1*) each other". A plant sprouts in spring and withers in autumn, and by spring it is full of life again.

This cycle repeats itself, and we must know the cycle to appreciate the underlying principle of existence. With awareness of the reality, there is no fear of death. Death is dreaded, because people hate to lose. But, when we understand the cycle and the underlying forces, we know that death is not a dead end, and thus not a loss. On the contrary, death is where new life begins. For a person of Tao, it can even be an ascension to a higher order. Knowing this, a person of Tao worries no more and has no fear of death.

Most people, unfortunately, don't see life this way. They care only about being: What they are doing now and the years ahead in their current life, rather than something perpetual. When they know how being and non-being engender each other, they will see the non-being and extend their vision of life beyond the decades of which they are living. They don't just see years but hundreds and thousands of years ahead that span many lives.

To do this, we have to jump out of the entrenched mindset. Of course, we cannot reverse what we have done in the past. We can, however, do something different for our future. Perhaps reading this book is a turning point. Or, maybe, we simply make a decision to be kind in everything we do from this point on. When we view life as a series of renewals, we cultivate our being in the present in order to refine our non-being for our future in this life and beyond. We must, therefore, make the most of every life and build upon each one; getting better and better in the long run.

Of course, being and non-being are not just about life and death. They are part of every existence and define every minute of our life. The money we make and the things we buy with it are being, the happiness that we bring to the family with the things we buy is a non-being. When we perform self-cultivation, the activities we conduct, such as meditation, are being. The refinement of our character is non-being.

Children are related to their parents through blood lineage. We may see this as being. The lineage, however, works only in the current life. There is another lineage that keeps them together beyond their current life. We may call this the qi lineage, which is in the non-being. The parent and child have to share a common qi lineage so that their link can go beyond the current life, or they may not be seeing each other again. Why? Because a blood lineage is temporal. A *qi* lineage, on the other hand, is based on *taihe* qi, which is Tao and the constant non-being. It is perpetual. Another good example of a *qi* lineage is that between a Master and their disciples. This is how my Master, Wu Tunan, myself and my disciples are linked together with the lineage that can be traced back to the great Taiji Master Zhang Sanfeng (born in 1247) and ultimately Laozi. It is long lasting. Cultivation of qi lineages is common across other spiritual practices and cultures as well. The only difference is in the names.

Difficult and easy complement each other

Difficult (难, *nan2*) and easy (易, *yi4*) sound contradictory, but they are two sides of the same coin, so they complement (相成, *xiang1cheng2*) each other. The relationship is mutually enhancing. Although adversity is tough, when we take steps to overcome it, we improve our problem-solving skills and, eventually, make the difficult easy. While it is important to see setbacks positively, we must not underestimate things that are easy. If there are inherent complications, things that are easy can turn nasty if we take it lightly. In the things we do, we must also see how the difficult and easy complement each other.

Long and short define each other

Long and short are relative. We cannot tell the long (长, *chang2*) from the short (短, *duan3*) without putting them side-by-side. They define (相形, *xiang1xing2*) each other. A foot is longer than an inch but shorter than a yard. Long and short, however, doesn't matter if we have no divides. When we notice how they enhance each other, their difference in length doesn't matter.

If long is strength and short is weakness, we can make ourselves stronger by not allowing the long and short to become mutually defeating. While we don't feel inferior for being weak, we are not conceited for being strong. Rather, we see how they can complement each other. We may, for example, work with others as a team so that they can make up for what we are weak in, and optimize our strength by improving ourselves to scale new heights. We enhance the long with the short and the short with the long.

High and low play off each other

The high and the low play off (相倾, *xiang1qing3*) each other to gain a foothold, so they are mutually defeating. The high (高, *gao1*) needs to step on the low (下, *xia4*) to become high, and the low cannot become high with the high on top. The relationship is, therefore, one of mutually defeating. We must see how we can turn it around. A way to do it is that when we are in a low position, respect the leadership of those above. When we are high up, win the people below over with our sincerity and virtue. With trust there is teamwork, and it turns the defeating relationship into one of enhancing. Instead of fighting, we allow the high and low to thrive together by complementing each other.

Sound and voice harmonize each other

Voice (声, *sheng1*), albeit sweet, is monotonous without a good accompaniment. When we harmonize (相和, *xiang1he2*) the strengths of voice with sound (音, *yin1*), we create a win-win relationship.

In self-cultivation, harmonization works in two ways: Being and non-being. We work on the "constant being" to harmonize the Yin and Yang energies. Smoothening the qi circulation in our body is one way to do this, and it helps us to stay healthy and live longer. At the same time, we work with the "constant non-being". We blend the air we breathe with the perpetual energy *taihe* qi. By doing so, we refine our souls and live our ultimate destiny.

Harmonization is important in all aspects of life. In geopolitical context, for example, it happens when countries work together for mutual benefits. When one country helps another in its development, both countries, their allies and all the citizens benefit. What if the harmony is jeopardized? The relationship becomes mutually defeating, and both countries, their allies and all their people lose.

Front and back follow each other

This relationship is evident between leaders and followers. It is mutually enhancing. First of all, the leaders lead at the front (前, *qian*2) and the followers follow at the back (后, *hou*4). At the same time, the leaders listen to the needs of the followers to make their leadership more effective. When I work with my disciples, this is what we do to keep our Taiji lineage alive. Master Wu Tunan was in front, and I followed him from the back. Now, I am in front, and my disciples are following me from behind. This is how the torch has been passed on from Laozi and other ancestors — to benefit the later generations. As teachers, on the other hand, we identify the strengths and weaknesses of our disciples and adjust the programs, so that they can progress better in their training.

Thus the Sage does by non-doing

"Non-doing" is a translation of 无为 (*wu2wei*2). It is, however, not about doing nothing. Rather, it is about how we can tap into the power of non-being to get things done. Like Laozi says later in the chapter: "Things are left to live by their nature, and the Sage rejects none. They create but possess not, do but seek no glory, grow but dominate not, accomplish but claim no credit." We flow with nature and live the non-being of Tao.

Teaches by not saying a word

Because the Sage works with non-being, it is hard for them to articulate what they do. Therefore, instead of relying on talking, the Sage "teaches" (教, *jiao*1) by "not saying a word" (不言, *bu4yan2*). They set themselves up as role models and inspire not only by what they say but also by what they do. At the same time, they help the followers to reflect on what they do.

Very often, to really learn a lesson, we must weather the storm ourselves and learn life's lessons "the hard way". The Sage can't work on our behalf. In order for us to learn, they must step aside and do nothing. It looks callous, but deep down, it is profound kindness. This is the most arduous aspect of "teaching by not saying a word".

Things are left to live by their nature, and the Sage rejects none

When "things are left to live by their nature" (作焉, *zuo4yan1*), they thrive with nature. Cycles of nature are unstoppable. We cannot stop winter from arriving because we don't like it. The Tao of Heaven allows things to grow and perish by following their own nature and by going with the flow of the law of the universe. Plants sprout, grow, wither, and conserve as the cycle of the seasons rolls on. The Sage accepts what is and "rejects none" (不辞, *bu4ci2*).

They create but possess not

Tao creates everything but owns nothing. Although we are a creation of Tao, Tao claims no credit for what it does. This is the virtue of Tao we find in the Sage that we must emulate.

Parents, for example, should not be possessive of their children. Children are the extension of blood lineage, so bringing them up and educating them is the heavenly duty of their parents. This doesn't, however, mean the children are their parents' property or that they should subject themselves to their parents' manipulation.

If we are a parent, we cannot deny our children's own destinies. They become our children for a variety of reasons that are out of our control. They could be here to pay their gratitude for our kindness to them in a previous life. If this is the case, they are naturally loving. They could, on the other hand, be here to seek revenge for our unkindness to them in a previous life. If this is the case, they can be reckless, and we must take the opportunity to pay what is due.

As the Chinese saying goes, "Every child has their own blessings." We must do our part and remember that blood lineage is short lived; only qi lineage lasts. Therefore, we must guide our children to take the path of Tao, so that we can extend the qi lineage to them.

Do but seek no glory

We practice non-doing and "seek no glory" (不恃, *bu4shi4*) for what we do. For example, the glory of this book is not mine. If you find this book helpful, the wisdom herein doesn't belong to me. I am just doing my part by sharing it with the world.

Accomplish but claim no credit

Things get done when conditions for their accomplishment are met. So, when the Sage "accomplishes" (功成, *gong1cheng2*), they see no reason to feel arrogant about it. They "claim no credit" (弗居, *fu2ju1*). Rather, they pay gratitude to the people and conditions that made the achievement possible.

Alas! As they claim no credit, Tao leaves them not

Alas! Since the Sage claims no credit for their success, Tao leaves them not (弗去, *fu2qu4*). Learning from the Sage, we must begin and end with Tao in all things we do. When we are one with Tao, Tao flows through us. When we claim credit and seek possession, self-interests set in and Tao stays away from us.

Laozi introduces the concept of non-doing, i.e., *wuwei*, for the first time in this chapter. Many people misinterpret non-doing to mean the Sage is apathetic or laid-back. However, after completing this chapter, it becomes clear that "non doing" is not about doing absolutely nothing. It is about doing by tapping into the power of non-being. If we and, better still, the entire human race, can practice true non-doing, stability and prosperity shall prevail. People of all countries will harmonize and live happily with contentment in enduring peace.

Chapter 3

Inspire the People, Lead the World
安民治世

Exalt not the eminent,
And people contend not.
Value not the precious goods,
There is theft no more.
See not the undesirable,
And the mind is not confused.
Thus the Sage leads by
Softening the mind,
Strengthening the belly;
Weakening the ambition,
And toughening the resolve.
They inspire people to stay
Not-knowing and not-desiring;
and they forbid the clever from interfering.
If we practice non-doing,
There is nothing that we cannot manage.

This is a highly controversial chapter, probably because of the sentence that says: The Sage "inspires people to stay not-knowing and not-desiring." Some readers interpret it as a promotion of ignorance in order to make people easy to govern. Is this the case? Hopefully, we can do our parts in dispelling the confusion.

Exalt not the eminent, and people contend not

Exalting the eminent is not wrong if the exaltation doesn't cause divides. Unfortunately, this is unlikely to be the case. When we single someone out and "exalt" (尚, shang4) them as "eminent" (贤, xian2), we are suggesting that others are not. So, we have divided people into classes of the eminent and otherwise, e.g., high and low. Furthermore, the eminent tend to enjoy prestige and superiority over others, making their positions even more coveted.

Given a choice, most people will want to join the league of the eminent. Obviously, this is not possible, or the privileged position would not exist. To prevent their privileges from being diluted, the incumbent erect barricades to ward off competition. The wealthy and powerful, for example, would strategically define "eminence" to keep the rest of the population poorer and powerless. This distorts the essence of eminence. It is based no longer on virtues, but the ability to compete.

When the focus is wrong, the quality of the eminent goes downhill. This is what happens to many high-sounding committees around the world. Their members use the positions to advance personal gains and political agenda, oblivious to the virtue of the eminent. What is worse is when the malicious pretend to be eminent to mislead. Quack doctor fakes reports to sell counterfeit medicine; self-proclaimed "investment advisor" swindles away people's hard-earned money with clever scams. Widespread social problems ensue, resulting in ruins of personal fortunes or even lives.

Exalting the eminent, therefore, is not just a matter of rhetoric. It creates divides and leads to agony. By not exalting the "eminent", we slow the spread of vice, sin, and thus, agony. Imagine if, instead of celebrating the superior, we focused our attention on self-cultivation and the attainment of Tao. If people don't feel inferior, and if they are content with what they have, they would naturally feel less inclination toward violence and other destructive or criminal behaviors.

Value not the precious goods, there is theft no more

Precious goods (难得之货, *nan2de2zhi1huo4*) command value because of scarcity, not because of their contribution to life. Are oysters, shark fin, lobsters, diamonds, and oil more valuable than water and air? Clearly not! Then, why are they coveted and command higher prices? It is because of our perception of them. The perceived difference between tasty and tasteless, valuable and cheap are not real. When the wrong perceptions persist, there is theft (盗, *dao4*).

What if we return to non-being and Tao? We eat just enough to stay healthy so that we can perform self-cultivation. We don't long for fancy foods, we don't covet possessions, and we don't envy others for having what we don't. Thus, there is no motivation to become thieves.

The "theft" Laozi talks about here is not only petty stealing, but it includes theft on a much larger scale that causes widespread suffering. For example, countless wars costing countless lives have been fought only because of perceived valuable commodities, including anything from spices to oil. Every one of them could have been averted if only the human race didn't value rare possessions.

See not the desirable, and the mind is not confused

When we don't covet things we don't have, our mind becomes clear. But, when we continuously desire that which we don't have, our thoughts become muddied, and we lose the composure. Therefore, if we don't want to become corrupt, don't put ourselves in a position to be bribed. If we don't want to be distracted by lust, stay away from pornography. By seeing not the "desirable" (可欲, *ke3yu4*), "the mind is not confused" (心不乱, *xin1bu4luan4*). Instead of being confused, we are directed by our true nature.

Thus the Sage leads by softening the mind, strengthening the belly

In this chapter, Laozi teaches us three things thus far: No competition, no theft, no confusion. What do we do if any of them is challenged? Laozi offers countermeasures in the following paragraphs.

First, we soften the mind. By "softening the mind" (虚其心, *xu1qi2xin1*), we are free of unnecessary baggage. We can do this by recognizing the ephemeral nature of things. Money, fame, status, etc. are not for us to keep forever. If not even life is permanent, how can any of our possessions be permanent? This awareness "softens the mind" and sets us free.

What about "strengthening the belly" (实其腹, *shi2qi2fu4*)? Many people find the word "belly" puzzling. One way to understand this is to refer to the *Yijing* and see how the hexagrams are structured. The *Yijing* uses 64 hexagrams as a means to explain the "System of Changes". Although the hexagrams vary, every one of them consists of six horizontal lines, either continuous or broken, stacking from bottom to top. We can use the hexagrams as metaphors for things in the universe. If we use them as an analogy for our body, the first two lines on the bottom are our legs (implying Earth). The subsequent two lines in the middle are the belly (implying human), and the remaining two at the top are the head (implying Heaven).

By seeing the third and fourth lines as a symbol of human, in contrast to Heaven and Earth, "Strengthening the belly" can be interpreted as protecting our human body from harm. To do that, we must keep to the center and live our life around Tao. Yet another connotation of the third and fourth lines of a hexagram implies "adversity" and "fear". Strengthening the belly, in this sense, can mean to guard against adversity and fear by being vigilant at all times. As if treading on thin ice, we remain alert so that we don't misstep or unknowingly commit bad karma.

Some people also interpret "Strengthening the belly" to mean we should stop eating before we are full because indulging in creature comforts invites gluttony. This interpretation is not wrong, but it is not as profound as the above interpretations suggest.

Weakening the ambition, and toughening the resolve

The "ambition" (志, zhi4) here refers to the aspirations for earthly achievements, such as the pursuit of glory and wealth. These goals are fine, but we must bear in mind that such accomplishments are ephemeral, because the materialistic gains that we obtain are not for us to keep forever. As such, we must not be obsessed with them. Laozi is moderate. He does not say that we should give up *everything*; only that we should be "*weakening* the ambition" (弱其志, ruo4qi2zhi4).

"Resolve" paraphrases 骨 (gu3), which means "bone". It is spiritual in this context and refers to the attainment of Tao. We must weaken the ambition for earthly gains but toughen our resolve for the attainment of Tao.

"Weakening the ambition" and "Toughening the resolve" complement each other. Together, they make us humble but firm; so that we are not easily thwarted by adversity. Worldly ambition is like desire, and it is illusory. "Resolve" is like bone, and it is resolute. We can't physically touch our desire, but we can touch our bone. We need to pay attention to both.

They inspire people to stay not-knowing and not-desiring

The word "people" (民, min2) here refers not to just a country's people but also community members. For example, as a Taiji master, my students are my "people".

Why, as a leader, must we ensure that our people "stay not-knowing and not-wanting"? Is Laozi promoting deception?

"Not-knowing" (无知, *wu2zhi*1) has an unusual connotation here, and it doesn't mean being ignorant or idiotic. The word "not" is not a denial. It refers to non-being, i.e., the non-being of Tao. So "not" knowing is to know the "nothingness" of Tao. It is knowledge of Tao and the true wisdom with an insight into the mystery of Heaven and Earth and the power of Tao Core. It sheds light on the true meaning of life and answers questions like: Why are we here? What happens when we die? How do we cultivate true wisdom?

Similarly, "not-desiring" (无欲, *wu2yu*4) is not *only* about not wanting. Again, the "not" here refers to non-being. It is a desire enriched by the power of non-being. By "softening the mind, strengthening the belly, weakening the ambition, and toughening the resolve", we are ready to have less desire. Gradually, it becomes a desire for non-being.

And they forbid the clever from interfering

Those who are "clever" (智者, *zhi4zhe*3), in this context, are not persons of wisdom. Instead, they are persons of divides and selfishness. They fight to be the "eminent". They are ready to steal precious goods to fulfill their insatiable desires. They deploy clever scams to trick people out of their hard-earned money.

Greedy people are easy targets. If we can "stay not-knowing and not-desiring", they cannot fool us. Even if we are promised the moon, we will not be swayed. By "not-knowing", we walk the path of non-being and become "not-desiring". We are indifferent to gimmicks that "the clever" design to trap us. We forbid them "from interfering" (不敢为, *bu4gan3wei*2).

If we practice not doing, there is nothing that we cannot manage

In the summary of the chapter, Laozi again stresses the importance of practicing "non-doing". As mentioned, it is not about doing absolutely nothing; but doing things by tapping into the power of the non-being of Tao. This further explains what Laozi says in Chapter 2 when he says the Sages "… create but possess not, do but seek no glory, accomplish but claim no credit." By tapping into the nature of non-being, we are able to do by not doing.

When people practice non-doing, they find no reason for contention, to be a thief, or to feel confused. They soften their mind, strengthen their belly, weaken their ambition, and toughen their resolve. By so doing, there is nothing in the world that they "cannot manage" (不治, *bu4zhi4*).

Chapter 4
Fusion of Yin Yang
道冲

*Tao is like
Emptiness in a cup (Tao fuses).
Use it, and it never
seems to fill up
(it is hard to be filled).
Deep as an abyss,
It is like the origin of all things.
Blunt the sharpness,
Untangle the knot,
Blend in with the light,
Merge with the dust.
So translucent,
It doesn't seem to go away.
I don't know whose child it is;
It seems to predate the sage king.*

Two versions of the opening sentences of this chapter are included here, with the second in parenthesis. The first elaborates on the emptiness of a cup, or the formlessness of Tao. The second addresses the fusion of Yin and Yang or the use of Tao. They are different but not conflicting, and both are profound.

Tao is like emptiness in a cup, use it, and it never seems to fill up

Let's look at the first. "Emptiness in a cup" paraphrases 道盅 (*dao4zhong1*). 道 is Tao, and 盅 refers to "a handleless cup", primarily used for wine or water. When given a cup, we tend to look at its physical features, such as the body, handle, or material. They are critical but insufficient to be useful on their own. The cup also needs a "real body": Its emptiness. The emptiness is invisible but indispensable. Just imagine the cup without it! It would not be able to hold anything, and what use is the cup? Although we cannot see the emptiness, it's the purpose of the cup's existence.

Tao, in us, is like the emptiness of a cup. We cannot see it, but it is what we really are. It makes our life useful and enables us to live our true nature. By adhering to its emptiness, we are receptive, compassionate, welcoming, and loving. Without it, we are, then, the opposite: bigoted, selfish, and judgmental.

To live the emptiness, we must not allow ourselves to be "filled up" (盈, *ying*2), i.e., feeling conceited, as Laozi advises in Chapter 41: "The richness of Te looks inadequate." When we fill a cup to the brim, there is no space for the content of Tao to go in. Therefore, we must keep the cup empty so that it can be filled with the proper content and keep Tao alive.

Tao fuses, use it and it is hard to be filled

Now, let's take a look at the second version. "Tao fuses" paraphrases 道冲 (*dao4chong1*). The pictogram 冲 (*chong1*) consists of radical 冫 on the left, and the sub-character 中 on the right. The radical is made up of two components: A dot and a tick. The dot "丶" moves downward, and the tick "✓" moves upward. Together, they symbolize Yin and Yang. The dot is Yang, and the tick is Yin. As for 中 on the right, it means "middle" or "center". When we put the two parts together, the pictogram implies the blending of Yin and Yang.

Yin and Yang are two aspects of the energy that permeate Heaven and Earth. They are contrasting forces within every being. Yang is creative and Yin destructive. We see the interplay of Yin and Yang in the four seasons. Spring and summer are Yang, which flourishes with life. Autumn and winter are Yin, which withers the liveliness away. The transition is gradual. From the warmth in spring to heat in summer, then coolness in autumn to frigidity in winter. Laozi uses the pictogram "fusion" (冲) to describe the ebb and flow of energy. "By blending the Yin and Yang, they produce harmony," Laozi says in Chapter 42. The cycle is unstoppable, moving on and on, and is "hard to be filled" (久不盈, $jiu3bu4ying2$).

The two versions of opening sentences offer different perspectives of the ways Tao works: Emptiness of a cup, and fusion of Yin and Yang. Emptiness is about the non-being. The fusion of Yin and Yang is about being. We need both of them. When we are in emptiness or the constant non-being, we are in the formlessness of Tao Core. We cannot stay in it forever, however, because we have a life to live. We must come out of it and stay in the present, i.e., the being, to meet the daily challenges. We are, therefore, constantly oscillating between the non-being and being. In the scenario of the cup, both the emptiness and its physical features are One. Being and non-being coexist, and they complement each other.

Let's see how we can use fusion in a life situation. If, say, someone attempts to pick a quarrel with us, what should we do? Being empty takes us back to the constant non-being, and we are accommodative. With the non-being, it is hard for us to feel angry even during a quarrel. Then, we are back to the being of the present to manage wane and wax of the Yin and Yang of the energy. To counter the aggressive energy of Yin, we inject into the situation brightness of Yang. We are respectful and forgiving, never mind who is right and who is wrong. With humility and patience, we turn a big problem into a small one and probably a small one into a non-issue. As the saying goes, "No one fights a smiling face."

Deep as an abyss, it is like the origin of all things

Although Tao is difficult to describe, it does not stop Laozi from attempting to do so. In this line, Laozi compares Tao to an "abyss" (渊, *yuan*1), which is unfathomable, far-reaching, and uncontainable. This is an apt analogy of Tao, which has no confines and bigger than Heaven and Earth.

"It is like the origin of all things," says Laozi. Like? It sounds hesitant. Why can't Laozi be more affirmative? Throughout the *Tao Te Ching*, Laozi talks in this tone, because "the Tao that can be described is not the eternal Tao". So the Sage is not unsure. There is a limit to what we can express through words, so we must always give room to things unsaid. Although Tao is elusive, it is "the origin" (宗, *zong*1), or the founding ancestor of all things.

Blunt the sharpness, untangle the knot, blend in with the light, merge with the dust

Laozi enumerates here four tenets that help us to put into practice the art of non-doing. It is amazing how Laozi can so succinctly put together an extensive body of thought in just a few words.

First, sharp edges hurt, so in our daily dealings, we must "blunt the sharpness" (挫其锐, *cuo4qi2rui4*). We file the sharp edges down so they don't hurt. By doing so, we surround ourselves with happy and supportive people and allow positive and vibrant Yang energy to permeate our life. In Taijiquan, we make every movement round, so we don't easily injure others while defending ourselves.

The roundedness is an attitude, not a technique. A teacher can be harsh when pointing out the students' mistakes, and that criticism can be painful to receive. It might sound as if the teacher is speaking with a sharp tongue. But, if the students know the teacher has a round heart, they will understand the teacher's genuine concerns and not be injured by the criticism.

Second, "untangle the knots" (解其纷, *jie3qi2fen1*). The knots here refer to both inner and outer predicaments. When we intervene to stop a quarrel, we are untangling an outer knot. Inner knots, on the other hand, are inner struggles and worries that are, more often than not, results of fixations and refusal to let go. This explains why before we can untangle the knots, we must be ready to accept the ephemeral nature of life.

To some parents, their children can be their "tangled knots". To untangle the knots, they may begin by working internally, and see that their children are with them either to repay kindness or to collect a debt, as prescribed by karma. This awareness helps them accept any behavioral problems with patience and tolerance. It doesn't mean that they are callous, only that they get to see whatever happens realistically. If the children are here to collect a debt, they take the opportunity to pay it off. As parents, they don't dominate; neither do they give up on the children.

Untangling outer knots improves our ability to handle the inner ones, and they both temper our character. We must bear in mind the three basic rules for change management, as mentioned in the *Yijing*, when untangling knots: Know what changes, what doesn't, and see how we can make the changes easy. By doing so, we are both principled and flexible. We can deftly move between the non-being and being and come up with solutions that are simple and effective.

Third, "blend in with the light" (和其光, *he2qi2guang1*). The "light" here refers specifically to divine lights, which is also known as the radiance of Tao. It is the halo we see in portraits of founders of major religions. It is not something we can get from just anybody, because only the completely enlightened have it. It is a fusion of Tao Core and *Yuanyang* the Primordial Yang Energy, as mentioned in Chapters 1 and 25. To "blend in with the light" is to blend in with the divine light, which can be approached in two ways:

First, we seek blessings. We soften our minds to establish the connection. When the mind is softened, we're inclined to see the ephemeral nature of existence and are more ready to let go of baggage, allowing us to bask in the divine light and enjoy its blessings.

Second, we learn from the sages. In addition to seeking blessings, we emulate the sages and assimilate their virtues and compassion. We learn to "create but possess not, do but seek no glory, grow but dominate not, accomplish but claim no credit". In the process, we see how we can "blunt the sharpness, untangle the knot, blend in with the light, and merge with the dust". The more we emulate what the sages do, the nearer we are to Tao, and the deeper we are when blending in with the divine light.

Now, the fourth tenet: "Merge with the dust" (同其尘, tong-2qi2chen2). We identify with those who are trampled like dust, such as the disabled, elderly, impoverished, and the diseased. We care for them as much as we care for ourselves. We don't lose our patience when an elderly or disabled person takes time to cross the road. We feel compelled to help when seeing an orphan who has no one to turn to. In the faces of victims of disasters, we feel their pain. While people turn a blind eye to them and see them as "dust", our hearts go out to them.

By observing the four tenets, we are in both non-being and being. We are in non-being because we walk the path of the formless Tao. We flow with nature and admire its harmony. We look up to the sky and marvel how the millions of stars can live side-by-side with others. There is no fear of collision. So orderly, so peaceful! Also, we see how the light of the sky blends in the dust of Earth, so soft, harmonious, and natural.

When we are in being, we appreciate what we have and are grateful to the abundance of the universe. It is, unfortunately, such a regret that appalling damage have been inflicted upon Earth. Nature erects forests to feed all living things oxygen and to prevent erosion. And, when we cut the forests down to make wood and paper products, we suffocate all living beings, while inviting soil erosion and dust-storms. Out of the human's greed for "the precious goods", we wreak havoc upon the natural order of things and then complain when nature becomes unbalanced. It is disturbing, but we must do what we can to help the world regain its balance.

By seeing the difference between being and non-being, we incorporate non-being into being in all things we do. We call the practice "non-doing". The more competent we are in its practice, the more progress we make in our attainment of Tao.

So translucent, it doesn't seem to go away

"Translucent" is a translation of 湛 (*zhan*4). The word consists of radical 氵 on the left, which means water, and the sub-character 甚 on the right, which means "a quantity of something". This pictogram creates an image of a large body of flowing water and implies the state of ever-flowing and eternity. It is elusive in that "It doesn't seem to go away". The clause paraphrases 似或存(*si4huo4cun2*), which means "as if in existence". If we say it is there, it doesn't seem to be there. If we say it is not there, it seems to be there. It is evocative of the formlessness of Tao.

I don't know whose child it is; it seems to predate the sage king

This sentence is spoken in the tone of an enlightened person. The indication is the use of the word 吾, rather than the usual word for "I" — 我. 吾 is made up of two Chinese characters: "five" (五) at the top and "mouth" (口) below. In the *Yijing*, the number five means "the center". So, it implies the speaker is a person who is "in the center", i.e., enlightened and wise.

I don't know "whose child it is" (谁之子, *shei2zhi1zi3*). It seems to "predate the sage king" (帝之先, *di4zhi1xian1*). It looks like it predates the modern god(s) we know, or Heaven and Earth, and all sages. Thus, it would behoove the sages of all religions to gain an understanding of Tao.

Chapter 5

Keep to the Center
守中

Heaven and Earth are unbiased;
They treat all things as straw dogs.
The Sage is unbiased;
They regard every person as a straw dog.
The space between Heaven and Earth is like a bellows.
Stay hollow and bend not.
Keep moving, and we are carried away.
Excessive words exhaust the reckoning.
It is better to find the center and hold on to it.

Heaven and Earth are unbiased; they treat all things as straw dogs. The Sage is unbiased; they regard every person as a straw dog

A straw dog (刍狗, *chu2gou3*) is an offering made of dry grass or thatch used in ancient times. It is inexpensive, but the devotion it embodies is invaluable.

Offerings are often used during worship of Heaven, Earth, and the sages. The ultimate goal of the practice is to establish a connection with Tao. The world of divides that we are in keeps us away from Tao and inflicts in us anxiety and endless worry. Deep in us, we long to be reconnected with the innocence of Tao. The connection, however, is only possible when there is an induction. This is what Heaven, Earth, and the sages can do for us, and rituals have been developed for us to seek the induction. All spiritual practices have such rituals.

How is this induction established? First, let's see how we can do this with the sages.

We obtain blessings from the sages by "blending in with the light", as mentioned in Chapter 4. For that, faith is fundamental. It is the faith that makes our interaction with the sages possible. An excellent way to demonstrate our faith is to present offerings. The offerings don't need to be expensive. So long as they are offered with all sincerity from the depths of our heart. Even something as inexpensive as a straw dog can do the job.

"The Sage is unbiased". "Unbiased" is a translation of 不仁 (*bu4ren2*). 不 means "not". 仁 usually means "benevolence", but has a special connotation here. The pictogram is made up of radical 亻, which means "human", and the sub-character 二, which means "two" or "divide". So, when we say "the Sage is unbiased" or without 仁, we're saying that the Sage has no divides. "They regard every person as a straw dog." Even when the straw dog we use is inexpensive, as long as we are sincere, the Sage responds. By the same token, if we cannot even offer something as inexpensive as a straw dog, the Sage will not take us seriously.

Similarly, we can seek induction from Heaven and Earth. It is said that there is a spirit in everything, be it a tree, the river, or the mountain. The spirits long to return to their roots, and implore Heaven and Earth for the induction. Again, they have to show their faith, and, in this case, there is no better way than making themselves a straw dog. To be a straw dog, they faithfully follow the law of nature. In response, Heaven gives them their blessings. What if the spirits refuse to be a straw dog? There are no blessings, and they risk elimination from existence. This is survival of the fittest: Those who follow Tao thrive, and those who go against it perish. It is the simplest form of evolution.

Both Heaven and Earth and the sages see it as their mission to free all sentient beings from suffering, so they are eager to help. They regard those with faith as straw dogs and are ready to help them with their transformation. The more devoted the worshipper, the quicker is their attainment of Tao.

The space between Heaven and Earth is like a bellows

A "bellows" (槖籥, *tuo2yue4*) is an air-box that pumps and draws air. The space between Heaven and Earth is where the being and non-being mingle, which behaves like a bellows. When we draw or suppress it, we make being and non-being work for us. Non-being is all-embracing. When it is transformed into being, things arise. From nothing to something and something to nothing: This is how Tao works.

Stay hollow and bend not

When a water hose "stays hollow" (虛, *xu1*), there is no obstruction to the flow of water. When we "bend" (屈, *qu1*) it, a blockage is formed, and the flow of water is disrupted. Similarly for the bellows. A blockage impedes the free flow of air, and it can render the bellows useless. It is, therefore, imperative that we keep the movement of air smooth, without obstruction. These apply to the flow of Tao, which must not be impeded. It has to be as fluid as the revolving seasons.

Unfortunately, bending and the resultant blockages happen all too often in life. They include emotions like bigotry and fixation. We must eliminate them as soon as they arise. This can be achieved by performing daily self-renewal. It is a continuous effort. When an old bend is cleared, a new one can emerge. Even when we are deep in stillness, there are moments of trial. All of a sudden, flashing through our minds are thoughts that steal our focus. They can be a treasure trove of gold or a beautiful lover that draw our attention away, leaving us fixated and stuck. We must be careful.

A way to avoid blockages is to recognize the fleeting nature of life and see existence as images in a mirror. When we are in front of a mirror, our image is there. When we walk away from it, the image vanishes. All forms of existence are as illusory as the images. They vanish when we step aside. With the understanding, there are no more fixations that disrupt our daily energy flow. "Stay hollow and bend not." "Hollow" in this context is the flow of the energy of Tao. It must not be bent.

Keep moving, and we are carried away

When we perform self-cultivation, we move from the divides to the Oneness of Tao. It is, however, not always smooth sailing. We can be distracted by greed that generates movement in the bellows, and we are confused by divides such as the highs and lows, good and evil, and gain and loss. If we "keep moving" (动, *dong*4), they can drag us down deeper and pull us further and further away from Tao. We must be careful not to keep moving and allow ourselves to be "carried away" (愈出, *yu*4*chu*1).

Excessive words exhaust the reckoning

"Words" (言, *yan*2) refers to our thoughts and actions. They become "excessive" (多, *duo*1) when we want more and more, and are carried away by desires for things like glory and wealth. "Reckoning" (数, *shu*4) refers to the use of numbers for figuring things out, similar to what we do when consulting the *Yijing*. When we have "exhausted the reckoning" (数穷, *shu4qiong2*), we cannot achieve anything more by being calculative. The best thing to do is to stop wanting more and return to our center.

It's better to find the center and hold on to it

"Center" is a translation of 中 (*zhong1*). Keeping to it means conforming to Tao. The *Tao Te Ching* teaches us to flow with nature and to do the right thing at the right time. Priorities change as we move on through the various stages in life. As a child, we learn hard like the plant sprouting in spring. As an adult, we work hard like growing plants in summer. When we have built our career, we harvest like what farmers do in autumn. As we grow older, we move on to the winter of conservation. We must be situational and adaptive to changes while keeping to the center and walking the journey of Tao. We adhere to the law of the universe, and waste no energy on the "excessive words" that don't add value. In this way, we "find the center and hold onto it" (守中, *shou3zhong1*).

Chapter 6
Mysterious Feminine
玄牝

Spirit of the valley never dies;
It is the Mysterious Feminine.
The gateway to the Mysterious Feminine
Is the root of Heaven and Earth.
Ever-flowing, it is as if present.
Use it sparingly when need to.

Spirit of the valley never dies

Shouting from the top of a valley, we can hear an echo. It is the emptiness of the valley that responds to us. Laozi uses this as a metaphor for getting a response from the absolute nothingness, and we may call it the "spirit of the valley" (谷神, *gu3shen2*).

If we see the emptiness of the valley as Tao Core, then the "spirit" is its use and "spirit of the valley" a transformation of non-being to being. Since both Tao Core and Tao Use are inexhaustible, spirit of the valley "never dies" (不死, *bu4si3*).

It is the Mysterious Feminine

"Mysterious" is a translation of 玄 (*xuan2*), which refers to things that are beyond our comprehension. What do you think is holding the entire universe together in such perfect order? This is one of the "mysterious" that we are talking about here. To put it simply, anything the sciences cannot explain is a "mysterious". Are they not mysterious? "One mystery after another, the gate to all wonders," says Laozi in Chapter 1.

"Feminine" is a translation of 牝 (*pin4*), which means a female and refers to motherliness. Every living organism is made up of both male and female populations, where the female is responsible for procreation. In this context, we may see the "Mysterious Feminine" (玄牝, *xuan2pin4*) as a mysterious process of procreation. It may be seen as the Tao Use we mentioned earlier in the "spirit of the valley", which creates the myriads of things in the universe.

The gateway to the Mysterious Feminine is the root of Heaven and Earth

At birth, newborns carry with them a strong layer of *taihe* qi. This means that, outside of cultivation, a person is rarely ever closer to Tao than when they are born. It is no wonder, then, that newborns are so natural and innocent. If the umbilical cord is our conduit to the "quantum entanglement" — a phenomenon described by modern quantum physicists — cutting it off severs our direct connection to Tao Core. As a result, we gradually lose our innate innocence and slide into an inextricable state of confusion. If we want the innate innocence back, we must return to Tao Core, and for that, we need to have the severed connection re-established.

This reconnection is never easy. Fortunately, although our umbilical cord was cut off, the part of our body responsible for the connection, the "life gate", is still within us. Every school of spiritual practice has its approach to the reconnection. We have it, too, in Taijigong.

First, we must know where the "life gate" is. It is located on our back, directly opposite the navel. To perform the reconnection, we link the navel back to the "life gate", so that we are back to a state as if before the severance of the umbilical cord. We do this through techniques such as "waist dominance" (主宰于腰) and "relaxing the abdomen to quietly generate the vibrancy of qi" (腹内松静炁腾然). Having restored the conduit, we are ready to connect the qi in our body with the *taihe* qi of the universe. In Taijigong, we call this "Integration of human and Heaven" (天人合一).

When this is done, the "life gate" is back to its innate state (先天). In Tao literature, we change its name back to what it was initially known: the "Mysterious Feminine" (玄牝, xuan2pin4). Now, the life-gate as if the receiver of an "antenna" is reinstalled, and connects our body with the universe. This is why Laozi calls the "Mysterious Feminine" "the root of Heaven and Earth". It allows the qi energy to surge from the soles of our feet to permeate our entire body. At the same time, by connecting to the universe, we harmonize the internal organs of our body with the energy from Heaven.

The reconnection is vital. It is, however, just the beginning of a long journey. In addition to maintaining the conduit by performing the regimen that integrates ourselves with the universe, we must complement it with the tempering of the mind and distillation of our innate nature. At the same time, apply non-doing in everything we do. Tao attainment is a long process. With perseverance, however, we will arrive.

Ever-flowing, it is as if present. Use it sparingly when need to

The *taihe* energy is "ever-flowing" (绵绵, *mian2mian2*). Although it is there for everybody to tap, the uninitiated are not aware of its presence. Laozi thus says it is "as if present" (若存, *ruo2cun2*).

For a trained Tao cultivator, practicing "integrating of human and Heaven" is a regimen that boosts our energy by infusing vitality from the sages. It is good for health and longevity, and it instills wisdom in us. For a Taiji practitioner, it has an added advantage of enabling mastery of advanced techniques of Taijiquan. Laozi, however, reminds us to use the energy only sparingly (不勤, *bu4qin2*). We must not overdo it. The energy is meant for us to attain enlightenment, so we must conserve it and use it for the right purpose. Only when we have fully attained Tao are we as powerful as the universe, and the energy inexhaustible.

Decoding Note: Instead of "use it sparingly", some translations of the *Tao Te Ching* use the word 觐 (*jin4*). In ancient times, this word meant "being summoned to the king". Understandably, the king would summon someone rarely and only when necessary. The use of 觐 is, therefore, not incorrect.

Chapter 7
Cling Not to Self
无私

Heaven and Earth are long-lasting.
They are long-lasting
because they are in Oneness;
And so, they live for a long time.
So the Sages put themselves last,
And they end up ahead.
They cling not to their self,
And their self lasts.
Is it not because they are selfless
That they fulfill their true self?

Heaven and Earth are long-lasting

In terms of time and space, nothing in this world lives as "long" (长, *chang2*) as Heaven, or is as "lasting" (久, *jiu3*) as Earth. We know of trees that live tens of thousands of years. Their ages, however, pale in comparison to Heaven and Earth's, which are in the order of billions of years.

They are long-lasting because they are in Oneness; and so, they live for a long time

Heaven and Earth are long-lasting, because they came directly from the convergence of Tao Core and *Yuanyang*, as explained in Chapter 1. They are not a product of Yin-Yang, so there is no procreation. They retain the Oneness of Tao and "live for a long time" (长生, *chang2sheng1*). "Oneness" paraphrases 自生(*zi4sheng1*), which means "self-born".

In contrast, the human being is a creation of divides and Yin-Yang. We don't derive directly from Tao Core. If we want to be as long and lasting as Heaven and Earth, we must return to the Oneness of Tao through consistent cultivation. We must cultivate our physical body to refine the perpetual body so that we can return to Tao Core.

So the Sages put themselves last, and they end up ahead

As mentioned in Chapter 5, the Sages see freeing the sentient beings from suffering as their mission. Humble and modest, they motivate with compassion and humility and inspire with their quiet devotion. The Sages "put themselves last" (后其身, *hou4qi2shen1*). They don't compete for benefit and attention. Furthermore, pampering their temporal body is, to them, never a priority. Their primary focus is the refinement of the soul and attainment of Tao. Although the Sages remain behind, people are awed by them and willingly follow their lead from behind. As a result, they "end up ahead" (身先, *shen*1*xian*1). In a nutshell, the Sages put their physical self behind, and allow their real self to be ahead and lead.

They cling not to their self, and their self lasts

There is a repetition of the word "self" (私, *si*1) in this line. The first "self" refers to things temporal, and the second to things perpetual. Knowing the importance of self-cultivation, the Sages regard the temporal body as transient, seeing it only as a tool for refining their perpetual self. The Sages are, therefore, indifferent to glorifying the temporal body with fame and wealth. Because they don't cling to their temporal "self", their perpetual, or real, self lasts. "Cling not to their self" paraphrases 无私 (*wu*2*si*1), which means "selfless". "Lasts" paraphrases 成 (*cheng*2), which means "succeed" or "complete".

Is it not because they are selfless that they fulfill their real self?

Being selfless, the Sages "fulfill their real self" when they have achieved the complete attainment of Tao.

Chapter 8

The Highest Good is Like Water
上善若水

The highest good is like water.
Water benefits everything yet contends not.
It stays at low places that all disdain
And it is near to Tao.

Stay in a good place.
Carry the heart of an abyss.
Treat others with kindness.
Speak with sincerity.
Govern with fairness.
Work with competence.
Watch timing for actions.
Since it contends with no one,
It thus has no worries.

The highest good is like water

"The highest good" is a translation of 上善 (*shang4shan4*). 善 is usually translated as "good", but it has a special connotation here. Tao is formless. It relies on Te, its manifestation, to work. For example, through water, we see the benevolence of Tao. Water is selfless; it is willing to travel to and stay at the low and filthy places where everybody dreads to go. Through the Te of water, we see the selflessness of Tao.

Te is described as "good" here. There are, however, various degrees of goodness as far as Te is concerned. Not to overeat is good, but is nowhere when compared to the goodness of a saint who devotes entire life to helping the poor. When Laozi talks about the best quality of Te, he uses the word 善. So not only is 善 good, it is a fine quality of Te. "The highest good", therefore, is the finest quality of Te. Even then, "the highest good" is not Tao. It is only a manifestation of Tao. It is Tao Use, but not the formless Tao Core. It is like water (若水, *ruo4shui3*), which is only close to Tao, not Tao itself.

Water benefits everything yet contends not

Although water is vital to the survival and growth of the myriads of things, and it "benefits everything" (利万物, *li4wan4wu4*), it treats all things as equal and claims credit from none of them. It "contends not" (不争, *bu4zheng1*).

It stays at low places that all disdain and it is near to Tao

Water flows downward and is known for its modesty and humility. It is ready to go anywhere, including low places like a basin of sludge where all things "disdain" (所恶, *suo3wu4*). Water doesn't avoid situations that people loathe to go. It is this "highest good" that allows its Te to be "near to Tao" (几于道, *ji4yu2dao4*).

This virtue is reminiscent of the hexagram "Humility" of the *Yijing*, which comes with the trigram of Earth on top and Mountain below. All of the 64 hexagrams in the Yijing prophesy both fortune and misfortune — except this one. Delightfully, hexagram "Humility" prophesies only good fortune. Indeed, a truly humble person doesn't go wrong when the "highest good" of Te shines through them.

In addition to humility, water boasts seven other virtues that take it to the proximity of Tao.

Stay in a good place

The first of such virtue is to "stay in a good place" (居善地, *ju*1*sh-an*4*di*4). Water is modest. It flows downward and is always ready to go low. Although it benefits everything, it contends with nothing. What is more, it brings the quality of its virtue to places where it gathers.

If we can behave like water, we bring good energy to places wherever we are. When we stay close to Tao by, say, immersing ourselves in fine scriptures, observing good spiritual practices, and performing good deeds, we change the qi energy — also known as feng shui — of the place we live. "If we conform to Tao, the power of Tao flows through us," says Laozi in Chapter 23. The home becomes a place of the "highest good" blessed with good fortune.

Carry the heart of an abyss

The "heart" (心, *xin*1) of water is like an abyss (渊, *yuan*1): So deep and open and is confined by neither time nor space. It is accommodating, ready to accept everything, and calls any part of the world its home. It is happy wherever it is, all the time. It "lets the heart go deep".

Treat others with kindness

Water showers everything with "kindness" (仁, *ren*2). The pictogram consists of radical 亻, which means "human"; and the sub-character 二 (*er*4), which means "two". 二 is made up of two horizontal strokes, which, in this context, may be seen as Heaven and Earth. In an ancient oracle bone script, these horizontal strokes are equal, and together they imply "Oneness of Tao". 二, in this instance, symbolizes equality (quite unlike the divides that we talk about in Chapter 5). It treats everything equally. Talk about kindness! There is hardly anything else in the world that is as kind as water. It nourishes and moisturizes everything it rains upon.

Unfortunately, while water is kind, it showers ill omens as well. This is not the water's fault. When the balance of the world is tilted, water must do something to restore it, resulting in calamities like floods and droughts. Therefore, these "natural disasters" are karmic retribution for what the sentient beings have done. Remember the two horizontal strokes of the character 仁? These strokes correspond with each other: The one above is Heaven, and the one below is the sentient beings on Earth. Water is the measure of balance. If the sentient beings conform to Tao, and the world is peaceful and in balance, so is water. When they disrupt the order, and the balance is tilted, water responds with calamities to make the correction.

Speak with sincerity

Water ebbs and flows as scheduled, and it never goes back on its word. It announces the arrival of winter with the glisten of frost and heralds the advent of spring with the melting of ice. Water "speak(s) with sincerity" (言善信, yan2shan4xin4).

Govern with fairness

Water is fair. It always calls a spade a spade. Builders rely on its bubble to level the ground and wall, and it never incorrectly says the ground is level. If we "govern" (政, zheng4) with the fairness of water, the people are never difficult to govern (治, zhi4).

Work with competence

Water is pliable. Ever ready to serve, it is square when we need it to be square, and round when we need it round. It makes the food we cook safe and delicious, the herbs we boil efficacious, and the tea we brew aromatic. With the "highest good" of water, things work better. Water helps us "work with competence" (事善能, *shi4shan4neng2*).

Watch timing for actions

Water adapts to changes. Should there be a departure from Tao, it brings itself back on track with adjustments that can be as drastic as a natural disaster. "Water can float a boat. It too can capsize it," says one Chinese proverb. Sensitive to changing circumstances, it freezes into ice at low temperature and evaporates into vapor when heated. It acts when the time is right, and "watches timing for actions" (动善时, *dong4shan4shi2*).

Since it contends with no one, it thus has no worries

If we can practice the "seven virtues" of water mentioned above, even when we are still far from the attainment of Tao, we are in its proximity.

"The highest good is like water." The key takeaway, here, is non-contention. When we consider each of the seven virtues, we are inspired to abstain from contending. Tao is formless and has no divide. If we behave like Tao and see everybody as equal, we will feel no need to contend with anyone.

Since it "contends with no one" (不争, *bu4zheng1*), it thus has "no worries" (无尤, *wu2you2*). When there is no contention, there is peace. Although the principle is easy to understand, it is rarely practiced. Not only do people fight for valuable commodities and possessions, but we also quarrel over trivial matters. Isn't it ridiculous?

Taoist Lu Dongbin of the Tang Dynasty said, "Man goes along, and the sages go against. We stumble along the way in between." Ordinary folks follow the crowd, but not the sages. The masses want glory and wealth, but the sages are indifferent to them. People want more, yet the sages want less and practice non-being. What the people see as a loss, the sages view as gain. To understand the merits of non-contention, we need a reverse mindset. It looks disadvantageous in the short run, but how long must we suffer? Wouldn't it be worth it if, in order to attain a higher level of Tao, we only had to suffer for 100 years?

In a fable of Zhuangzi, the little sparrow, puzzled by the actions of the enormous *peng*, a legendary bird of prey, asks, "Why must you fly to the South Heaven Gate that is tens of thousands of miles away? You have enough to eat and a lot of fun here. Why bother to fly so far?" Unfortunately, the tiny bird can't imagine the ambition of the *peng*. The *peng* flies to the South Heaven Gate to attain enlightenment, while the little bird lives only a dozen years and is satisfied by eating worms. How can it even comprehend the *peng*, whose ambition is so much bigger?

To assimilate the virtues of water, we contend not and go to places people loathe. While doing so may sound silly, it takes us to the proximity of Tao and lays us a sound foundation for the final attainment, giving us a hidden advantage.

Chapter 9

Step Back When the Job is Done
功成身退

Hold and fill to the brim;
Better to stop in time.
Sharpen it non-stop,
Can make the blade thin and weak.
Fill the house with gold and jade,
And there is a problem with safekeeping.
Arrogance in prestige and wealth,
Sow the seeds of one's downfall.
Step back when the job is done and glory earned
Is the way to flow with Tao of Heaven.

Hold and fill to the brim; better to stop in time

To "hold" (持, *chi2*) here means clinging on to something, and implies a refusal to let go. We need things to live a life. So there is nothing wrong with desiring. It, however, doesn't mean that we should overdo it. Once we are fixated with having more and more, we become greedy. When we allow the greed to go unbridled, we fill our minds "to the brim" (盈之, *ying2zhi1*) with desires, and this is problematic.

Should this happen, "stop it in time" (已, *yi3*)! Let go of unhealthy desires! Stop the pursuit! I often ask my disciples to find out what they need to sustain them for the rest of their life. Once they have got enough, they should let it go, and focus on self-cultivation for the attainment of Tao.

Sharpen it non-stop, can make the blade thin and weak

The sentence refers to the insatiable greed for things we don't deserve. It is as if we are never happy with the blade, and keep sharpening it. "Sharpen it incessantly" paraphrases 揣而锐之 (*chuai3er2rui4zhi1*). 揣, here, refers to "plotting", which implies obtaining something one doesn't deserve. 锐之 means to "sharpen something", and suggests resorting to harming to achieve one's goals. These are against Tao. Even if we get what we want, the ill-gotten wealth is fleeting. It is not for us to keep forever. "Make the blade thin and weak" paraphrases 不可长保 (*bu4ke3chang2bao3*), which means "cannot last". Heaven is unbiased. We reap what we sow.

Fill the house with gold and jade, and there is a problem with safekeeping

A house full of gold and jade is alluring, but it is unreal. However much wealth we have, we can't take it along when we die. Nothing in this world is permanent. "Fill the house" (满堂, *man3tang2*) with "gold and jade" (金玉, *jin1yu4*), and "there is a problem of safekeeping" (莫之能守, *mo4zhi1neng2shou3*). This is because, eventually, we are going to lose it. Learn to let go early!

The most significant value of life is not to accumulate wealth, but to take the opportunity to cultivate our temporal body for the refinement of our perpetual self. One life builds on another. What we attain in this life makes the next life stronger. Every life cycle is an occasion for refinement. If we don't make the best use of the opportunity to bring us closer to Tao, it is a real loss.

Arrogance in prestige and wealth, sow the seeds of one's downfall

The biggest potential ruin to "prestige and wealth" (富贵, *fu4gui4*) is arrogance (骄, *jiao1*). Looking down on others and feeling self-congratulatory for what we have is to throw our weight around. Wealth is ephemeral. If it vanishes one day, we can't be arrogant anymore. What is left is only sorrow and regret. Even if we don't see any retribution in this life, it is going to weigh on us in our lives to come. We are "sowing the seeds" (自遗, *zi4yi2*) of our "own downfall" (其咎, *qi2jiu4*).

Step back when the job is done and glory earned is a way to flow with Tao of Heaven

Things in the universe move and repeat in cycles. Following spring and summer are autumn and winter. The cycle goes on and on. When "the job is done" (功成, *gong2cheng2*), we have accomplished our goals. When "the glory is earned" (名遂, *ming2sui4*), we have enjoyed the recognition. What comes right after? We must "step back" (身退, *shen1tui4*). After spring and summer are autumn and winter. It is time to leave the success behind, and turn our attention to self-cultivation. Go with the flow of nature. Do the right thing at the right time. This is the way to flow with "Tao of Heaven" (天之道, *tian1zhi1dao4*).

It is, nevertheless, easier said than done. Few can truly let go to "flow with Tao of Heaven". Like what the *Yijing* says, clinging onto the past glory results in us being "a lonely dragon of regret". It is not unlike insisting on wearing thin summer clothes in winter. Not only does it hurt us, if we are a leader of a country, it is also a torment to the people.

Success is the vibrancy of summer, and glory is the harvest of autumn. When winter comes, the best thing to do is to step back and go into conservation. It is Tao of Heaven that no one can go against. We must know when to step back and devote ourselves fully to self-cultivation. One life builds on another. It brings us closer to the attainment of Tao.

Chapter 10
Mysterious Te
玄德

Can we embrace our
Vigor and soul as one,
With no gap between them?
Can we focus our life energy and become
Supple, like a newborn baby?
Can we feel throbbing of a baby
when we reverberate the life energy to attain emptiness?
Can we cleanse our inner vision,
Until not a stain is found?
Can we love our country
And manage our people
By not forcing our will on them?
Can we interact with the universe,
With (without) femininity?
Can we stay not knowing,
When acquiring true wisdom?
It gives birth to it, nurtures it.
It creates but does not possess,
Does but does not seek glory,
Grows but does not dominate,
Accomplishes but does not claim the credit.
This is the Mysterious Te.

This is a very important chapter of the *Tao Te Ching*, where Laozi asks a series of fundamental questions of Tao cultivation. If we can aptly answer them and put the wisdom into practice, we will have no problem experiencing the "Mysterious Te" (玄德, *xuan2de2*) and the Oneness of Tao.

Can we embrace our vigor and soul as one, with no gap between them?

Before we look at the translation, let's go back to the original text, one word at a time. It is hard to appreciate the depth of the sentence without some knowledge of it.

Here you are: "载营魄抱一，能无离乎？". 载 (*zai3*) means "to carry". Here, it refers to the way we carry ourselves. 营 (*ying2*) literally means "to operate", but refers to the qi energy, or vigor, of our body. 魄 (*po4*) may be interpreted as the "soul" or "spirit". 抱一 (*bao4yi1*) is "to embrace as one".

The second part of the question, 能无离乎 (*neng2wu2li2hu1*) simply means: "Can there be no gap between them?"

As a whole, the question means: "Can we get our life energy and spirit aligned and in One, so that they can connect us to Tao effectively?" It is important to feel the undertone of the question. We often think of aligning the body and mind for health. But Laozi wants us to think beyond that. We don't just invigorate our body with energy; we must also nurture it with qi. We not only keep our mind healthy; we must also refine our soul. In this way, not only do we have a healthy body, but also a spiritually fulfilled self.

Can we focus our life energy and become supple, like a newborn baby?

"Focus our life energy" paraphrases 专气致柔 (*zhuan1qi4zhi4rou2*), which means to "cultivate the qi energy within our body". It involves not only breathing, but also the circulation of the qi energy. Doing it properly, we will become as supple as "a newborn baby" (婴儿, *ying1er2*).

Stress, which stiffens our body and blocks the flow of energy, is a common cause of many illnesses. It can develop lumps — the embryo of severe conditions like cancer. Keeping our body supple releases stress and prevents blockages in our body, and it can help us steer clear of the many problems caused by stress. At the same time, it boosts our energy and vigor. This is evident in a newborn baby. Staying relaxed and supple is clearly a key reason why infancy is the stage of a human's life marked by the fastest growth.

In Taijigong, we introduce a series of exercises that help us retain our vibrancy by staying supple through qi cultivation. Yangshenggong, meaning "health nurturing exercise", is one of them. Before starting the exercise, which is for beginners, many trainees can't bend at their waists. After just a few sessions, most of them can touch their toes. My Master Wu Tunan was able to stand on one leg as in the posture of a "golden rooster" (金鸡独立) when he was 102 years old. This is because his qi energy was so strong he was able to remain supple despite the advanced age.

Can we feel throbbing of a baby when we reverberate the life energy to attain emptiness?

Not every edition of the *Tao Te Ching* includes this question. It highlights some critical aspects of Tao cultivation, and is well illustrated by the practice of Taijigong. It is elaborated in the Chapter: Apply the Wisdom to Taijiquan.

Can we cleanse our inner vision, until not a stain is found?

"Inner vision" is a translation of 玄览 (*xuan2lan3*). 玄 means "mystery of the universe". 览 refers to the senses of the six sensory organs, including eyes, ears, nose, tongue, body, and the mind. Drowning our senses in worldly pursuits make us end up in total confusion. It can be derailing and takes one further away from Tao. To prevent it from happening, we must "cleanse our inner vision" regularly. It purifies our heart and prevents the external distraction from disrupting our inner peace. With tenacity, we go deep, and this brings us close to our true selves.

Can we love our country and manage our people by not forcing our will on them?

"Country" (国, *guo2*) here refers not only to a nation but also a community such as a company, a school, or a family. The people are thus not just citizens of a country but also members of a community, such as employees, students, or children.

As a leader of a country, we lead our people to walk the path of Tao and let them experience the benefits. When they know that it is good for them, they will naturally love the community. "Not forcing our will on them" paraphrases non-doing. My disciples follow me to enjoy the benefits of a healthy body by practicing Taijigong that I teach. They are grateful and naturally love the community.

Some editions of the *Tao Te Ching* put the question as: "Can we love our people and lead our country?" From a Tao cultivator's point of view, I prefer the word "manage", instead of "love". When we "manage" the people, we guide them to walk the path of Tao.

This is what I do as a teacher. In addition to teaching Taijigong, I also advise my more-financially-successful students to step back from their work and think beyond just about making more money. They are disciples who are near or past the retirement age, with no reason to keep wanting more. They are metaphorically moving from harvesting in autumn to conservation in winter. The progression is inevitable, and they must be ready for it. In this way, they are less likely to stray from Tao.

Can we interact with the universe with (without) femininity?

"Interact with the universe" paraphrases 天门开阖 (*tian1men2kai1-he2*), which literally means "to open and close the gate to Heaven".

As an individual, we are in the realm of a Small Taiji, and there is a longing to communicate with the Large Taiji, i.e., Tao Core as if a child talking to their parent. This is what we do in Taijigong all the time. Although specific techniques are used, the principle applies to the non-Taiji situation as well.

To benefit from the interaction, we must first be receptive. This explains why in Taijigong, we begin the interaction by performing "With femininity" (为雌, *wei2ci2*). We keep our body relaxed and supple and put ourselves in a state of Yin. This allows us to assimilate a tremendous amount of Yang energy from the universe when the connection is established. In the process, we permeate our body with qi, making our body warm and energized, elevating the level of Yang in us.

The takeaway here is that, contrary to what many people believe, we cannot "stay hard" to assimilate the good energy from the universe. The good energy is Yang, and we cannot attract the Yang energy by hardening our body. We don't attract Yang with Yang; we attract Yang with Yin, and it means softening our body. The more relaxed we are, the more Yang energy we can assimilate, and the warmer our body becomes.

Apply the principle to life; it underlines the importance of listening. When we interact with the universe, we must not keep doing the talking. There must be an adequate space of silence so that messages from the universe can trickle in. When we are in silence, we are "With femininity" and in a state of Yin.

In the parenthesis of the sentence, there is the word "without". It indicates another state of interaction with Heaven — "Without femininity" — when there is only Yang and no Yin. This is a far more advanced stage, and few people, if any, can do it. So it is introduced here as a reference only. It is an ideal state when we integrate ourselves with the Primordial Yang. In this state, there is only Yang and not a bit of Yin. We are back to Oneness. It is the pinnacle of Taijiquan, and only a few people throughout the history of humanity have achieved that.

Can we stay not knowing, when acquiring true wisdom?

"Attaining true wisdom" paraphrases 明白四达 (*ming2bai2si4da2*). The pictogram 明 consists of two sub-characters: 日 and 月, meaning "the sun" and "the moon", respectively. It thus implies "clarity". The second pictogram 白 means "white", which suggests plainness and purity — before the white is dyed into other colors. It is a metaphor of our nature that stays forever with us, even when our physical body perishes. 明白, in this context, is a realization of our true nature.

Additionally, 四 means "four", and 达 means "reach". It implies that if we have attained true wisdom, we can reach out to all four directions — Heaven, Earth, the past, and the future. But, the question Laozi asks is still perplexing: "Can we stay not knowing, when acquiring true wisdom?" What has "not knowing" (无知, *wu2zhi1*) got to do with the true wisdom? In fact, "not knowing" is not about knowing nothing. It is about knowing with the non-being of Tao. If we can live the nature of non-being, we are truly in the know.

Attaining true wisdom in this context, therefore, is never easy. So, we must be wary of people who claim to be truly knowing. Many mystics do that. Although they claim to know the unknown, they are nothing more than self-proclaimed prophets, and can even be a demon. They are unlike sages like Laozi, who have withstood the test of nothingness and truly know. We must be discerning.

It gives birth to it, nurtures it. It creates but does not possess, does but does not seek glory, grows but does not dominate, accomplishes but does not claim the credit. This is the Mysterious Te

Although Tao creates the myriads of things and nurtures them, it possesses and dominates none. This is the virtue of the "Mysterious Te" (玄德, *xuan2de2*).

We talked about the word "Mysterious" in Chapter 1. It is a translation of 玄, which is both Tao Core and Tao One, and another name of Tao. We may, therefore, see the "Mysterious Te" as the virtue of Tao.

Chapter 11

The Non-Being that We Use
虛中

Thirty spokes converge on a single hub;
It is the nothingness within
That moves the cart.
Molding clay into a vessel;
It is the nothingness within
That allows it to be filled.
Making doors and windows;
It is the nothingness within
That makes the house inhabitable.
So, while being brings us benefits,
it is non-being that we use.

This is a simple but insightful chapter. Laozi vividly explains here the concepts of being and non-being and how they are related to each other.

Thirty spokes converge on a single hub; it is the nothingness within that moves the cart

In Laozi's times, the wheel of a horse cart was made up of "thirty spokes" (三十幅, *san1shi2fu2*) that converged on "a single hub" (一毂, *yi4gu3*). No matter how elaborate the wheel was, its hub had to be empty so that the spokes could connect to it to turn the wheel. In the context of Tao, the nothingness (无, *wu2*) in the hub is the non-being that "moves the cart" (有车之用, *you3che1zhi1yong4*). If the hub is filled up, the spokes would have no room to converge, and the wheel cannot turn, rendering the cart useless.

Molding clay into a vessel; it is the nothingness within that allows it to be filled

We mold "clay" (埏埴, *shan1zhi2*) into "vessels" (器, *qi4*) of various shapes and sizes. Although the features of a vessel are important, it is the empty space within it that "allows it to be filled" (有器之用, *you3qi4zhi1yong4*). Without the nothingness, the vessel cannot be filled with any content, and the vessel is no longer a vessel. The nothingness is non-being, and the vessel, being. The being is useful only when there is non-being.

Making doors and windows; it is the nothingness within that makes the house inhabitable

"Doors and windows" are translations of 户 (*hu4*) and 牖 (*you3*), respectively. When building a house, doorways and window frames must be left empty, or the house is inaccessible. Besides, there must be empty space in the house, or no one can live in there. The structure of the home is the being, but it is the empty spaces within, the "non-being", that "makes the house inhabitable" (有室之用, *you3shi4zhi1yong4*).

So while being brings us benefits, it is non-being that we use

This final sentence summarizes the chapter: Both being and non-being are important. One of them brings us substance, and the other provides actual use.

It underlines the fundamental of self-cultivation. Our physical body is the being that makes self-cultivation possible. If we look at our body as a vessel and leave it full, no wisdom can go in, and the cultivation would be of no benefit. Therefore, we must focus on keeping our vessel empty and unfilled so that it can remain useful. The ultimate use, however, is not with the physical body; but the perpetual body that we are cultivating. "So while being brings us benefits (利, *li4*), it is non-being that we use (用, *yong4*)," says Laozi.

Chapter 12
Focus on the "Belly"
为腹

The five colors blind the eyes,
The five tones deafen the ears,
The five flavors numb the palate,
Chasing and hunting madden the mind,
Precious goods lead one astray.

Thus the Sage focuses on the belly,
Not the eyes.
Hence they choose one and
Reject the other.

The five colors blind the eyes. The five tones deafen the ears. The five flavors numb the palate

The five colors (五色, *wu3se4*) — red, yellow, blue, black, and white — brighten the world. It sounds strange that Laozi says they "blind the eyes" (目盲, *mu4mang2*). Just imagine how boring the world would be without the colors. There is no doubt that the colors add to the excitement of life, but when we are fixated on them, we lose sight of Tao, and this is what Laozi means by blinding the eyes. Laozi uses them as metaphors for distractions. Similarly, for the "five tones" (五音, *wu3yin1*) and "five flavors" (五味, *wu3wei4*). When we indulge ourselves in them, we become distracted from our primary goals of self-cultivation and metaphorically become blind, deaf, and lose our sense of taste.

Chasing and hunting madden the mind

When we are "chasing" (驰骋, *chi2cheng3*) and "hunting" (田猎, *tian2lie4*), we are obsessed with catching the prey. We are controlled by the external pursuits, which "madden the mind" (心发狂, *xin1fa1kuang2*). It takes away the calmness that is essential to self-cultivation.

Precious goods lead one astray

We treasure "precious goods" (难得之货, *nan2de2zhi1huo4*) because of divides and selfishness. Obsession with materialistic pleasures inspires us to be greedy. And, all too often, we also do unscrupulous acts to satisfy the desires. "Astray" paraphrases 妨 (*fang2*), which means "obstacle", and implies hindrances in the pursuit of Tao.

Thus the Sage focuses on the belly, not the eyes. Hence they choose one and reject the other

The Sage keeps themselves fed for self-actualization, not to satisfy the external distractions that meet their eyes.

Of all external perceptions, our eyesight is the most detrimental and distracting. Seeing is not only believing; it also stimulates our perceived desires. When we see something we like, we want it and are thus distracted from our focus on Tao. Here, Laozi uses the eyes as a metaphor for all kinds of external desires.

A sage is a sage because they are directed by Tao rather than external distractions. The Sage chooses to focus on their "belly" (腹, *fu*4), rather than allowing themselves to be misguided by their "eyes" (目, *mu*4).

As explained in Chapter 3, the word "belly" has a special connotation in the *Tao Te Ching*. From the perspective of the human body, the belly is in the middle. It thus implies "keeping to the center". In the hexagrams of the *Yijing*, "belly" is represented by the third and fourth lines of the hexagram, known as the humanity lines. They are in the middle, implying the center and Tao. Focus on the belly is, therefore, to keep to the center and follow Tao.

Decoding Note: As far as life-energy cultivation is concerned, the belly plays a unique role. It is where the *dantian*, also known as the reservoir of qi energy, is located. In Taijigong, several techniques help us focus on the belly. Among them are "closing the eyes to nurture the mind" and "looking inward to conserve energy".

Chapter 13

Greet Praises and Insults with Alarm
宠辱若惊

Greet praises and insults with alarm.
Nourish our body
As if there is imminent danger.

Why greet praises and insults with alarm?
Praises lift us up,
Insults press us down.
Getting them is alarming,
So is losing them.
This is to greet praises and insults
With alarm.

Why nourish our body
As if there is an imminent danger?
We are faced with danger because of our bodies.
If we had no body,
What danger do we have?

Thus those who treasure the world
As their own body
Are worthy of guarding the world
Those who love the world
As their perpetual self
Are worthy of governing the world.

Greet praises and insults with alarm

To most of us, praises (宠, *chong*3) and insults (辱, *ru*3) are antithetical. In the eyes of the Sage, they are not. It is the sense of divides that creates the difference between them. If we have to struggle with them, it shows that we are yet to hold to the Oneness of Tao. It is alarming (惊, *jing*1).

To a person of Tao, praises and insults exist alongside each other and are part and parcel of life. When there are praises, there are insults and vice versa. If we can take them in stride, we are in calmness — a state of mind that is essential to our pursuit of Tao.

Like everyone else, I have experienced a fair share of praises and insults. This is one of them. Teaching Taijigong is pleasant, and I am rewarded with praises from my disciples and the likes. It, nevertheless, brings me insults as well. I was once even called a "liar"! It is prompted by my performance of the *"lingkongjin"* (凌空劲), an advanced Taiji technique that allows me not only to lift an opponent without touching him but also to toss him in the air like a big ball. It sounds miraculous, but it is a genuine technique. Not everybody understands it, though. As a result, some of them clamored on the Internet that it was fake. How should I react to it? I accept it as no different from the praises and see it as a motivation for me to do better and remain humble. Even if the insults are untrue, they are trials of my tolerance. There is no need for me to feel angry or hit back.

Nourish our body as if there is imminent danger

The sentence sounds perplexing. Why "nourish our bodies" (贵身, *gui*4*shen*1) as if there is an "imminent danger" (大患, *da*4*huan*4)? Nourishing our bodies is not wrong. We need a healthy body for self-cultivation, and we must take good care of it. We must, however, know where the limit is. When the body is pampered with creature comforts, we may lose the motivation for self-cultivation, which is the primary purpose of our life. We must not miss the forest for the trees. Again, Laozi uses the word "as if" (若, *ruo*4) here. He is telling us that although we must be wary, it doesn't mean that we are in danger, especially if we can nourish our bodies without overindulgence. Only when the balance is lost that the danger is imminent.

Why greet praises and insults with alarm? Praises lift us up; insults press us down. Getting them is alarming, so is losing them. This is to greet praises and insults with alarm

If we can see things in Oneness, then there is no difference between praises and insults. While one "lifts us up" (上, *shang*4) and the other "presses us down" (下, *xia*4), neither of them is permanent. We can bask in praises this moment and drench in insults the next. Greet both with alarm and respond to the situations appropriately. We must bear in mind the 11th hexagram of the *Yijing*, Pervading, that says: "Energy of Heaven flows downward, and that of Earth moves upwards." Allow the two energy to mingle and find their harmony, and we are in peace.

Why nourish our body as if there is an imminent danger? We are faced with danger because of our bodies. If we had no body, what danger do we have?

When we have a body, there is always danger associated with it, be it physiological or psychological or both. On the one hand, we must take good care of it because we need it for self-cultivation. On the other, we must not over pamper it and distract ourselves from the ultimate goal of refining our soul. As long as the balance is maintained nourishment will complement, rather than hamper, our cultivation of the perpetual self and there will be no imminent danger.

What if we had "no body" (无身 *wu2shen1*)? Then there is no danger. The "no body" here refers to having a body of non-being, i.e., the perpetual body. If we are focused on cultivating the perpetual body and perturbed not by the temporal body, then there is no danger. The perpetual self is fine, no matter what has happened to the temporal body.

Thus those who treasure the world as their own body are worthy of guarding the world. Those who love the world as their perpetual self are worthy of governing the world.

The two sentences sound alike, but paint two very different scenarios. They are distinguished by the words "treasure" and "love"; and "guard" and "govern".

"Treasure" is a translation of 贵 (*gui4*). When we treasure the world, we take care of it as if it is our temporal body. What we do to it, however, is primarily in forms. We help the poor, care for the old, provide for the orphans, and offer relief to disaster victims. Unlike the formless Tao, however, we are also hungry for fame and recognition. The good deeds earn us a good fortune but don't add much to our attainment of Tao. Even then, we can be trusted for "guarding" (寄于, *ji4yu2*) the world.

"Love" is a translation of 爱 (*ai4*). When we love the world, we are devoted to it as if it is our perpetual self. It is like nourishing our bodies to attain a bigger purpose. Not only do we provide for the people when governing the world, but also help them to refine their soul and walk the path of Tao. We are, therefore, "worthy of governing the world". "Governing" paraphrases 托于 (*tuo1yu2*), which means to be "entrusted with the mission to do something".

Chapter 14
Discipline of Tao
道纪

Look at it, yet it cannot be seen,
We name it "ji".
Listen to it, yet it cannot be heard,
We name it "xi".
Grab it, yet it cannot be grasped,
We name it "wei".
These three are indefinable,
So we see them as One.

High up, it is not bright,
Down under, it is not dark.
Unceasing like an unbroken thread,
It cannot be named.
To the nothingness it returns.
It is in the shape of no shape,
And the form of no form,
It is transient and shimmering.
Face it, and we cannot see its front,
Follow it, and we cannot see its end.

Keep to Tao of the primordial,
To guide our lives today.
Knowing how the universe began,
we know where the discipline of Tao is engraved.

Look at it, yet it cannot be seen, we name it "*ji*". Listen to it, yet it cannot be heard, we name it "*xi*". Grab it, yet it cannot be grasped, we name it "*wei*". These three are indefinable, so we see them as One

As we have discussed previously, Tao is formless, so we can neither see, hear, nor grasp it. Laozi, however, gives each of the scenarios a name. "*Yi*" (夷) or "*ji*" (几) refers to its invisibility. "*Xi*" (希) about its inaudibility. "*Wei*" (微) depicts its intangibility. Be it *ji*, *xi*, or *wei*; each refers to the formless Tao and its use.

Despite the name, all three are still "indefinable" (致诘, *zhi-4jie2*). They are, after all, non-being, and we cannot define them precisely. Laozi, therefore, "sees them as One" (混而为一, *hun4er-2wei2yi1*). The word "One" here has two implications. First, the very one source that all three of them were derived from. Second, the Oneness that manifests the formless Tao.

In Taijiquan practice, we are in the state of One when we permeate our entire body with the qi energy. When this happens all three of them, *ji*, *xi*, and *wei* become tangible and robust enough for us to rely on them for self-defense. Even if we don't practice Taiji, we can perceive them if we are truly relaxed, and the feeling becomes stronger after some practice. We can even connect to Tao through them.

My Master Wu Tunan used to say, "Oh, *wei*, *ji*, *xi*! They are full of wonders!" In Taijigong sparring, we listen to each of them to decide how to counteract. As previously discussed, if we are competent, we can even control an opponent without touching their body. From *wei* to *ji* to *xi*, it is indeed a journey of wonders.

High up, it is not bright. Down under, it is not dark

Although Tao is invisible it resides in us as a constant, known as the "essence of Tao" (道性, *dao4xing4*). Since it is a constant, we cannot add or subtract anything from it. Even when we have advanced in our attainment of Tao, it does not change the essence. By the same token, the essence of Tao in a sage is not necessarily better than that of an average person. "Bright" is a translation of 皦 (*jiao*3), and "dark" is a translation of 昧 (*mei*4). It doesn't mean that it is bright when it is high up (其上, *qi2shang*4), and "dark" when it is down under (其下, *qi2xia*4). It is a constant.

Unceasing like an unbroken thread, it cannot be named

Tao is ever-present. It is like an unbroken thread (绳, *sheng*2) which has been around since the beginning of time. It is still around today and will extend its presence into the future with no end in sight. "It cannot be named" (不可名, *bu4ke3ming*2). A name makes it specific and lose many of its nuances. This highlights the peculiarity of learning Tao. We cannot treat Tao like an object. We have to feel it with our hearts. Similarly, if we want to learn from the sages, we must assimilate their wisdom and learn from what they do. There must be faith, and we must be prepared to behave like straw dogs, as discussed in Chapter 5. The straw dogs are worthless, but the faith they convey is golden.

To the nothingness it returns

Although all things return to the "nothingness" (无物, *wu2wu4*), not all returns (复归, *fu4gui*1) are the same. There are three different realms of nothingness or non-being: The Large, Medium, and Small Taiji. The "Taiji" here is not the same as Taijiquan, the exercise we practice for health. Literally meaning "the supreme ultimate", it is a state of Tao where various forms of existence reside. The Large Taiji is the formless Tao, which is larger than the universe and constrained by neither time nor space. It is where a person who has attained Tao returns to. The Medium Taiji is the universe that we are in, and the Small Taiji is what we are. Depending on their situations, all things return to their respective realms of nothingness. Even the universe goes through its life-cycle and eventually return to the nothingness.

From nothing to something, then something to nothing, the cycle goes on and on. For the myriads of things, most of them return to the small Taiji.

The ultimate aim of a person of Tao is to return to the Large Taiji. It is very unlikely that we can do it within a life-cycle. The returns are cumulative. We have to go through many cycles of Small Taiji and have one cycle improved upon the last. This is why the primary objective of a person of Tao is self-cultivation. By refining our souls life after life, we may one day arrive at the Large Taiji.

It is in the shape of no shape, and the form of no form

Essentially, every existence is in "the shape" (之状, *zhi1zhuang4*) of "no shape" (无状, *wu2zhuang4*), and "form" (之象, *zhi1xiang4*) of "no form" (无象, *wu2xiang4*). As a human being, before we came into existence in our current shape and form, we had been no shapes and forms. When we perish one day, we return once again to no shape and form. So the shape and form that we have now are, in essence, neither shape nor form. They are temporal.

It is transient and shimmering

"Transient and shimmering" paraphrases 惚恍 (*hu1huang3*). They are a reflection of a phenomenon like a flickering light. Now we see it, and now we don't. Both pictograms consist of radical 忄, which means "heart". It implies that they are related to our original self. 恍 also consists of the sub-character 光, which means "light". It refers to the *taihe* qi energy that lights us up and keeps us alive in the present. When the light goes off, we vanish. This is what happens when 惚 takes place. The pictogram consists of the sub-character 忽, which is made up of 勿 and 心, which may be interpreted as "having no heart". With the heart disappearing, we are in the nothingness.

We are "now in the non-being, and now in the being". It is another way of saying "in the shape of no shape, and form of no form". This is what we experience during meditation. Transient is in the state of non-being and shimmering, being. It depicts the brevity of life. Whether it is a person who lives a hundred years or a mosquito that survives only a week, they all eventually return to nothingness and back to no shape and no form. Knowing this makes us even more determined to make the best use of our temporal body to refine our perpetual self.

Face it, and we cannot see its front. Follow it, and we cannot see its end

No one knows when Tao began. It has been around since the dawn of time and is older than the universe we know. Although it is extremely old, it is here to stay. There is no end of it in sight. Tao, therefore, has no beginning and no end. This is why you can see neither its "front" (首, *shou*3) nor its "end" (后, *hou*4).

Keep to Tao of the primordial, to guide our lives today. Knowing how the universe began, we know where the discipline of Tao is engraved

If we know the Tao of "primordial" (古, *gu*3), which since the beginning of time is the underlying principle of the universe, we are able to use it to guide (御, *yu*4) us in our daily lives today. We will get to see the timeless secrets and treasures of all of existence, leading us onto the path toward the full attainment of Tao. If we know "how the universe began" (古始, *gu*3*shi*3), we know how the universe was created and cannot help but to marvel at the Oneness of Tao. Through it, we will see how the law of the universe operates, and adhere to the "discipline of Tao" (道纪, *dao*4*ji*4).

Chapter 15

Seek Not to be Filled to the Brim 不盈

*The ancient masters of Tao were
Subtle and profound.
They were unfathomable.
As they were unfathomable,
They can only be remotely described.*

*Watchful, as if crossing a river of thin ice;
Wary, as if surrounded by hostile neighbors;
Cordial, as if receiving a guest;
Fluid, as if ice about to thaw;
Plain, as if wood yet to be carved;
Accommodating, as if an empty valley;
Opaque, as if muddied water.*

*Who has the patience to wait
Till the mud settles, and the water is clear?
Who can remain unmoving
Till the moment of action arises by itself?
Those who embrace Tao
seek not to be filled to the brim.
Since they are never filled,
They can wear out and renew
(return to be what they actually are).*

The ancient masters of Tao were subtle and profound. They were unfathomable. As they were unfathomable, they can only be remotely described

Nothing seems to baffle the "ancient masters" (善为道者, *shan4wei-2dao4zhe3*), whom Laozi describes here as "subtle and profound". They were able to read the situations that they were in with accuracy and identify a strategy for change in time. They were composed, calm and unruffled even under daunting circumstances, and always in control. "Subtle" is a translation of 微妙 (*wei1miao4*), where 微 implies Tao; and 妙 refers to its use. "Profound" paraphrases 玄通 (*xuan2tong1*), where 玄 means "mystery of the universe"; and 通 means "discerning".

How exactly the ancient masters manage to do the extraordinary things they did is anybody's guess, and so they were known to be "unfathomable". Fortunately, Laozi depicts here what they could have been by having them "remotely described" (强为之容, *qiang-2wei2zhi1rong2*) in the passages below.

Watchful, as if crossing a river of thin ice

"Watchful" is a translation of 豫 (*yu2*). To understand what it means, we may refer to the 16th hexagram of the *Yijing* that shares the same name. The hexagram is made up of two trigrams: "Thunder" on top and "Earth" below.

Essentially, the hexagram is about celebration. Instead of talking about having a good time, Laozi suggests that we must remain watchful. This is what made the ancient masters unique. They never let go of their vigilance, even at the time of celebration. It is like walking on a frozen river in winter. While it is fun, any misstep on the thin ice can mean a tragic fall into the icy water. The same applies to other things in life. The path of self-cultivation, for example, is supposed to be joyous and peaceful. We must, however, remain vigilant so that we will not fall into the perilous sea of distractions.

Wary, as if surrounded by hostile neighbors

"Wary" paraphrases 犹 (*you*2), the name of a small animal which is timid and always on its guard. "Surrounded by hostile neighbors" paraphrases 若畏四邻 (*ruo*4*wei*4*si*4*lin*2), which means "as if afraid of the neighbors". Apparently, Laozi is not suggesting that we must be nervous all the time. What he is telling us is that we must remain alert and conscientious, even when no one is watching.

Cordial, as if receiving a guest

"Cordial" is a translation of 俨 (*yan*2), which carries the connotation of "dignity". The ancient masters were discreet, heedful and attentive all the time, as if "receiving a guest" (若客, *ruo*4*ke*4). They were not just polite but genuinely friendly and warm.

Fluid, as if ice about to thaw

"Fluid" is a translation of 涣 (*huan*4). To understand what the word means, let's refer to Hexagram 59 of the Yijing. It is the same Chinese word, but in Yijing it also means "Dispersion" when interpreted in English. It has trigram Wind on top and Water below. When the wind blows over the water, it creates waves, and this implies lurking danger. If the pursuit of Tao is a voyage, the ancient masters were careful when helming the boat.

"Thaw" is a translation of 释 (*shi*4), the process that sees ice melt into water. The ancient masters were "fluid" (涣, *huan*4). When any distraction intrudes, they steer clear of it like allowing ice to melt into water and remain firmly anchored to their pursuits.

Plain, as if wood yet to be carved

"Plain" is a translation of 敦 (*dun*1), which means "authenticity". The ancient masters were as plain (朴, *pu*3) as a piece of wood yet to be carved, where the authenticity of Tao is still alive within them.

They were kind to everybody and accomplished without contending with anyone.

Accommodating, as if an empty valley

"Accommodating" is a translation of 旷 (*kuang*4). The pictogram is made up of two sub-characters: 日, and 广, meaning "the sun" and "broadness", respectively. So the ancient masters were warm and broad-minded. They were like "an empty valley" (谷, *gu*3), which is echoic and thus responsive. It implies that the masters were always ready to serve when people approached them for help.

Opaque, as if muddied water

"Opaque" is a translation of 浑 (*hun*2). It is reminiscent of the state of chaos before Heaven and Earth emerged. Although opaque, like the muddied (浊, *zhuo*2) water, the ancient masters never lost their authenticity. "The lotus coming out from the mud unsoiled," the Chinese saying goes. They were in control of situations, not the other way around. Despite their extraordinary capabilities, they looked no different from others. They valued the essence, not the appearance.

Thanks to Laozi, with the depictions above the ancient masters are no longer totally "unfathomable" to us. It helps us put their wisdom into practice.

Who has the patience to wait till the mud settles, and the water is clear?

"Mud" is a translation of 浊 (*zhuo*2). It is a metaphor of things that mar our vision. When our mind is filled with greed, for example, our cultivation suffers. It bogs us down and derails our course. When it happens, shaking the muddy water does not help. Instead, we must keep it calm to allow the sediments to settle. We wait till "the mud settles" (浊以澄, *zhuo*2*yi*3*cheng*2) and "water is clear" (徐清, *xu*2*qing*1). By the same token if distractions strike, we must not worry about them. Rather, calm ourselves down, acknowledge their existence, know their sources, but refuse to pay any attention to them. By calming our mind and returning to a state of no-thought we regain clarity.

Who can remain unmoving till the moment of action arises by itself?

When there are no thoughts, there is peace. With the peacefulness 安 (*an*1), we enter into a state of absolute tranquility. Moments later, "the moment of action" arises by itself. "Action" is a translation of 动 (*dong*4), and "the moment of action" paraphrases 生 (*sheng*1), which means "alive". The law of reversal has it that at the extreme, things take a reverse course. When we remain unmoving (安以久, *an*1*yi*3*jiu*3) we are in the deep tranquility, and "action arises by itself" (动之徐生, *dong*4*zhi*1*xu*2*sheng*1) when time is right. New messages trickle in, and the *taihe* energy in our body is stabilized, thereby transforming the tranquility into "absolute stillness".

Those who embrace Tao seek not to be filled to the brim. Since they are never filled, they can wear out and renew (return to be what they actually are)

In the state of "absolute stillness", we embrace Tao and are in harmony with it. "Embrace" paraphrases 保 (*bao*3), which means "to protect". It is important, however, that we must not have ourselves "filled to the brim" (盈, *ying*2) with desires. Only then can we continually improve, so as to "wear out and renew". "Wear out" is a translation of 敝 (*bi*4), which means "obsolete"; and "renew" 新成 (*xin*1*cheng*2). When an old life perishes, a new life begins. With continuous effort from one life cycle to another, we transcend from the Small to the Middle and then the Large Taiji. When we are at the Large Taiji, we are back to the core of Tao. Since the core of Tao is the origin of all things, anything in it is in its original form; hence providing credence for the phrase "what they actually are" (敝不新成).

Chapter 16
Fulfillment of Destiny
復命

Toward absolute nothingness,
Hold fast to tranquility.

In the bustle of all things,
I see them returning to their origin.

Despite the diversity,
All things to their roots, they return.

Returning to the root is tranquility.
Tranquility is a Fulfillment of Destiny.
Fulfillment of Destiny is constancy.
Knowing constancy is insight.
Not knowing constancy
leads to disaster.

Knowing constancy, we accept what is.
Accepting what is, we are impartial.
By being impartial, we understand the universe.
Understanding the universe,
We know the Greatness of Tao.
The Greatness of Tao is eternal.
If we are as formless as Tao,
We are never in danger.

Toward absolute nothingness, hold fast to tranquility

This chapter is, in itself, an excellent guide to Tao cultivation.

"Toward" (致, *zhi*4) points to a direction. "Nothingness" (虚, *xu*1) refers to a state of mind. "Nothingness" emerges with the realization of the impermanence of being. Things in life are unreal. They don't follow us at our passing. With the realization, there is no fixation on things. It is, however, just a beginning. Nothingness by itself is insufficient to help us attain Tao. We have to go further and move toward "absolute nothingness" (虚极, *xu*1*ji*2), which is the formlessness of Tao Core.

The direction, however, is important. When the direction is clear, we are calm and able to "hold fast to tranquility" (守静笃, *shou*3*jing*4*du*3). We keep to the calmness and are totally undisturbed. With calmness, we dive deep into the "absolute nothingness", which is similar to the profound stillness of Zen. There is no desire, no thoughts. We are on the path to witnessing Tao.

In the bustle of all things, I see them returning to their origin

While the Sage is in profound stillness, the rest of the universe continues in their hustle and bustle (并作, *bing*4*zuo*4). The Sage observes in silence the enigma of changes that return all things to their origin.

Despite the diversity, all things to their roots, they return

Trees grow taller; grasses color themselves green. Livestock is docile, unlike the ferocious tiger and wolf. In the meantime, a bird flies high up in the sky, and fish swim freely in the water. The universe enjoys its diversity (芸芸, *yun*2*yun*2) when all things live their nature and destiny.

However varied they are, "all things to their roots they return", a process Laozi describes as *Guigen* (归根, *gui1gen*1). The ways things return to their roots are not homogeneous. They can be broadly divided into three levels, corresponding to the realms of Taiji, which we mentioned in Chapter 14: Large, Medium, and Small. The Large *Guigen* takes us back to the Large Taiji, or the Tao Core. The Medium *Guigen* returns us to the Medium Taiji, or nothingness of the universe. In most cases, things return to the Small Taiji, before they are reborn and begin another cycle in the Small Taiji.

The level of *Guigen* one takes is not always a matter of choice. Why is a mosquito a mosquito? No one can say for sure. It seems to us there is a predestined path for it to follow, something not within its control. In comparison to beings like mosquitoes, the human is lucky because we enjoy a certain level of choice. We are gifted with the intelligence for self-cultivation, making attaining the Large *Guigen* possible. It is thus lamentable if we don't make the best of the opportunity. Even then, achieving the Large *Guigen* is not something that we can complete in a lifetime. Not even a few. It can be countless Small *Guigens* before we arrive at the Medium, and then Large *Guigen*. What is important, however, is that the first steps are taken. In the passage below, Laozi gives us some pointers on how we can get started.

Returning to the root is tranquility

Tranquility is an extreme Yin, something like the depth of winter or stillness in meditation. Using a seasonal plant as an illustration, it sprouts in spring and flourishes in summer when the Yang energy is intense. Having reached its peak, the law of reversal sets in, and the Yang energy begins to sap, ushering in autumn and winter when the plant matures and, before long, perishes into the tranquility of extreme Yin. A return to the root of Small *Guigen* has drawn a full circle.

This is the pattern in which things in the universe evolve. When a cycle comes to an end, a new one begins. More often than not, however, things don't move beyond the confines of the Small Taiji. Completion of a Small *Guigen* brings about another cycle within the Small Taiji. The breakthrough takes place only upon consistent self-cultivation. For that to happen, not only must we repeatedly "hold fast to tranquility", but also move on to the "absolute nothingness" to witness the core of Tao.

Tranquility is a Fulfillment of Destiny

"Fulfillment of Destiny" (复命, *fu4ming4*) is a very important concept in the *Tao Te Ching*, and it is more profound than "returning to the root", or *Guigen*. Tranquility takes us into the state of "absolute nothingness" for *Guigen*, and "Fulfillment of Destiny" brings back to us our true nature.

A major milestone of Tao attainment, "Fulfillment of Destiny" can be achieved at two levels: Large and small. A large fulfillment is an accumulation of an infinite number of small fulfillments. As we mentioned earlier in this book, it is said that the Buddha went through 500 reincarnations before he attained complete enlightenment. We are unlikely to take anything less. The accumulation is gradual. In the case of the Buddha, every life he lived was a small fulfillment built on the last. In Taijigong, we call it "returning is an accretion of cycles (往复需有折叠)". We begin a new cycle on the foundation of the last. Then, there is another cycle, yet another cycle.

Fulfillment of Destiny is constancy

Fulfillment of Destiny is "constancy" (常, *chang2*). We don't do it once, and then forget about it. We keep at it constantly. We don't only do it in this life, but life after life. It is a process of refinement, where we temper our nature and purify our soul. It builds us the foundation for attaining Large Fulfillment of Destiny, allowing us to be in One with the constant Tao.

Knowing constancy is insight

"Insight" paraphrases 明 (*ming2*), which means "clarity". With the constancy, we "light up our heart" (明心, *ming2xin1*) that guides us in "realizing our true nature" (见性, *jian4xing4*).

Not knowing constancy leads to disaster

If we don't know the constancy, we face the dire consequences of deviating from Tao. It can be a "disaster" (凶, *xiong1*).

Knowing constancy, we accept what is. Accepting what is, we are impartial. By being impartial, we understand the universe. Understanding the universe, we know the Greatness of Tao. The Greatness of Tao is eternal. If we are as formless as Tao, we are never in danger.

The passage elaborates on the nature of the constancy of Tao.

Knowing the constancy, we bask ourselves in the benevolence of Tao, which teaches us to be tolerant and to "accept what is" (容, *rong2*). By doing so, we are no longer bridled by prejudices. We are broad-minded and accommodating.

When we accept the ways things are, we treat everything fairly. We are selfless and "impartial" (公, *gong1*).

Being impartial, we don't impose our will on others. We know that we are just a tiny part of the universe. "Understand the universe" paraphrases 王 (*wang2*), which means "Kingly". The pictogram 王 consists of three horizontal lines and a vertical stroke. Each horizontal line symbolizes a realm — Heaven, Humanity and Earth. The vertical stroke links the three lines together. By knowing how the three realms are interacting with one another, we know the law that governs the universe.

The realization brings us closer to the Greatness of Tao. "Greatness" implies an infinity of hugeness and the formlessness of Tao. It has no boundary and is gigantic beyond imagination.

The Greatness of Tao is eternal (久, *jiu*3). If we can live the Greatness of Tao, we are "formless". "Formless" here paraphrases 没身 (*mo*4*shen*1), which literally means "without a body". When we are without a body, there is no death, and thus we are never in danger.

Chapter 17
The Supreme 太上

The Supreme
Know the unknowable.
Next is one whom
People love and praise.
Next comes the one they fear.
Next comes the one they despise.

Those who don't trust enough
will not be trusted.

Nonchalant and reticent.
When the work is done,
And goal achieved,
The people say,
"We did it all naturally!"

This chapter is often interpreted from the leadership perspective. Obviously, it is not the only way to read it. Since this book is on "decoding" the *Tao Te Ching*, let's look at it from the perspective of spiritual cultivation.

The Supreme know the unknowable

"The Supreme" paraphrases 太上 (*tai4shang*4), which refers to a person who has fully attained Tao. This is how Laozi is sometimes revered as. First-century Taoist Zhang Daoling, who turned Taoism into a religion, addressed Laozi as the "Supreme Old Gentleman" (太上老君). Tang Taizong, Emperor of the Tang Dynasty from 626 AD to 649 AD, wanted a historical sage to honor his imperial family. He was delighted to have found Laozi, with whom he shared a common family name, and thus honored him as his ancestor and addressed him as "The Supreme".

"Unknowable" paraphrases 不知 (*bu4zhi*1). It literally means "not" knowing. As mentioned in Chapter 3, the "not" here is not a negation, but a noun that describes the non-being of Tao. In this context, "unknowable" refers to Tao, and thus the true wisdom. The word "know" is used here to paraphrase 有之 (*you3zhi*1), which literally means "having it". Reading the sentence as a whole, the "unknowable" is, to the sages, knowable. Having fully attained Tao, they are able to put the invisible into visible use.

Next is one whom people love and praise

Second to The Supreme are the accomplished person of Tao who brings peace and happiness to people. "Love and praise" is a translation of 亲 (*qin*1) and 誉 (*yu*4), respectively. In mythology, they are portrayed as deities who always respond to the sentient beings' pleas for help. They are, therefore, loved and praised.

Next comes the one they fear

Next comes the righteous, who are impartial and intolerant of any wrongdoing. In mythology, they are portrayed as the deities of justice who punish anyone who acts against Tao. It explains why they are the ones whom the people fear (畏, *wei*4).

Next comes the one they despise

Then, there are the despicable whom the people despise (侮, *wu*3). They have no qualms about hurting people in the name of Tao to fulfill their selfish desires. People are fearful of them, but the fear is different from the fear people have for the righteous. It is more a fear of detestation than awe.

Those who don't trust enough will not be trusted

Trust (信, *xin*4) is the basis of Tao cultivation. If we have trust in Tao, we are able to feel it and be awed by it. We are like an empty cup, always ready to imbibe its nourishment. The greater the trust the stronger is the connection. Even when we are still far from the level of "the Supreme", we get better and are likely to become an enlightened person whom people "love and praise". In contrast, when there is not enough or no trust at all, there is hardly any connection, and we enjoy no blessings.

Nonchalant and reticent

"Nonchalant" is a translation of 犹 (*you*2), which also means "hesitation" and thus implies "calmness". "Reticent" paraphrases 贵言 (*gui*4*yan*2), meaning "something hard to explain". When there is no trust in the listener, it makes no difference no matter how hard we try to convince. Tao has to be internalized, and not everybody is ready for it. We must be patient.

When the work is done, and goal achieved

"Work is done" is a translation of 功成 (*gong1cheng2*), and "goal achieved" 事遂 (*shi4sui2*). If we are consistent in our practice, we will get the work done and eventually achieve our goals of Tao attainment.

The people say, "We did it all naturally!"

If we go with the flow of Tao, we are blessed by it. If we don't, we suffer a lack of it. This is only natural. A person of Tao is aware of the implications. Thus, when they accomplish their goals, they say, "We did it all naturally".

Chapter 18

When Great Tao is Lost
大道废

When Great Tao is lost,
Self-righteousness arises.
When wisdom is missing,
The great pretense comes close behind.
When kinship falls apart,
People talk of filial piety and love.
When the country is in chaos,
There are praises of loyal ministers.

When Great Tao is lost, self-righteousness arises

The "Great Tao" (大道, *da4dao4*) refers to both the Tao Core and Tao Use. It "creates but doesn't possess, acts but doesn't seek glory, grows but doesn't dominate, accomplishes but doesn't claim credit". When it is "lost" (费, *fei4*), self-righteousness arises, and it governs the world with divides. Now, the rights and wrongs are determined not by Tao, but by ego and self-interests. Conflicts arise, and people suffer.

    Decoding Note: Levels of Tao attainment are named differently. Sometimes, similar things are given different names, even within the *Tao Te Ching* itself. Cross-references are useful to avoid such confusion. The "Great Tao" of this chapter, for example, is similar to the "Supreme" mentioned in Chapter 17, as well as Te and "non-doing" in Chapter 38. The "self-righteousness" mentioned here corresponds to the enlightened whom "people love and praise" in Chapter 17. "Propriety" and "chaos" of Chapter 38 are related to what people "fear" and "despise" in Chapter 17, respectively.

When wisdom is missing, the great pretense comes close behind

With the abandonment of the Great Tao wisdom (智慧, *zhi4hui4*) is discarded, and the "great pretense" (大伪, *da4wei3*) comes close behind. Now, people's intelligence is channeled not to the cultivation of Tao, but deception and artifice. If we want society to prosper, we must not allow the distorted wisdom to rule and fool people.

When kinship falls apart, people talk of filial piety and love

"Kinship" is a translation of 六亲 (*liu4qin1*). 六 mean "six", and 亲 means "kinship". It refers to one's closest relatives, including parents, siblings, spouses, and children. When the Great Tao prevails, everybody is like a family, even for people who are not part of the kinship. On the other hand, when the Great Tao is lost, even the closest of relatives cannot get along. No wonder there is a lack of "filial piety" (孝, *xiao*4) and "love" (慈, *ci*2) when the kinship "falls apart" (不和, *bu*4*he*2).

When the country is in chaos, there are praises of loyal ministers

"Loyal ministers" is a translation of 忠臣 (*zhong*1*chen*2). A country is in chaos (混乱, *hun*4*luan*4) when the Great Tao is lost. Divisive rulers, however, always call on their ministers to stay "loyal" when that happens. If the ministers die for such rulers, they are helping the rulers to go against Tao. What is more, they miss their golden opportunity for cultivating their souls. The "loyalty" is, in fact, foolishness.

Chapter 19

Bring Down the Ego, Desire Little
少私寡欲

*Give up "sanctity" and cleverness,
People profit a hundredfold.
Say no to self-righteousness,
People return to filial piety and love.
Abandon guile and greed,
No longer are there robbers and thieves.*

*These three are more than rhetoric.
About them, attention is drawn to the tenets below:*

*Live plainly, embrace simplicity.
Bring down the ego, desire little.*

This chapter complements the previous, elaborating further on ways to deal with the chaos resulting from the abandonment of the Great Tao.

Give up "sanctity" and cleverness, people profit a hundredfold

A leader of a country with the Great Tao bears the best interests of the people close to their hearts. Unfortunately, when the Great Tao is lost, in their place are leaders who are divisive and self-centered. They will do anything to cling on to power and wealth, even if it means deception and plunder. Many such leaders, ironically, want people to believe that they are sacred and saintly. "Sanctity" is a translation of 圣 (*sheng*4), "cleverness" 智 (*zhi*4), and "profit" 利 (*li*4). If people can see through their lies, they "profit a hundredfold".

Say no to self-righteousness, people return to filial piety and love

Similarly, as mentioned in the previous chapter, self-righteousness is used by reckless leaders to whitewash their selfish qualities. By rejecting the self-righteousness, it helps return the society to the Oneness of Tao. People are equal and respect one another. When this happens, love for families is spontaneous without force or pretense. There is no need to preach filial piety and love.

Abandon guile and greed, no longer are there robbers and thieves

"Guile" here paraphrases 巧 (*qiao*3); and "greed" 利 (*li*4). Eager for quick gains, the people of guile turn to deception and thievery. They bribe to make a fast buck or flatter to cheat a promotion. If they are in control of the country's vital resources, the extent of their corruption can dent the country's economy. If the people can reject those with guile the Great Tao will be back. Everybody is then contented with what they have and perceives not the need to become "robbers or thieves" (盗贼, *dao4zei2*).

These three are more than rhetoric

The damage resulting from the three types of behavior mentioned above are so tremendous, and we can go on and on to talk about them. They are, however, more than "rhetoric" (为文, *wei2wen2*). Rather than arguing in words, concrete counter-actions are needed.

About them, attention is drawn to the tenets below:

Here, Laozi admonishes in the tone of a teacher. "Attention" paraphrases 令 (*ling4*), which is a command. "Tenets" paraphrases 所属 (*suo3shu3*), which implies "what has been agreed on".

Live plainly, embrace simplicity

"Live plainly" is a translation of 见素 (*jian4su4*), and "embrace simplicity" 抱朴 (*bao4pu3*). In this context, 朴 also means Oneness of Tao. If we can "live plainly", we are happy and content. We enjoy abundance in whatever situations of life. If we can "embrace simplicity", we are in harmony with the universe and are in the proximity of the formless Tao.

Bring down the ego, desire little

"Bring down the ego" is a translation of 少私 (*shao3si1*). Laozi doesn't expect us to become selfless overnight, so he suggests that we begin with having less (少) ego. "Desire little" is a translation of 寡欲 (*gua3yu4*). Similarly, there is no need for us to practice total abstinence to follow Tao. Just avoid overindulgence and distraction. What is important is to get started. By following it up with one concrete step after another, we are in the state of tranquility before moving "toward absolute nothingness", as mentioned in Chapter 16. It makes the attainment of Tao achievable.

Chapter 20

The Mother of Wisdom
食母

Learn the eternal wisdom
And there are no worries.

What is the difference
Between being polite and rude?
What is the difference
Between being good and evil?
What people fear,
We cannot afford not to fear.
Desert the wisdom,
And we lose the Center.

Others are bustling,
Feasting heartily and
Walking up the terrace in spring.
I alone am indifferent, not knowing where to go
I am innocent like an infant yet to smile.

I am drifting as if knowing nowhere to go.
Others have more than what they need,
While I seem to be left alone.
I cherish the heart of a fool.

*Simple and humdrum.
Others look knowing and bright,
While I alone look gloomy and depressed.
Others are savvy and sharp,
While I alone look muddled and dull.
Transient, it is like an unsettling sea.
Shimmering, it is as if having no end.*

*Others are engrossed,
While I alone am stubborn and uncouth.
I alone am different from others,
Faithfully imbibe nourishment from
The Mother of wisdom.*

Learn the eternal wisdom, and there are no worries

This is a very confusing chapter. Many translations begin it by saying, "Give up learning". But is learning wrong? The confusion is probably caused by the word 绝 (*jue2*), which usually means "ending". Since 学 (*xue2*) means "learning", then to say that 绝学 means "giving up learning" doesn't sound implausible. The advice, nevertheless, is incongruent with the rest of the *Tao Te Ching*. Something is missing.

To make sense of the phrase, we must know that 绝 has multiple meanings. In addition to "ending", it also means "ultimate" or "eternal". Seeing in this light, we may then also interpret 绝学 as the "ultimate knowledge" or the "eternal wisdom". Since Tao is ultimate and eternal, could it be that the Sage is urging us to learn the teachings of Tao? Does the phrase make more sense now?

There is a critical difference between eternal wisdom and practical knowledge. We rely on practical knowledge to earn a living, but the eternal wisdom to refine our soul. A doctor needs medical knowledge to treat a patient; a farmer must know the soil and the seeds to grow the crops. No matter how much we know about a subject and the number of academic degrees we earn, however, the usefulness of the practical knowledge fades with the passing of our life.

It is the eternal wisdom that provides continuity. It gives us clarity of the meaning of life and leads us to see the ephemeral nature of things. Now that we are no longer constrained by gain and loss, we are free of stress and anxiety. "There are no worries" (无忧, *wu2you1*). Once we have acquired eternal wisdom, we can benefit from it life after life. It plays a crucial role in our attainment of Tao.

What is the difference between being polite and rude?

When talking to people, we tend to enjoy polite rather than rude reply. Can we, therefore, conclude that one is showing more respect than the other? With the eternal wisdom, we go beyond. Respect is not in what we say, but in what is deep in us. Here, Laozi uses 唯 (*wei*2) to denote a polite response, and 阿 (*e*1) a rude one. A cordial reply or even a ninety-degree bow isn't necessarily more respectful than a rough response. If we cannot see the underlying intent, we cannot see the essence and are still remote from Tao.

What is the difference between being good and evil?

Again, with the eternal wisdom, we don't rely on the worldly standards to define good and evil. Since Tao is formless there is ultimately no difference between them. "Good" is a translation of 善 (*shan*4), and "evil" is 恶 (*e*4). Like Laozi says in Chapter 18, when the Great Tao is lost, self-righteousness prevails. So do the divides such as good and evil. These are judgments based on ego and self-interests rather than Tao. If we can return to the formlessness of Tao everything is in Oneness, and no longer are there good or evil.

What people fear, we cannot afford not to fear. Desert the wisdom, and we lose the Center

This is another confusing passage of the chapter. For clarity, let's refer back to the original text.

Let's look at the second sentence first. "Desert the wisdom, and we lose the Center" is a translation of 荒兮，其未央哉. Because it begins with 荒 (*huang*1), which means "desert", it tends to grab more of our attention. Thus some translators see it as a negation of the preceding statement "what people fear, we cannot afford not to fear". In fact, 荒 is not the anchor here. The primary word of the sentence is 央 (*yang*1), which means "the Center". With the new focus, the meaning becomes clear: If we lose our center, we are going to neglect the primary pursuit.

Let's use the story of the Buddha to explain what it means. Before the Buddha attained complete enlightenment, he was Prince Siddhartha, and he had a wife and son. When Siddhartha deserted everything to pursue his spiritual interests, his father, the king, sent troops after him. The determined prince refused to turn back. Exasperated, the king wrote him a letter of reprimand, which read: "Your father is getting old, and the country needs you back to succeed the throne. You refuse to come back; this is "disloyalty". You defy your parents' will; this is impiety. You abandoned your wife and son; this is inhumane. I sent the guards to take you back, and you'd rather let them be beheaded for failing the mission; this is lack of righteousness. From disloyalty, impiety, inhumanity to being unrighteous, you commit the four sins all at once. Are you good or evil?"

But was it good or evil? Had Prince Siddhartha regarded what he did as evil, he would have "deserted the wisdom and lost the center", and wouldn't have attained complete enlightenment in the end. It would have been a great loss to the world as we wouldn't have had his blessings for the past centuries! Was the Buddha wrong?

Following the question on the difference between good and evil, Laozi concludes: "What people fear, you cannot afford not to fear." Had Prince Siddhartha been fearful of what other people feared, he would have succumbed to the demands of the mundane world — spending his life with his wife and son and succeeded the throne. This world, as a result, would have been deprived of the spiritual beacon. While the Buddha had to endure being an "evil" for 82 years, the sacrifice paled in comparison with the tremendous contributions he made. Most of us tend to be far too short-sighted as worldly pleasures blind us. So, we should be wary of what most people fear.

Others are bustling, feasting heartily and walking up the terrace in spring

People are busy indulging in worldly pleasures. They feast away heartily and enjoy the breathtaking landscape by walking up the terrace. "Bustling" is a translation of 熙熙 (*xi1xi1*). "Feasting heartily" paraphrases 享太牢 (*xiang3tai4lao2*). 享 means "enjoy", and 太牢

refers to "beef, mutton, and pork". "Terrace in spring" is a translation of 春台 (*chun1tai2*).

I alone am indifferent, not knowing where to go. I am innocent like an infant yet to smile

The worldly pleasures, nevertheless, are no allure to the Sage. "Indifferent" paraphrases 泊 (*bo2*). Since the Sage is indifferent, people don't really notice him. To them, judging by the worldly standards, the Sage appears "not knowing where to go" (未兆, *wei4zhao4*). It is a misunderstanding. The Sage does not follow the norm. He has no divides. He is as pure and innocent as "an infant who is yet to smile" (未孩, *wei4hai2*).

I am drifting as if knowing nowhere to go

Here, the Sage describes himself as a tiny boat, which drifts along in the wind, without an itinerary in mind. "Drifting" is a translation of 乘乘 (*cheng2cheng2*).

Others have more than what they need, while I seem to be left alone

Most people work hard for the accumulation of wealth. They are thus better off and have more than enough to spare (有余, *you3yu2*). The Sage is different. He doesn't keep more than what he needs, so he is an odd one out. "Left alone" is a translation of 遗 (*yi2*). Not being part of the world, the Sage is disregarded.

I cherish the heart of a fool

Most people cannot understand the Sage. To them, it is difficult to comprehend how a person can be indifferent to worldly pursuits. They thus take him as "a fool" (愚人, *yu2ren2*). The Sage simply laughs it off. They are not wrong: "I cherish the heart (心, *xin*1) of a fool". The Sage is indeed foolish in the eyes of others.

Simple and humdrum. Others look knowing and bright, while I alone look gloomy and depressed

"Simple and humdrum" paraphrases 沌沌 (*chun*2*chun*2). While others look "knowing and bright" (昭昭, *zhao*1*zhao*1), the Sage appears to be "gloomy and depressed" (昏昏, *hun*1*hun*1). Since most people are financially better off, they look smart. In contrast, the Sage's "career" is nothing but the cultivation of Tao. His focus is not on the temporal existence but the perpetual self, and there is nothing much for him to crow about. It makes the Sage look as if a person with no future.

Others are savvy and sharp, while I alone look muddled and dull

People are "savvy and sharp" (察察, *cha*2*cha*2). They are, however, at the same time, petty and calculative. In contrast, the Sage looks "muddled and dull" (闷闷, *men*1*men*1). The use of 闷 is interesting. The pictogram is made up of 门, which means "door" and 心, which means "heart". It implies that the Sage "discreetly keeps the heart indoors". When the heart is kept indoors, it doesn't roam about. This is another way of saying "keeping to the center". Since his focus is on inner peace, he contends with no one and is not calculative.

Decoding Note: To decipher the *Tao Te Ching*, we often have to resort to disassembling the Chinese pictograms, rather than looking at dictionary definitions of the words. The character 闷 is a case in point. Seeing it, the heart being kept indoors is more vivid than interpreting it as "boring", as defined in dictionaries. The approach brings us deep into the underlying nuances, and it can be done when we are spiritually connected to Laozi.

Transient, it is like an unsettling sea. Shimmering, it is as if having no end

We use "transient and shimmering" to paraphrase 惚恍 (*hu1huang3*) in Chapter 14 for the illustration Small *Guigen* — a returning to the root in the Small Taiji. Here, we use the same pictograms again, but to describe Big *Guigen*, a return to the Large Taiji or the formless Tao.

Although the pictograms are the same, the interpretation is different because of the different context here. The first pictogram 惚 means "vacillation" and implies fickleness of mind, which wavers "like an unsettled sea" (若海, *ruo4hai3*). This is what happens to most of us in the mundane world. The second pictogram, 恍, in contrast, implies the "light in the heart". It refers to the heart of Tao. While we cannot avoid being fickle-minded at times, if we can be consistent in the cultivation, we will one day experience a sudden convergence with the radiance of Tao. This is the Big *Guigen*, i.e., a major return to the destiny that greatly elevates our attainment of Tao. We must keep the heart of Tao shimmering. The pursuit is as if "having no end" (无所止, *wu2suo3zhi3*).

Others are engrossed, while I alone am stubborn and uncouth

"Engrossed" paraphrases 有以 (*you3yi3*), which means "having something to rely on". Most people are engrossed in the pursuit of worldly pleasures. "Stubborn" is a translation of 顽 (*wan2*), and "uncouth" paraphrases 鄙 (*bi3*). Since the Sage is indifferent to worldly pleasures, he is not well off and thus has no social status to crow about. In the eyes of the ordinary folks, he is uncouth. It, however, doesn't stop the Sage from his pursuit of Tao. As mentioned in Chapter 28: he "knows the honor, and shns not the insult."

A story of the highly-revered monk Sixth Patriarch illustrates this well. He lived with a group of hunters for fifteen years. Because he was relying on them for a living, he had no status to talk about.

Everyone looked down upon and bullied him. The disdain didn't seem to bother him at all. He did what he ought to. While others were feasting on fish and meat, he ate only the vegetables that were meant to complement the meat. He looked "stubborn and uncouth", but was, in fact, wiser than any of the hunters around him.

I alone am different from others. Faithfully imbibe nourishment from Mother of wisdom

The Sage is unique. He is different from others. "Faithfully" paraphrases 贵 (*gui*4). The pictogram consists of three components: 中, 一, and 贝; meaning, respectively, "middle", "Oneness", and "treasure". Putting them together, it denotes a pure, trusting, and sincere devotion. "Imbibe" is a translation of 食 (*shi*2), which means "food" or nourishment. In this context, it is the blessings of the Mother of wisdom. As mentioned in Chapter 1, "Mother" refers to Oneness and Use of Tao, which created the universe. We may, therefore, paraphrase the sentence as: "We sincerely seek blessings of Oneness of Tao." Tao is formless, and it is through Oneness that we return to it.

Chapter 21

Now We See It and Now We Don't
恍惚窈冥

A glimpse of Te
Reflects the nature of Tao.

Tao as a thing,
flickers like a light.
Now we don't see it, and now we do,
There is a form in it.
Now we see it, and now we don't,
There is a thing in it.
Empty and silent,
There is the essence in it.
The essence is real,
There is faith in it.

From the beginning of time till today,
Its name is not lost,
By means of it, I read all creations.
How do I know the behaviors of all creations?
By means of these!

A glimpse of Te reflects the nature of Tao

"A glimpse of Te" paraphrases 孔德之容 (kong3de2zhi1rong2). The phrase literally means "seeing Te in a hole". Metaphorically, since Te is a manifestation of Tao, it comes directly from Tao, and so they are from the same "hole". In other words, if we want to describe Te, we must know the nature of Tao. While Te comes in all forms and shapes, we can always trace it back to Tao. The only difference is that Tao is formless, while Te is with form.

Tao as a thing, flickers like a light

When manifested in things, Tao is like a flicker of light. Now you see it, and now you don't (惚恍, as explained in Chapter 20). It vacillates between the being and non-being. In the non-being, it is a "return to the root"— known as *Guigen*, as mentioned in Chapters 16 and 20. If it is a Small *Guigen*, our temporal body vanishes into the non-being. If it is a Large *Guigen*, our eternal body returns to its true nature. Then we are back to the being of the mundane world again. Between the two states of existence, we witness the wonders of the universe.

Now we don't see it, and now we do, there is a form in it. Now we see it, and now we don't, there is a thing in it

"Now we don't see it" is non-being, and "now we do" is being. Between non-being and being, the myriads of things are born.

Here, Laozi groups the presence of being into "form" and "thing". "Form" (象, *xiang*4) is a living being, such as a human. "Thing" (物, *wu*4) is a non-living being, such as a mountain or a river. In the "flickers" of Tao, the "form" and the "thing" take shape, and they bring into existence the diversity of the universe. They are the myriads of things from One Source. Like Laozi says, in every being, "there is a form in it" and "there is a thing in it".

Together they shape the world that consists of both the sentient and non-sentient beings.

Empty and silent, there is the essence in it

"Empty" refers to an utmost emptiness (窈, *yao*2), and "silent" the utmost serenity (冥, *ming*2). In Buddhism, they contribute to the "Chan (Zen) stillness". In Taijigong, we call it "absolute stillness". It is a state of mind Laozi depicts in Chapter 16 as "Toward absolute nothingness, hold fast to tranquility". When we are in absolute nothingness and silence where distracting thoughts are absent, actions arise. Within the actions, there is "the essence (精, *jing*1) in it". When the essence is connected to our "original spirit" (元神), which we inherited from our previous life, we move on to a cycle of *Guigen* that takes us back to the root source and our true nature.

Decoding Note: The "essence" is similar to a form of mystical energy that we can feel at places of worship. Generally, good energy with substantial Yang is beneficial, and bad energy with substantial Yin is harmful. We must, therefore, be wary of the type of energy we assimilate. Accumulation of the Yang energy brings us wisdom to become a person whom people "love and praise", as mentioned in Chapter 17. In contrast, accumulation of the Yin energy can turn us wayward, making us a person people "despise".

The essence is real; there is faith in it

As previously discussed, the "essence" returns us to our root by way of the *Guigen*. Every cycle of return further refines the essence, contributing to the eventual complete attainment of Tao. The essence is "real" (甚真, *shen*4*zhen*1). What is even more important is that "there is faith in it". Faith (信, *xin*4) is a conduit where the divine intelligence can be routed to us, making the messages audible and helping us with our Tao attainment. When the essence is added with the faith, our commitment becomes unshakeable. We are connected with the "original spirit" of our previous lives, and have completed another cycle of "Fulfillment of Destiny". It takes us closer to the complete attainment of Tao.

From the beginning of time till today, its name is not lost

"The beginning of time" (古, *gu*3) is a time of the past. It is non-being. In contrast, "today" is the substantiality of being. "Its name is not lost". The "name" refers to Tao. Be it being or non-being, it is never "lost" and is always in existence.

By means of it, I read all creations

"All creations" (众甫, *zhong*4*fu*3) refers to the myriads of things generated by One Source. Having attained Tao, the Sage is able to read (阅, *yue*4) the nature of every creation and the karma associated with it.

How do I know the behaviors of all creations? By means of these!

How does the Sage know the behaviors of all creations? The Sage is already at the levels with "the essence" and "the faith". At the same time, the Sage is well-versed with Te. These allow him to know the law of nature that governs "the fate of all creations" (众甫之然, *zhong*4*fu*3*zhi*1*ran*2).

Chapter 22
Embrace Oneness 抱一

Yield to preserve the whole,
Bend to become straight,
Empty to fill,
Decay to renew.

Less is gain,
More is in disarray.
The Sage thus embraces One,
As a model of the world under Heaven.
Those who are not bigoted, see the light,
Those who are not conceited, shine.
Those who are not haughty, earn the glory,
Those who are not complacent, grow.

As they contend not,
The world cannot contend with them.

Is the ancient saying
"Yield to preserve the whole"
Empty words?
No. Those who sincerely do so
Are made complete.

In this chapter, Laozi teaches us how, in the world of divides, we can attain completeness by complementing one quality with another.

Yield to preserve the whole

Can a straight line be turned into a circle? We can do so by bending the line and have its two ends meet. By "yielding" (曲, *qu*1), a full circle is formed to preserve the "whole" 全 (*quan*2).

This is a preferred way to handle conflicts. When there is a willingness to yield or concede, the chances of leading to a happy resolution are high. It is, however, possible only when there is a common goal. Otherwise, the two ends have no basis to converge. This explains why we must avoid countering force with force. When one of the parties is willing to yield, the other should explore common ground for a solution. Divorce is an example. Divorce is getting more common these days, but many of the cases could have been averted. The differences very often can be ironed out by the willingness to yield and find common ground. As a rule, the stronger party — be it the husband or wife — must take the initiative. This is Tao of humility.

Bend to become straight

"Bend" paraphrases 枉 (*wang*4), which means "being wronged". We tend to put up an intense defense when we think we are wronged. A person of Tao, however, is ready to pull through a raw deal if need be. In a world that is illusory, they see no absolute difference between praises and insults. Although being wronged is hard to swallow, it tempers their character. By bending, they can straighten the path to the attainment of Tao. We must learn to bend so as to be "straight" (直, *zhi*2).

The story goes that the old monk Guangqin was once accused of stealing money from the donation box he was entrusted with. Because his conscience was clear, he saw no need to argue and took the accusation in his stride. When the truth finally surfaced to prove that he had been wronged, his disciples were all praise for his exceptional virtue of "bending to be straight".

Empty to fill

The word "empty" paraphrases the pictogram 洼 (*wa*1), which literally means "a pit". The deeper the pit, the more water it can hold. It implies the more humble we are, the more capacity we have to "fill" (盈, *ying*2) ourselves with wisdom.

Decay to renew

"Decay" is a translation of 敝 (*bi*4). As part of a life cycle, things age and decay, taking them to an end of the cycle before a renewal (新, *xin*1) takes place. The vitality of spring and summer declines when autumn and winter set in, but reinvigorates as the new spring approaches. Death needs not to be an end in itself. For a person of Tao, it ends the temporal life but also enables a new beginning, paving the way to higher attainment.

Less is gain

"Less" is a translation of 少 (*shao*3). It refers to earthly desires, which are insatiable. "Gain", on the other hand, is a translation of 得 (*de*2), which refers to growth in Tao attainment. They are two sides of an equation. The time and effort we spend on the worldly pursuits are at the expense of that for self-cultivation. By having less earthly desires, we enjoy more spiritual gains.

    Decoding Note: Remember that, in Chapter 1, Laozi says, "Thus in the constant non-being, there is a desire to see its wonders." The "constant non-being" is signaled by having less. "Wonders" is a translation of 妙 (*miao*4). As explained in Chapter 1, the pictogram consists of two sub-characters: 女, which means "female" or "soft"; and 少, which means "less". Putting the two of them together works marvels. The five virtues we learn in this chapter — to yield, bend, empty, renew, and having less — are all related to the "wonders". They are critical to the realization of our true nature and a fulfilled life.

More is in disarray

"More" here refers to insatiable desires. If we do not know when to stop, we will want ten million when we have a million, and then more or more. In the end, we are going to be swamped by nothing but our desires and push the pursuit of Tao aside. The more desires we have, the more we want, and the more we are "in disarray" (惑, *huo*4).

The Sage thus embraces One, as a model of the world under Heaven

What we learn in this chapter may be summarized in one word: "One" (一, *yi*1). It refers to Tao One. "The world under Heaven" (天下, *tian*1*xia*4) is derived directly from Tao One. We find much of how it works in the unspoiled nature. It makes an excellent "model" (式, *shi*4) for emulating the practice of Tao.

    The Sage embraces One (抱一, *bao*4*yi*1), rather than the Zero of Tao Core. Tao Core is formless; it does not help the myriads of things directly. It has to rely on Tao One, its manifestation, to do the work. One has forms and shapes to interacts with things. By the same token, the Sage cannot help anyone when he is in the stillness on a remote mountain as he is in Tao Zero. He has to come out of it to "embrace One" so that he can take concrete actions to help. To the Sage, "embraces One" is *the* mode of working, not Zero.

Those who are not bigoted, see the light

A person who is "bigoted" (自见, *zi*4*jian*4) cannot see the merits of the tenets taught in this chapter. Because they are not ready to yield, bend, empty, renew, and have less, they are like a cup filled to the brim that refuses the infusion of wisdom. Only when they can let go of the bigotry that they can "see the light" (明, *ming*2) and understand how, through the practice, they can discover their true self.

Decoding Note: Bigotry also happens to people who see their spiritual path as The ONLY correct path. In truth, all spiritual paths lead to enlightenment and are, thus, equal. We choose a path based on our inclination for better results, not that it is the only path. When we are not bigoted, it enables us to "see the light" and have clarity on the path to attain Tao.

Those who are not conceited, shine

Bigotry is about thoughts. Conceit mentioned in this sentence is about behavior. When we are conceited (自是, *zi*4*shi*4), we are arrogant. We think what we do must be right and refuse to change. As a result, we don't open up to the teachings of Tao. If we are not conceited, we are prepared to adopt the practice of Tao to be part of us and begin the self-cultivation. Only through the practice can we allow the wisdom to "shine" (彰, *zhang*1) through us.

Those who are not haughty, earn the glory

"Haughty" paraphrases 自伐 (*zi*4*fa*2). 伐 has a connotation of starting a fight. Here, it implies having a big ego. Haughty people want everything their ways. Driven by divides, they are selfish, pretentious, dominating, and hungry for credit. These qualities conflict with Tao and are hindrances to Tao attainment.

Those who are not complacent, grow

"Complacent" is a translation of 自矜 (*zi*4*jin*1), which means thinking too highly of oneself. It is similar to conceit, but with a slight difference. When a person is conceited, they insist on doing what they do, even if it is harmful. When a person is complacent, they are just thinking highly of themselves. So, if we are not conceited, we don't do things that are harmful. Rather, we practice Tao cultivation. In this way, we illuminate Tao through us. We shine. When we are not complacent, we know we are still not good enough and find room for improvement. We "grow" (长, *zhang*3).

As they contend not, the world cannot contend with them

This chapter is basically about the Tao of non-contention. Since Tao is formless and has no divide, there is no difference between you and me and everyone else. What is there for us to contend with? Because a person of Tao "contend not" (不争, *bu4zheng*1), the world "cannot contend with them" (与之争, *yu3zhi1zheng*1). Seeing it from the spiritual perspective: Since the world is derived from Tao One, it must not compete with Tao.

Is the ancient saying "Yield to preserve the whole" empty words? No. Those who sincerely do so are made complete

The wisdom of yielding "to preserve the whole" is so enduring that it has been passed down for generations since ancient times. Are they "empty saying?" Of course not. True, some unscrupulous people pretend to "yield" to trick the innocent. But, remember: Only "those who sincerely do so (诚全, *cheng2quan*2) are made complete (归之, *gui1zhi*1)".

Chapter 23
What Is! 自然

Talking about nature.
A strong wind does not blow all morning,
A huge storm does not last all day.
Who is dispensing these? Heaven and Earth!
If all things, including Heaven and Earth,
Cannot last forever,
What about a person?

Therefore, in the pursuit of Tao,
Those who conform to Tao,
Are one with Tao.
Those who conform to Te,
Are one with Te.
Those who conform to loss,
Are one with loss.

If we conform to Tao,
The power of Tao flows through us.
If we conform to Te,
The power of Te flows through us.
If we conform to loss,
The power of loss flows through us.

There are those who don't trust enough
And those who don't trust it.

Talking about nature

"Talking" paraphrases 希言 (*xi1yan2*). The first pictogram 希 has a double-meaning. First, it means "hope". Second, it is another name of Tao. In Chapter 14, Laozi uses the word *xi* (希) to describe the inaudibility of Tao. As for the second pictogram 言, it is straightforward and means "talk". 希 is thus non-being, and 言 being. "Nature" (自然, *zi4ran2*), in this context, is a manifestation of Tao, so it refers to Tao. Reading the phrase as a whole, we may interpret it as saying: We hope we can explain nature. Unfortunately, since "the Tao that can be mentioned is not the eternal Tao", it is very hard for us to do so. Although it is difficult to talk about the formless Tao, we must do it to our best ability, only bear in mind the limitations that we have.

A strong wind does not blow full morning. A huge storm does not last all day

Changes in weather are gradual. There are occasions of gusty winds or even tornadoes to adjust environmental imbalances. Just like the eruption of a person's temper, however, they don't last long. "Strong wind" is a translation of 飘风 (*piao1feng1*), and "huge storm" 骤雨 (*zhou4yu3*). So long as the balance is regained, normality is back. In reality, however, devastations of the environment, such as massive deforestation and air pollution, is ongoing and getting more rampant. They wreak havoc to the environment, and there are a lot more drastic adjustments. When the time comes, human beings suffer the effect collectively. If we are remorseful and don't repeat the mistakes, the nightmare is short-lived. Be it gust or tempest; it will soon subside. A strong wind blows not "all morning" (终朝, *zhong1zhao1*), a huge storm lasts not "all day" (终日, *zhong1ri4*)," says Laozi.

Who is dispensing these? Heaven and Earth! If all things, including Heaven and Earth, cannot last forever, what about a person?

Who is dispensing the strong wind and massive storm for the correction? Heaven and Earth. Heaven and Earth are creations of Tao One, and so is humanity. If humanity continues to do damage, we hasten the demise of Heaven and Earth and will perish alongside them.

The Sage uses the weather as a metaphor to illustrate the impermanence of things. While a gust of wind doesn't last all morning, neither are Heaven and Earth immune to impermanence. Like all things, although they may take longer, they, too, will eventually cease to exist. Therefore, Laozi reminds us that we, too, will eventually cease to exist. It is only with the attainment of Tao that we can enjoy the longevity of Tao and outlive Heaven and Earth. This explains why we must adhere to Tao and be consistent in our self-cultivation. Laozi uses this sentence to set up the wisdom conveyed in the rest of this chapter.

Therefore, in the pursuit of Tao, those who conform to Tao are one with Tao. Those who conform to Te are one with Te. Those who conform to loss are one with loss

"Those who conform to Tao" (道者, *dao4zhe3*) are "one with Tao" (同于道, *tong2yu2dao4*). They are the supreme, as mentioned in Chapter 17, who "know the unknowable". Life after life, they remain focused on the cultivation to accumulate their attainment for the realization of the full attainment. "Those conform to Te" (德者, *de2zhe3*) are one with Te (同于德, *tong2yu2de2*). They are the enlightened who help free people of their suffering. There are, however, also those who conform to neither Tao nor Te. They are selfish and greedy. On the surface, they seem to be gaining but are in fact suffering because they have missed the opportunities for self-cultivation. In other words, they are "those who conform to loss" (失者, *shi1zhe3*) and are "one with loss" (同于失, *tong2yu2shi1*).

If we conform to Tao, the power of Tao flows through us. If we conform to Te, the power of Te flows through us

If we align ourselves with Tao, we emulate the Supreme and internalize the wisdom of Tao. They are happy to help us further in our attainment of Tao. Similarly, when we live in accordance with Te, we exude Te in all we do. We are trusted and relied upon, loved, and praised for our selflessness.

If we conform to loss, the power of loss flows through us

If we conform to loss, we lose both Tao and Te and become wayward. As previously explained, in this state, we are greedy and selfish. We may even be drawn to the evils. Although the evils are eager to help us, they do so not without conditions. We will have big trouble extricating ourselves from their influence later on. The consequences are grave.

There are those who don't trust it enough and those who don't trust it

This chapter has shown a stark divide between those who trust (信, *xin4*) Tao and those who don't. Most people are the "average person" Laozi describes in Chapter 41. They are the skeptical, i.e., "those who don't trust it enough" (信不足, *xin4bu4zu2*). There are also those "who don't trust it" (不信, *bu4xin4*). Also, in Chapter 41, Laozi describes them as "the ignorant", who roar with laughter upon hearing Tao. Without faith, we can't make the best of Tao. If we don't trust it enough or, worse still, don't trust it at all, it becomes a hindrance to the realization of Tao.

Chapter 24
What People of Tao Avoid
道者不处

Those who stand on tiptoes
Are not steady,
Those who overstretch their steps
Do not walk far.
Those who are bigoted
Cannot see the light.
Those who are conceited
Do not shine.
Those who are haughty
Earn no glory.
Those who are complacent
Do not grow.

In the eyes of Tao,
These are "gluttonous and
Wasteful acts".
They may be detested by others,
And thus avoided by people of Tao.

Those who stand on tiptoes are not steady

No one can stand on their tiptoes for long. Similarly, anyone who pretends to be more superior than they actually are cannot sustain the facade for long. "On tiptoes" is a translation of 跂 (qi3) and "steady" paraphrases 立 (li4). It is unnatural and against Tao. When we realize that nobody is better or worse than anyone else, we see there is no need to "stand on tiptoes", and anyone who does so is merely being foolish.

Those who overstretch the steps do not walk far

By the same token, when we "overstretch the steps" (跨, kua4), we might gain speed, but we will tire quickly and soon run out of breath. We do not "walk far" (行, xing2). This is a metaphor for impatient people, who bulldoze their ways to get what they want. It is unnatural and against Tao, and their victory is short-lived. But, when we accept and appreciate what we have, take our time and progress in accordance with nature, we are in the proximity of Tao.

Those who are bigoted cannot see the light. Those who are conceited do not shine. Those who are haughty earn no glory. Those who are complacent do not grow

Here, Laozi reiterates what he says in Chapter 22, although in a different tone. This reiteration highlights the importance of the messages and reminds us that being bigoted, conceited, haughty, and complacent hinder our attainment of Tao. Some intellectuals and academics find Tao cultivation difficult because they believe they already know the answers to life's questions. They equate worldly knowledge to wisdom, making the former a stumbling block. The reality is many of those who are highly enlightened have little or no formal education.

The following four sentences briefly remind us of the lessons from Chapter 22.

Those who are bigoted cannot see the light

Those who are bigoted cannot let go of their prejudices and fail to see the merit of Tao cultivation. As a result, they drift further and further away from Tao.

Those who are conceited do not shine

Those who are conceited are stubborn in both thoughts and actions. They think too highly of themselves and refuse to open up to possibilities. As such, there is no light of Tao that shines from within them.

Those who are haughty earn no glory

Those who are haughty bulldoze their ways and earn no glory. Even if they win, the victory is short-lived.

Those who are complacent do not grow

Thinking too highly of themselves, those who are complacent are unjustly self-satisfied, thus seeing no reason to grow or improve themselves. As a result, they are stagnant and do not grow.

In the eyes of Tao, these are "gluttonous and wasteful acts"

The aforementioned behaviors deviate from Tao. "Gluttonous" paraphrases 余食 (*yu2shi2*), and "wasteful acts" paraphrases 赘行 (*zhui4xing2*). They are like excessive food that doesn't add nutritional value or acts that contribute not to the attainment of Tao. The behaviors enumerated above are examples.

They may be detested by others, and thus avoided by people of Tao

"Others" paraphrases 物 (*wu*4), and refers to "the myriads of things". If such behaviors "may be" detested by others, it implies that not everyone finds them detestable. This is understandable. To the person of Tao, however, they are behaviors that have to be avoided.

Chapter 25
Naming Tao 曰道

Something nebulous was present,
before the birth of the universe.
In ultimate silence and emptiness,
It was on its own and unchanging,
Ever revolving and enduring,
It is Mother of the universe.

Not knowing its name,
I call it Tao.
Clumsily, I name it "Great".

Great is timeless,
Timeless is far,
Far is returning.

Therefore,
Tao is Great,
Heaven is Great.
Earth is Great, and
The Kingly is also Great.
In the universe, there are four Great powers,
And the Kingly is one of them.

Humanity follows Earth,
Earth follows Heaven;
Heaven follows Tao;
Tao follows what is naturally so.

Something nebulous was present, before the birth of the universe

Before the birth of the universe, there was "something" (有物, *you3wu4*) "nebulous" (混成, *hun4cheng2*). It was a mass of energy and contained what we may call the *taihe* qi. It was formless, without judgment and liking, and was beyond description. It was Tao, and we may call it Tao Core or Tao Zero. Scientists today use terms like protons, atoms, or dark matter to describe the unseen. Laozi, however, did not have this privilege, so he described it simply as "something nebulous".

Then, there came the moment like what was described in The Big Bang Theory. The *taihe* qi converged with *Yuanyang*, or the Primordial Yang, and ignited a flash of mystical light that beamed millions of miles. *Yuanyang* was full of creative energy, and the convergence generated Tao One that created Heaven and Earth and then the myriads of things.

After so many years, the primordial *taihe* energy is still there, and will always be there. In the Taijigong training, how we can connect to and receive the *taihe* qi is an exercise of fundamental importance. The more *taihe* qi we assimilate, the more potent is our energy. We need faith, emptiness, and sincerity to establish the connection, and efforts life after life to accumulate the *taihe* qi for the attainment of Tao Core. Although the journey to the complete attainment is long, every connection brings us a step closer to our goal. It is said that the Buddha took not less than 500 rebirths to do that, and we are unlikely to be any quicker.

In ultimate silence and emptiness

The clause suggests how we can integrate with Tao Core. "Ultimate silence" is a translation of 寂 (*ji4*), which means "silent to the extreme". "Emptiness" paraphrases 寥 (*liao2*), which means "empty to the extreme". Since Tao Core is formless and totally silent, we can only be in its proximity if we can do likewise. In fact, this is done whatever spiritual path we take. Staying silent and empty are, without exception, the pre-requisite for connection with the divinity.

It was on its own and unchanging

Tao Core was on its own (独立, *du2li4*) and totally unfettered. It was constant, unchanging (不改, *bu4gai3*), formless, and with no beginning or end.

Ever revolving and enduring

The phrase is about Tao Use. Everything in the universe moves in a cycle, revolving (周行, *zhou1xing2*) unabated. Some cycles are big, others small, and may be known as Large, Medium, and Small Taiji. The life cycle of the universe is perhaps the largest of all Taiji. The four seasons are a medium one. And, a human's life cycle, along with the lives of the myriads of things, is Small Taiji. Every cycle, be it big or small, moves continuously. There is no beginning or end. The beginning is end, and the end is beginning. It never stops.

"Enduring" is a translation of 不殆 (*bu4dai4*), which means "without going into decay or in danger". All material things decay and die. When there are transformation and renewal, a new cycle starts all over again. As far as reincarnation is concerned, the cycles only come to an end upon the complete attainment of Tao.

Decoding Note: Revolving and unabated cycles takes us back to our root, again and again, to fulfill our destiny, as illustrated in Chapter 16.

It is Mother of the universe

Tao Core is the source from which everything in the universe is derived. It is, therefore, "Mother of the universe" (天下母, *tian1xia4mu3*).

Decoding Note: Only through the realization of "ultimate silence and emptiness" and repeating the cycles of "Fulfillment of Destiny" that a person of Tao is able to return to Tao One — Mother of the universe — gradually.

Not knowing its name, I call it Tao

Before Laozi, Tao had no name. In order to illustrate its wonders, Laozi had no choice but to give it a name. He "calls it Tao" (曰道, *yue*1*dao*4). It is for this reason that the Sage is also revered as the Founder of Taoism.

Clumsily, I name it "Great"

Clumsily (强为之, *qiang*2*wei*2*zhi*1), Laozi also "names it Great" (曰大, *yue*1*da*4). Tao is often known as "Great Tao" (大道). Why Great? What is the greatest thing in the world? Anything that has form or shape, be it the moon, the sun, or the galaxy, can never be great enough. In comparison, Tao is formless with no boundary, and it is indefinitely big. Laozi thus names Tao also as "Great".

Great is timeless. Timeless is far. Far is returning

"Timeless" paraphrases 逝 (*shi*4), which implies the flow of time. Tao is Great, and it is timeless. "Far" is a translation of 远 (*yuan*3), which refers to space. Tao is limited not by distance, so it is boundless. "Timeless is far." It's now and forever, or the so-called "a split-second of eternity". The mystical light that radiates from Tao can be defined by neither time nor distance.

Far is "returning" (反, *fan*3). A person who has fully attained Tao is, just like Tao, constrained not by time and distance. They, however, come back to the present of the mundane world to help the sentient beings now and then, and traverse between non-being and being. They keep returning to the non-being of Tao Core when they are in being, so they don't indulge in the worldly pleasures while in the mundane world. "Returning is the way Tao moves", says Laozi in Chapter 40.

Therefore, Tao is Great, Heaven is Great, Earth is Great, and the Kingly is also Great

"Tao is Great" is a translation of 道大 (*dao*4*da*4). Things that have form and shape are measurable; they can never be great enough. Tao is formless, so it is Great.

"Heaven is Great." is a translation of 天大 (*tian*1*da*4). Heaven is great because it was derived directly from Tao One, and it is its first creation. No one can measure how big the universe is. We don't even know how many stars there are in the sky. So it is Great.

"Earth is Great" is a translation of 地大 (*di*4*da*4). Tao One created Heaven, followed by Earth. So Earth is considered a direct creation of Tao One. Everything on Earth, be it the living or non-living things, all rely on it for survival. Earth, therefore, is Great.

"The Kingly is also Great" is a translation of 王亦大 (*wang*2*yi*4*da*4). Many editions of the *Tao Te Ching* use the version "Humanity is Great", but I prefer this one. Bestowed with intelligence, humans are endowed with the potential of living the greatness of Tao, although those who live the full potential are few and far between. We may call the few who have attained Tao "the Kingly". It paraphrases 王 (*wang*2), which literally means "a king", as explained in Chapter 16.

Visually, the character 王 is made up of three horizontal lines and a vertical stroke. The three horizontal strokes represent Heaven, Humanity, and Earth, respectively. The vertical stroke connects the three of them as one. So "the Kingly" is a highly-enlightened person who knows the ins and outs of the ways Heaven and Earth work. The greatness of "the Kingly" is not determined by their size, but their depth of Tao attainment. While it grounds them firmly on Earth, it also allows them to reach out to Heaven. They are in the proximity of Tao Core.

Although most of us are not "the Kingly", we are endowed with the potential. As long as we are consistent in our practice, we will be as enlightened as the Kingly someday.

In the universe, there are four Great powers, and the Kingly is one of them

There is an important implication: To be "kingly", one must first be a human being. Plants and animals cannot be Kingly because they cannot perform self-cultivation. Legend has it that Master Zhang Sanfeng, the illustrious Taiji ancestor, used to be a Celestial Crane. My Master Wu Tunan used to tell me that he was a leopard in Heaven. Like animals, they could not read the divine scriptures, and this prevents them from being enlightened. They had to be reborn into human form to cultivate themselves and aspire to kingship.

Humanity follows Earth. Earth follows Heaven. Heaven follows Tao. Tao follows what is naturally so

These are various levels of Tao attainment.

"Human follows Earth": The Tao cultivator emulates the humility of Earth, known to be accommodating, tolerant, humble, and yielding.

"Earth follows Heaven": Now we elevate from the virtue of Earth to that of Heaven. We have no prejudices and readily accept whatever that happens.

"Heaven follows Tao": By now, we are in the proximity of the formless Tao. We understand the impermanence of things. We are ready to let go of baggage, so as to "hold fast to tranquility" and move "toward absolute nothingness".

"Tao follows what is naturally so": At this level, we are in the state of "ultimate silence and emptiness", as mentioned earlier in this chapter.

Chapter 26
Calm and Rooted 静重

The heavy is the root of the light.
Calmness prevails over restlessness.

Thus the Sage travels all day;
Not losing sight of their profound calmness.
Notwithstanding their splendid abode,
They move freely as if a swallow.

Yet the lord of a thousand chariots,
Conduct themselves lightly in the world.
The light lose their root,
The restless lose their Master.

The heavy is the root of the light

"The heavy" (重, *zhong*4) and "the light" (轻, *qing*1) are used here to contrast our perpetual and temporal bodies. The perpetual body is weighty. It is what we are. The temporal body is frivolous, especially when inflated with worldly desires. The perpetual body is "the heavy" and, therefore, the root (根, *gen*1) of "the light", i.e., the temporal body. It does not mean that the temporary body is unimportant. Without it, we cannot cultivate our perpetual self. A person of Tao is given a new temporal body upon rebirth. Even then, it is "the light" in comparison to the perpetual body, which is being refined life after life.

Calmness prevails over restlessness

When we make whatever we do as a means to refine our perpetual body, we earn the calmness (静, *jing*4). With the calmness, we walk the path of Tao. If, on the other hand, whatever we do is meant to pamper our temporal body, then restlessness (躁, *zao*4) gets the better of us. We are inflicted with illusions, confusions, and worries. We need calmness to bring our true self back. It "prevails over" (君, *jun*1) restlessness.

Thus the Sage travels about all day; not losing sight of their profound calmness

Most versions of the *Tao Te Ching* use 辎重 (*zi*1*zhong*4), which means "military impediments", in this sentence. I prefer the version that uses 静重 (*jing*4*zhong*4), which means "calm and rooted" and implies calmness of the perpetual self. Whatever the Sage does, they do it with calmness and adherence to Tao.

Notwithstanding their splendid abode, they move freely as if a swallow

"Abode" (观, *guan*1) refers to a palace, temple, or home. A person of Tao "moves freely" (处超然, *chu*3*chao*1*ran*2) as if a "swallow" (燕, *yan*4). They go about helping people and promote the appreciation of Tao, constrained not by their abodes, however splendid they are.

Yet the lord of a thousand chariots, conduct themselves lightly in the world

It is really a pity! Look at the lord who has tens of thousands of horses and chariots. Despite the abundance, they "conduct themselves lightly" (身轻, *shen*1*qing*1), oblivious to the importance of self-cultivation. Despite the fortune bestowed on them, they show no gratitude and have no intention to repay the kindness. They blow the golden opportunity to cultivate their soul and squander the privilege of being a human being.

The light lose their root

If we pay excessive attention to "the light", i.e., the temporal body, we lose sight of self-cultivation, leading to the loss of our root.

The restless lose their Master

When we are restless, we need the calmness of our perpetual self, i.e., the "Master" (君, *jun*1), to bring the composure back. Why is the lord of thousands of chariots obsessed with the temporal body? They lose their calmness while chasing after glory and wealth. Not only do they lose the "Master" of calmness, but they also trample the opportunity for the refinement of the soul.

Chapter 27
Inheriting the Light 襲明

A good deed leaves no trails.
A good speech makes no blunder.
A good count needs no tally.

A good door needs no lock
Yet cannot be opened.
A good tie uses no knots
Yet cannot be untied.

Thus the Sage takes good care of everyone
And casts no one away.
They take good care of all things
And cast nothing away.
This is "inheriting the light".

Thus a good person is a bad person's teacher,
A bad person is a resource of a good person.
If a teacher is not respected,
Or a resource not treasured,
One is clever but grossly unwise.
Here lies the secret of the wonders.

Laozi uses the adjective "good" (善, shan4) repeatedly in this chapter: Good deed, good speech, good count, good door, and good tie. "Good" has a special connotation here. It refers to an ideal state of performance. It is an extension of Tao Core and an action of Te. Te is a manifestation of Tao, and "good" is what Te does. When Te is performed right from the bottom of one's heart, it is "good". If we want to assess the Te of a person, we see whether they are kind and compassionate. A "good deed" is a thing done by a person of Tao, and a "good speech" is what they say.

A good deed leaves no trails

A "good deed" (善行, shan4xing2) is what a person of Tao does. It leaves no "trails" (辄迹, zhe2ji1), which refers to "marks left by a wheel on the path". Wheels in the ancient days were made of wood and tended to leave traces wherever they went. It is used as a metaphor here to depict a person of Tao who claims no credit for the good deeds they perform. Knowing that nothing is permanent, they cling to nothing.

A good speech makes no blunder

"Blunder" paraphrases 瑕谪 (xia2di2). 瑕 means "blemishes", while 谪 means "rebuke". The words spoken by a person of Tao have no divides. They are absent of self-interests and intend only to help and cause no harm. They thus have no blemishes and make no blunder.

A good count needs no tally

Although a person of Tao "counts" (计, ji4), they are not calculative. They don't use "tally" (筹策, chou2ce4), because they are not preoccupied with gain and loss. They go with the flow of Tao. Do by non-doing, they put in the best efforts, but leave what can happen to Heaven.

A good door needs no lock yet cannot be opened

We use a lock (关键, *guan1jian4*) to secure a door to keep away unwanted intrusions. Metaphorically, "a good door" is locked to ward off divides and distractions. When, say, greed arises, we shut the door tight so that it will not distract our attention. If it arises again the next day, we lock the door again to keep it out. This is, however, not necessary for a person of Tao. They are in Oneness. Even when there is no lock, the door "cannot be opened" (不可开, *bu4ke3kai1*), and divides and distraction will not be able to go through it. "A good door" paraphrases (善闭, *shan4bi4*), which means "securely closed".

A good tie uses no knot yet cannot be untied

The "good ties" is a translation of 善结 (*shan4jie2*). Here, it refers to an affinity with Tao. A person of Tao is spiritually connected to Tao, and the affinity is reaffirmed life after life. The tie gets stronger in the process. Even when there is no "knot" (绳约, *sheng2yue1*) to tie them down, the knot "cannot be untied" (不可解, *bu4ke3jie3*). What is more, Tao is formless, and thus there is no such thing as untying it from an affinity.

In my case, it applies to the continuation of the qi lineage that I have inherited. The lineage ties the ancestors, me, and my disciples tightly together. The tie cannot be untied, and it continues beyond my current life.

Thus the Sage takes good care of everyone and casts no one away

The Sage is compassionate. They do all they can to "take good care of everyone" (常善救人, *chang2shan4jiu4ren2*); and so "cast no one away" (无弃人, *wu2qi4ren2*). The Sage is always ready to guide the people who are willing to walk the path of Tao.

They take good care of all things and cast nothing away

Laozi uses "things" (物, *wu*4) here to describe non-human sentient beings, including animals and plants. The Sage takes good care of not only people but also all "things". Every sentient being is able to walk the path of Tao; it is just that the journey and time they take are longer because they are not endowed with the human's intelligence. Even then, the Sage does not cast any one of them away.

This is "inheriting the light"

"Inheriting" is a translation of 襲 (*xi*1), and "the light" 明 (*ming*2). It means inheriting the wisdom of Tao. Having learned the teachings of Tao, we put them into practice and pass it down to the later generations. The teachings are not complicated; what they say is basically to walk the path of the Oneness, and keep ourselves away from the divides. If we adhere to the teachings, there is neither knot to untie nor lock to unlock. Otherwise, there are knots and locks that perplex us. Reading the *Tao Te Ching*, again and again, is a way to learn the teachings. It sheds the light of the wisdom by providing broad outlines. If we can reflect on what it says time and again, we will see the light.

Thus a good person is a bad person's teacher

"A good person" (善人, *shan*4*ren*2) refers to a person of Tao. A "bad person" (不善人, *bu*4*shan*4*ren*2) is not necessarily "bad"; it is just that they are yet to be awakened to Tao. Because of their ignorance, they may be unknowingly doing bad things. A person of Tao must do what they can to help them.

A bad person is a resource of a good person

A person who is yet to be awakened to Tao is a resource (资, *zi*1) for a person of Tao. The more people a person of Tao helps, the more resourceful they are. Accumulation of resources is an important task leading to the attainment of Tao.

If a teacher is not respected, or a resource not treasured, one is clever but grossly unwise

If people don't treasure the wisdom of Tao and respect (贵, *gui*4) their teachers, or the teachers fail to treasure (爱, *ai*4) their resources and provide them with guidance; they are clever (智, *zhi*4) but grossly unwise (大迷, *da*4*mi*2) and thus highly confused.

Here lies the secret of the wonders

Because no one can attain Tao overnight, it is all the more important that we understand "the secret of the wonders" (要妙, *yao*4*miao*4). If we can't see the relationship between teachers and their resources, or we don't have the desire to help free the sentient beings from their suffering, we will not know the "secret". While we are clever enough to know the worldly matters, we are confused about the essence of Tao. By reiterating the importance of "the wonders", Laozi points us to the secret of success for Tao cultivation. To this end, readers may wish to refer back to Chapter 1 for an explanation of the Chinese character 妙 (*miao*4).

Chapter 28

Great Governance Never Disintegrates 大制不割

*Know the masculine,
But keep to the feminine,
And become a brook under Heaven.
Being a brook under Heaven,
The constant Te leaves us not,
And we resume to be a baby newly born.*

*Know the white,
But keep to the black,
And become a pattern under Heaven.
Being a pattern under Heaven,
The constant Te falters not,
And we return to infinity.
Know the honor,
But shun not the humiliation,
And become a valley under Heaven.*

*Being a valley under Heaven,
The constant virtue of Te prevails,
And we return to the state of pu.*

*With pu, things are formed,
The Sage becomes their great governor
By employing it.
Thus great governance never disintegrates.*

"Enlightenment is by itself neither real nor unreal," the Buddha is quoted as saying. The "unreal" is in the non-being, i.e., the nothingness. The "real" is being, i.e., the substance. This may be translated into three levels of Tao attainment, which Laozi enumerates in this chapter: "Know the masculine; but keep to the feminine"; "know the white, but keep to the black"; and "know the honor; but shun not the humiliation".

Know the masculine, but keep to the feminine

"Know", in this context, goes beyond cognizance and refers to being truly aware and wise. "The masculine" is a translation of 雄 (*xiong*2). Although literally referring to "male", it is used metaphorically for strengths one has acquired through cultivation. When we are in a position of "the masculine", we must "keep to the feminine". "The feminine" is a translation of (雌, *ci*2). Although it literally means "female", it is used metaphorically to refer to softness and humility.

Let me relate a personal experience to explain this. Being a Taiji master. I "know the masculine", as far as attainment in the martial arts is concerned. It is, however, important that I must "keep to the feminine" and to remain humble.

One day, I drove to town and was stuck in a traffic jam caused by the blockage of a giant cement mixer. The driver, however, was oblivious to the chaos he had created and the anger of other road users. Feeling impatient, three young men yelped out loudly to him but faded into silence when they caught sight of the burly figure of his.

Feeling amiss, I got out of my car and saw the driver. Although he was big, I knew he was of no match to me should there be a fight. While I knew the "masculine", I kept to the "feminine". Instead of admonishing him, I remained polite. "Friend! Can you do us a favor by removing the truck?" I said. Unfortunately, he mistook the politeness as timidity and did not take me seriously. I had to show him the "masculinity" out of no choice. I walked toward him, held him up slightly, and infused a current of qi through his bones by employing a Taiji technique. I could have tossed him away but preferred to keep to my "feminine". Instead of flying into a rage, the driver was bewildered that this old man had been able to disrupt his balance with a simple stroke and, therefore, softened his tone, "Well, just for you, old man! I'll move the truck away!" What a relief! So he did, and the flow of the traffic went back to order.

What if I had not kept to the feminine? I would have clashed his masculinity with mine, ending the matter with grievances. Do note, however, that we cannot keep to the feminine if we don't have the masculine or cannot properly project it. Had I not been competent in Taiji, the truck driver wouldn't have compromised, and if he picked a fight with me, I would have landed myself in hot water. Keeping to the feminine without masculine is dangerous.

And become a brook under Heaven

Brook is a translation of 溪 (*xi*1). When we are like a brook, which flows down and is modest and humble, we enjoy support from people. When the traffic jam was cleared without ugly arguments, other commuters were thankful, and their gratitude formed "a brook under Heaven". With a dozen of people, the "brook" is of the size of a dozen of people. If the number is in the hundreds, thousands, or more, then the "brook" is a larger one.

Being a brook under Heaven, the constant Te leaves us not

The "constant Te" (常德, *chang2de2*) is the virtue of Te that is constant and enduring. It is derived directly from Tao. Tao is formless. Te is Tao manifested in concrete actions. "Know the masculine, but keep to the feminine" is an action. This was what I did when I talked to the cement truck driver. I was in a position of masculine, but I chose to stay soft. This is an act of embracing the constant Te, and Te "leaves us not" (不离, *bu4li2*).

And we resume to be a baby newly born

When we "resume" (复归, *fu4gui1*) to be "a baby newly born" (婴儿, *ying1er2*), we again have no divides and are as innocent and selfless as a baby. When I was driven by the constant Te, my focus was on clearing the traffic jam. A newborn baby is being, but their innocence is non-being. With the non-being in mind, we are on the path of the non-being of Tao. Although we cannot be in the proximity of Tao immediately, with the constancy, we are going to arrive there one day.

Know the white, but keep to the black. And become a pattern under Heaven

This sentence is about non-being. "White" (白, *bai2*) implies illumination. "Dark" is a translation of 黑 (*hei1*), which means "black". We may, therefore, interpret the sentence as "illuminating nature of innocence in a pitch-dark room".

Imagine that you are in a room pitch-black doing meditation, suddenly a flash of light brightens up the darkness. This is what "knowing the white" is like. It is a harbinger of a great realization of true nature. Despite the light, nevertheless, we must "keep to the black". We must remain in a low position, and ready to accept the black, which can be unpleasant things that come our way regardless of our success. We are never complacent. We constantly improve and renew ourselves. We remain in the "dark" and work just as diligently.

Being a pattern under Heaven, the constant Te falters not, and we return to infinity

Heaven derived directly from Tao One, so "under Heaven" (天下, *tian1xia4*) implies Tao. "Pattern" is a translation of 式 (*shi4*), which means a system. We may, therefore, interpret "a pattern under Heaven" as an approach to the pursuit of Tao. The approach, in this case, is to "know the white, and keep to the black". If we always cultivate ourselves and serve the world, we internalize the constant Te. Under such circumstances, we are unlikely to go astray. "Falter" is a translation of 忒 (*te*4). "Falters not" implies we are unlikely to fall into the wrong track. By adhering to the right path, we will eventually "return to infinity". "Infinity" is a translation of 无极 (*wu*2*ji*2), where the non-being in it helps facilitate the discovery of our real selves.

Know the honor, but shun not the humiliation. And become a valley under Heaven

"Honor" is a translation of 荣 (*rong*2); and "humiliation" is 辱 (*ru*3). The phrase describes the behavior of one who has fully attained Tao. They are in both non-being and being. The Buddha, who is highly revered, "know the honor". But he "shun not the humiliation" when he went round begging for alms. He could have asked his disciples to bring him the food but preferred not to do so. Begging is lowly in the eyes of the mundane, but not the honorable Buddha.

Why is it so? Highly enlightened, he is able to be in non-being at one moment and being the next. He moves freely between non-being of the formless Tao Core and being of Tao One. He is one moment with the non-actionable Tao, and the other with the actionable Te. If we can behave similarly, we are on the way to complete enlightenment. We see no difference between honor and humiliation and are always ready to help compassionately — like "a valley under Heaven" (天下谷, *tian*1*xia*4*gu*3).

Being a valley under Heaven, the constant virtue of Te prevails, and we return to the state of *pu*

"Valley" is echoic, so it is responsive. When a sage is "like a valley under Heaven", they are responsive to the sentient beings in helping them walk the path of Tao. By doing so, their Te is constant and rich. With the constant presence of the Te, the Sage returns to *pu* (朴, *pu*3) — a state of purity and simplicity of Tao. It is the One Source. When we are in it, we know the honor and shun no humiliation.

With *pu*, things are formed

Pu is Tao — the One Source where the myriads of things (器, *qi*4) are generated. Returning to the state of *pu* is to attain Tao fully. When we "know the masculine, but keep to the feminine", we are in being, i.e., Taiji (太极). When we "know the white, but keep to the black", we are in non-being, i.e., *wuji* (无极). When we "know the honor, but shun not the humiliation", we are in both being and non-being. We have returned to *pu*, the purity of Tao.

The Sage becomes their great governor by employing it

"Governor" is a translation of 官长 (*guan*1*zhang*3), which means the officials who govern the people. In this context, it refers to the great spiritual mentors. When the Sage uses *pu* to educate the people, they guide them spiritually as a great mentor.

Thus great governance never disintegrates

As mentioned in Chapter 25, formlessness is "Great", and "Great" in this context is another name of Tao. "The Great governance" (大制, *da*4*zhi*4), therefore, may be interpreted as the system for the attainment of Tao. It will never be disintegrated. We learn to be in the present, i.e., being, and in the nothingness, i.e., non-being. Then, we are in both being and non-being. It is a system to achieve the "Great".

Chapter 29
Give Up Control 不为不执

If we think we can
Take over the world under Heaven
And do what we like,
I am sure we cannot succeed.

The world under Heaven
Is a sacred vessel,
Controlling it, we fail.
Gripping it, we slip

There are those who lead
And those who follow;
Those who blow hot
And those who blow cold;
Those who are strong
And those who are weak;
Those who are the victor
And those who are the conquered.

The Master thus avoids
Extremes,
Excesses, and
Complacency.

If we think we can take over the world under Heaven and do what we like, I am sure we cannot succeed

To "take over the world" (取天下, *qu3tian1xia4*) is a selfish desire. The "world under Heaven" is devoid of divides and human desires. Do you think anyone can take it over and "do what they like" (为之, *wei2zhi1*)? In the view of the Sage, no one can.

The world under Heaven is a sacred vessel. Controlling it, we fail. Gripping it, we slip

The world is a "sacred vessel" (神器, *shen2qi4*). It was derived directly from Tao One, and retains the spirit of One Source. If we want to control it, we can only approach it with non-doing by aligning ourselves with nature. If we are going to impose our will on it, we are bound to fail. Even if we can grip it for a while, we are going to lose it eventually.

In the remaining part of the chapter, Laozi suggests how we can use the preceding principle to handle situations in life.

There are those who lead and those who follow

"Lead" paraphrases 行 (*xing2*), which means "moving". Here, it implies "walking at the front". "Follow", on the other hand, is a translation of 随 (*sui2*), which means to follow from behind. In life, there are those who inspire and those who follow the lead. This is a type of relationship between teachers and their resources, as explained in Chapter 27.

Those who blow hot and those who blow cold

"Blow hot" paraphrases 呴 (*xu3*), which means to blow the air slowly. This is what we do during cold weather to warm up our hands. "Blow cold" paraphrases 吹 (*chui1*), which means "to blow".

It is something like blowing our fingers softly when the weather is hot. We may see them as metaphors for handling praises and blames.

Those who are strong and those who are weak

"Strong" is a translation of 强 (*qiang*2), and "weak" paraphrases 羸 (*lei*2), which means "thin and frail". When we are strong, we feel spirited, happy and dignified. When we are weak, we feel worried, humiliated and insignificant. They are antithetical.

Those who are the victor and those who are the conquered

"The victor" paraphrases 载 (*zai*3), which means "to carry" and implies winning a total victory. "The conquered" is a translation of 隳 (*hui*1), which means "damage" or "collapse".

The Sage thus avoids extremes, excesses, and complacency

If we can remain calm and are unruffled by the ups and downs of emotions such as those mentioned above, we will always have peace of mind. It helps us attain a high level of Oneness. Although we can't be in a state of Oneness overnight, the direction must be right. As far as possible, remain modest and humble, and we rarely go wrong. "Extremes" paraphrases 甚 (*shen*4), "excesses" 奢 (*she*1), and "complacency" 泰 (*tai*4). If we can avoid these pitfalls we will have fewer worries and desires, and move closer and closer to the full attainment of Tao.

Chapter 30
Against Tao 不道

A leader who governs with Tao,
Uses no weapon to force the world.
Because every force used
Creates a counterforce.

Places rampaged by armies,
Thorns and briers grow.
In the wake of a fierce battle,
bad years follow.

A good commander stops
On striking a decisive blow;
Rather than forcing their will.

They don't win in conceit.
They don't win in haughtiness.
They don't win in arrogance.
They win with regret that the war had to be fought.
They win by not forcing their will.

When a thing is strained with force,
It perishes young.
As it is against Tao,
It is on its way to early decay.

Laozi is anti-war, and he is unambiguous about it. He is especially against people who force their wills on others and conquer with haughtiness. To him, "a country's weaponry should not be displayed to anyone" (Chapter 36), not to mention using them to destroy and conquer.

A leader who governs with Tao uses no weapon to force the world

"Govern" paraphrases 作人主 (*zuo4ren2zhu3*), which means "being a master of someone". For a person who doesn't follow Tao, they are directed by their desires, so their master is their desires. For a person of Tao, their master is Tao. "A leader who governs with Tao" is guided by Tao. When they govern people, they naturally adhere to the principles of Tao and have the interests of the people close to their hearts.

"Weapon" paraphrases 兵 (*bing1*), which means "army"; and "force" 强 (*qiang2*), which means "strength". Such a leader will not suppress or impose their will on people by using force. Instead, they convince with their virtue of Te.

Because every force used creates a counterforce

A country that invades another is repelled by the counterforce it generates, usually in proportion to the force it exerts. History is full of examples of such defeats, causing suffering to their people.

"Counterforce" paraphrases 好还 (*hao3huan2*). 好 means "good", and 还 means "return". 好 is made up of two sub-characters: 女 and 子, which mean "female" and "child", respectively. The "female" is Yin, and the "child" is Yang. It, therefore, carries the connotations of destruction and creation. It implies counterforce is a return to the force one exerts. It is another way of saying reaping what we sow.

Places rampaged by armies, thorns and briers grow. In the wake of a fierce battle, bad years follow

In times of war, people are displaced. After the war, the places rampaged by armies (师, *shi*1) become desolate, where "thorns and briers" (荆棘, *jing*1*ji*2) flourish. After an engagement of two armies, corpses of humans and animals dot the field. Plague spreads and what follows are "bad years". The end of a war doesn't end the problems it created. Laozi is against war because it always leaves the people suffering.

A good commander stops on striking a decisive blow, rather than forcing their will

"A good commander" paraphrases 善者 (*shan*4*zhe*3), which means "a good person". Having attained their ultimate aim of driving out the aggressor, a good commander stops giving chase. "A decisive blow" paraphrases 果 (*guo*3), which means "result". They have achieved their objectives, and do not want to exert further force.

They don't win in conceit

"Conceit" is a translation of 矜 (*jin*1). The commander is not conceited; even when a battle is won. Similarly, we must not go around challenging people so as to show off our prowess, even if we are excellent in the martial arts.

They don't win in haughtiness

"Haughtiness" is a translation of 伐 (*fa*2). Having won a battle, we must not press on to satisfy the ego. It is of little use to put others down just to feel good.

They don't win in arrogance

"Arrogance" is a translation of 骄 (*jiao*1). We must not become arrogant because of the victory. It is important to stay modest and humble at all times.

They win with regret that the war had to be fought

"With regret" paraphrases 不得已 (*bu*4*de*2*yi*3). The battle is won for self-defense, not aggression. It is fought because there are no better options. Taoists believe in self-defense and frown on invasions. So are Taiji practitioners. They live by the principle that says: "Effective self-defense is a total victory".

They win by not forcing their will

"Forcing their will" paraphrases 强 (*qiang*2), which means "strong" or "force". Winning a battle makes us stronger. We should, however, exploit the stronger position for self-defense, not to invade others.

When a thing is strained with force, it perishes young

"Strained" paraphrases 壮 (*zhuang*4), which means being "robust". "Perishes young" paraphrases 老 (*lao*3), which means "become old". Things take the reverse course when they reach the extreme. Things thrive in summer but go into decline with the arrival of autumn and winter. It is the inevitability of the law of nature. The only solution is to attain Tao. Then, even if our physical body perishes our perpetual self continues to thrive.

As it is against Tao, it is on its way to early decay

If we "use the weapons to force the world", we are faced with the consequences mentioned earlier. Because doing so is against Tao, it is on its way to "early decay" (早已, *zao3yi3*).

Chapter 31

Honor the Left 尚左

Weapons of destruction,
Are tools of ill omen.
Detested by all things,
A person of Tao avoids using them.

A fine person honors the left,
And a person of war the right.
Weapons are tools of ill omen,
Not instruments of a fine person,
Who uses them only as a last resort
And always with restraint.
Victory is not sweet.
Those who rejoice at victory
Take pleasure in killing.
Those who take pleasure in killing,
Earn no support from the world.

Good omen takes a left,
And the bad takes a right.
So the lieutenant takes a left,
And the General takes a right.
Orate as in a funeral.
For the many who are killed,
Lament with grief.

When a war is won,
Celebrate by mourning.

I prefer the version of the *Tao Te Ching* that begins the chapter with the pictograms 奪兵 (*xun*4*bing*1), rather than "佳兵". 奪, or *xun*, is a bird of colorful feathers. It is beautiful, nimble, and boasts mighty flying skills. It has a fatal weakness though: It likes to show off, now flying way up and now gliding low. The showiness makes it the target of bird hunters. Before long, it is in captivity.

Weapons of destruction, are tools of ill omen

"Weapons of destruction" (兵者, *bing*1*zhe*3) are flashy tools of ill omen, just like *xun*, the beautiful bird that cannot wait to flash its feathers. The military is meant for self-defense. If it is used to create discord or bully around, it spells "ill omen" (不祥, *bu*4*xiang*2) and will lead to something sinister.

Detested by all things, a person of Tao avoids using them

"All things" (物, *wu*4), in this context, are the myriads of things that include Heaven and Earth and everything within them. They cannot condone the flaunting of might. If it is "detested" (恶, *wu*4) by all things, including Heaven and Earth, how can a person of Tao accept them? They "avoid using them" (不处, *bu*4*chu*3).

A fine person honors the left, and a person of war the right

To understand the passage, we need to know the layout of a form of architectural structure for homes found widely in the olden days; many of them are conserved in China today. Known as a "three-in-one courtyard" (三合院), it is made up of three houses and a courtyard. When we face out toward the courtyard, the house on the left is thought to be filled up mainly with the Yang energy. Since

Yang gives life, it is auspicious and superior. The house on the right, on the other hand, is thought to have a strong presence of Yin energy. Since the Yin energy symbolizes killing, it is inauspicious and inferior. "A fine person" (君子, *jun1zi3*) is a person of Tao who deserves to be put up in the auspicious cluster of houses. They, therefore, "honors the left" (贵左, *gui4zuo3*). A military person who kills is more aptly put up in the house that is inauspicious — the one on the right — that is also used to receive the guests' attendants.

Weapons are tools of ill omen, not instruments of a fine person

"Weapons" (兵者, *bing1zhe3*) are tools that kill and are of ill omen. They are, therefore, not instruments of a fine person of Tao. A truly fine person wins people over with Te, not force. They may be carrying weapons, for example, a sword. But their weapons are meant strictly for self-defense and used only when someone forces their hand.

Decoding Note: Taiji is an art of Tao that is meant purely for self-defense, not offense. Taiji exponents always act only to counter an attack. They return the opponents' force to them, or to create an impasse where the opponents can neither advance nor retreat. Only when the opponents stop attacking do the Taiji exponents let go of the engagement.

Who use them only as a last resort, and a lways with restraint

The true gentle-person uses weapons only as a "last resort" (不得已, *bu4de2yi3*) for self-defense, and are always "with restraint" (恬然, *tian2ran2*). They prefer to settle disputes amicably. It is only when confronted with the ferocious that they would respond with their might.

Victory is not sweet. Those who rejoice at victory take pleasure in killing

Even when they win a battle, people of Tao are not joyous. They don't celebrate it as something "sweet" (美, *mei3*). Those who see it as something sweet are those who "take pleasure in killing" (乐杀人, *le4sha1ren2*). It is sinister.

Those who take pleasure in killing, earn no support from the world

Those who enjoy killing go against Tao, and earn no "support" (得志, *de2zhi4*) from the world. The world was derived from Tao One, which likes to give life and loathes to kill. So those who enjoy killing fly in the face of Tao and will face retribution sooner or later.

Good omen takes a left, and the bad takes a right

"Good omen" (吉事, *ji2shi4*) takes a left because, as explained earlier, the left-hand side gives life. It is auspicious in this context. "The bad" (凶事, *xiong1shi4*) takes a right, because the right-hand side kills, and is inauspicious.

So the lieutenant takes a left, and the General takes a right

The lieutenant (偏将军, *pian1jiang1jun1*) has no power to start a battle. They only follow orders. Although they are ranked lower than the General (上将军, *shang4jiang1jun1*), they are received in the superior house on the left. The General's commands can start a battle. Therefore, they are received in the inferior house on the right, despite their superiority in rank. The fine person of Tao denies the General the auspicious house. It serves as a reminder for the General to preserve peace. Conflicts must be avoided as they bring suffering to people.

Orate as in a funeral

In speeches, one should speak of the victory in the tone of a funeral (丧礼, *sang*4*li*3) and express bitterness. "Orate" is a translation of 言 (*yan*2). Every being has its own destiny. There is time for it to live and time for it to die. There is no reason for anyone to intervene.

For the many who are killed, lament with grief

When a battle is won, it is not an occasion for celebration, because lives have been lost. On the contrary, it should be treated with sorrow, like weeping at a funeral. "Lament" is a translation of 悲哀 (*bei*1*ai*1). "Grief" paraphrases 泣 (*qi*4), which means "to weep". Because it is out of no choice that we are engaged in a battle, what is there for us to celebrate?

When a war is won, celebrate by mourning

A country of Tao would not start a war easily. Even if we have to defeat our enemy out of no choice, "when a war is won" (战胜, *zhan*4*sheng*4), it is to be treated like a funeral. Waging war is not in the spirit of Tao.

Tao is constant and has no name. While it (*pu*) can be small, no one in the world can lord over it

Tao is constant (常, *chang*2) and unchanging. It is formless and "has no name" (无名, *wu2ming*2). Laozi named it "Tao" out of necessity, and subsequently gave it other names, such as "Mysterious Te" (玄德) and "Mysterious Harmony (玄同)". Tao One is a manifestation of the formless Tao Core. To describe it, Laozi uses the word "*pu*" (朴, *pu*3) here, which means "innocence or simplicity".

Tao One, or "*pu*" "can be small" (虽小, *sui*1*xiao*3). It is small for a few reasons. First, the number "One" is the lowest numerically. Only "Zero", another name of the formless Tao, is smaller. *Pu*, therefore, is tiny. Second, Tao One is Mother of all things. What it creates can be as small as a speck of dust. While Tao is great it can also be small when it resides in the myriads of things.

While *pu* is small, no one in the world can "lord over it" (臣, *chen*2). *Pu* is Tao One and thus Mother of all things, as Laozi explains in Chapter 1. Who dares to "lord over" Mother of the universe?

When rulers can keep to it, all things obey their command

"Rulers" is a translation of 侯王 (*hou*2*wang*2). It refers to "the Kingly" or 王 we explain in Chapter 25, who is a person connected to Heaven and Earth and truly knows Tao. The "rulers", being "Kingly", is thus a leader who "keep to" (守, *shou*3) the non-doing of Tao. "They create but possess not. Do but seek no glory. Grow but dominate not. Accomplish but seek no credit." All things "obey their command" (自宾, *zi*4*bin*1). They go with the flow of Tao and thrive naturally, contributing to the abundance of the universe.

Heaven and earth conjoin to have rain of the sweet dew formed

The preceding sentence talks about the myriad of things; this sentence is about Heaven and Earth. Heaven is Yang, and Earth is Yin. The Yang energy descends, and the Yin energy rises. When they meet, they conjoin (相合, *xiang1he2*) to form the "sweet dew" (甘露, *gan1lu4*) of wind and rain that moisten the world. When there is enough rainfall, they bring the world the sunshine it needs. With the interplay of Yin Yang, the myriads of things flourish and live peacefully together.

Despite an order from no one, it falls equally on everyone

Having talked about Heaven and Earth, now let's look at people. When the weather is good and the land is full of abundance, people are well provided for and live happily together. Despite "command from no one" (莫之令, *mo4zhi1ling4*), the country is in good order, and people find their own ways to balance the resources. When there is excess, they produce less and save the extra for the rainy days. They cultivate themselves spiritually after a hard day's work. The world is peaceful, and the bliss "falls equally on everyone" (自均, *zi4jun1*).

Since time primordial when things were given names, there are desires for more. Alas, one must know when to stop

"Time primordial" paraphrases 始制 (*shi3zhi4*), which means "the system that was in existence at the beginning of time". Upon the emergence of Heaven and Earth, "being" (既有, *ji4you3*) came into existence, and they were given names. "One generates two, two generates three, and three generates the myriads of things," says Laozi. Alongside the thriving of the myriads of things are the spawning of desires. Alas! One must "know when to stop" (将知止, *jiang1zhi1zhi3*) and return to Tao. Refining our perpetual self is the primary purpose of our life.

Knowing when to stop, keeps one away from danger

By "knowing when to stop", we will not steer off the path of Tao, and we are "away from danger" (不殆, *bu4dai4*). If, on the contrary, we allow our desires to run wild, we are drifting further and further away from Tao. Sooner or later, we will reach a point of no return, putting our perpetual self in danger.

The way Tao works in the universe is not unlike rivers flowing into the sea

A sea cannot be a sea without the infusion of water from countless waterways. Even then, it doesn't mean that the more the water, the merrier. If water keeps flowing in without restraints, it deluges the sea.

Tao gives birth to the myriads of things, and the myriads of things generate insatiable desires. If Tao is the sea, then desire is the flow of water. If the water keeps pouring in without restraints, Tao Core is risking a deluge. In other words, although indulgence in the worldly pleasures is fine, we must know when to stop. Once we have crossed the limit, it becomes dangerous. The sea is our real self, and the waterways are our desires. Insatiable desires can flood our real selves. When that happens, our real self is in danger.

Decoding Note: Laozi outlines the benefits of Tao at the beginning of the chapter. It allows people to live happily together in harmony. There must, however, be a balance. Remember: We cultivate the temporal body to refine the perpetual self, not to fulfill the insatiable desires. Putting the cart before the horse is dangerous. We can suffocate our perpetual self with overindulgence.

Chapter 33
Die but not Perish 死而不亡

Knowing others is clever;
Know our self is truly wise.
Mastering others is strong;
Mastering our self is mighty.

Knowing we have enough,
We are truly rich.
Perseverance is strong will.
Losing not our center,
We shall endure.
Dying without perishing.
We live forever.

Knowing others is clever; know our self is truly wise

People enjoy talking about others. They are "clever" (智, *zhi*4) when making witty comments and taking part in juicy gossips. The cleverness, however, is of divides and short-sightedness. A person of Tao is guided by true wisdom. They know their roles in the universe and the urgency of self-cultivation. Although they are not clever, they know their true self and are "truly wise" (明, *ming*2).

Mastering others is strong; mastering our self is mighty

"Mastering others" paraphrases (胜人, *sheng*4*ren*2), which means "conquering" or "winning" others. To prevail over others, we often resort to physical force or design, which are a display of strength. We are "strong" (有力, *you*3*li*4). The victory, however, is based not on the virtue of Te, and it adds little to our Tao attainment. "Mastering our self" (自胜, *zi*4*sheng*4) is different. We rely on a strong inner strength to overcome desires and rein back stray thoughts. The quality makes us "mighty" (强, *qiang*2) in the pursuit of Tao.

Confucius liked to sing praises of Yan Hui. The young disciple was so disciplined he would not repeat a mistake, and this inner strength alone was enough to make him stand out. Few of us can be like him.

Decoding Note: Laozi draws a similar comparison in Chapter 48. Knowing and mastering others are more like "acquire knowledge". We add something every day. Knowing and mastering our self, on the other hand, is like learning of wisdom. For that, we let go of something every day. One is about the outward strength, while the other is about inner wisdom.

Knowing we have enough, we are truly rich

It sounds simple, but knowing that "we have enough" (知足, *zhi*1*zu*2) is not easy. More often than not, we keep wanting more.

We tell ourselves we would be wealthy if we had a million spare dollars. But, once we have a million, we would only want more. If we never feel we have enough, we will never be satisfied. On the other hand, when we know the impermanence of wealth and stop being slave to it, we make the best of everything we have. Then we are truly wealthy in an instant.

Decoding Note: "To be rich" refers not to materialistic possessions, but the spiritual richness for the attainment of Tao. When a person of Tao knows that they have enough, they are distracted not by worldly pleasures. They let go of the superfluous so that they can devote themselves fully to their pursuit. It enriches their virtue, making them ever more resourceful in the attainment of Tao.

Perseverance is strong will

"Perseverance" paraphrases 强行 (*qiang2xing2*), which means "forging ahead". With perseverance, we are steadfast in our pursuit of Tao. We don't allow the intrusion of the "five poisonous afflictions": greed, anger, ignorance, arrogance, and suspicion. We are disciplined, and we persevere to stay the course.

"Strong will" is a translation of 有志 (*you3zhi4*). It refers to our ambition to attain Tao. If we cannot even quit small bad habits, there is no point for us to talk about Tao attainment. The pursuit of Tao requires unwavering commitment. We must bring down our ego and ward off unwarranted desires. If we can persevere in doing these, we demonstrate our strong will.

Losing not our center, we shall endure

"Our center" paraphrases 其所 (*qi2suo3*), which means "what it is for". The center of our life is the cultivation of the temporal body for the refinement of our perpetual self. It paves the way for the complete attainment of Tao that "endures" (久, *jiu3*). If we can fully attain Tao, we enjoy eternity, as Tao does.

Dying without perishing, we live forever

"Dying" is a translation of 死 (*si*3), and "perishing" 亡 (*wang*2). When we fully attain Tao, we live on in our perpetual body. We are not constrained by the demise of our physical bodies. We "live forever" (寿, *shou*4).

Chapter 34
Achieve Greatness 成大

*The Great Tao flows everywhere
Both to the left and the right.
All things thrive on it,
And it denies none of them.
It accomplishes,
Yet claims no ownership.
It loves and nourishes everything,
Yet seeks no possession.
Always without desires.
It may be named "Small".
All things return to it,
And yet it does not dominate,
It may be named "Great".
By not claiming to be Great,
It achieves greatness.*

The Great Tao flows everywhere, both to the left and the right

"Everywhere" paraphrases 泛 (*fan*4), which means "deluge of a river" or "being everywhere". Together they refer to the omnipresence of Tao. While the Great Tao is definitely big, it is next to us: "Both to the left and to the right" (其可左右, *qi2ke3zuo3you*4). It is infinitesimal.

This is what we see in the pictograms of Taiji (太极), which is used to describe the Great Tao. The first pictogram 太 is made up of the sub-character 大 and a dot. 大 means big, and the dot means small. The second pictogram 极 means "ultimate" or "extreme". So the word 太 implies both big and small to the extreme. It can be immeasurably big and infinitesimally small.

While we are in awe of the grandness of the Great Tao, do not forget that it also impacts everything, however trivial it is. A small bad habit, for example, can snowball into a big problem to torment us if we don't stop it in time.

All things thrive on it, and it denies none of them

Every one of the myriads of things is derived from Tao, and they "thrive on it" (恃之以生, *shi4zhi1yi3sheng*1). Tao "denies" (辞, *ci*2) none of them. Everything comes and goes naturally; Tao forces none of them and allows them to live and grow in accordance with their destiny. This is the spirit of One Source that generates the myriads of things.

It accomplishes, yet claims no ownership

This sentence underscores the nature of Tao. "Accomplishes" is a translation of 功成 (*gong1cheng*2). "Claims no credit" paraphrases 不名有 (*bu4ming2you*3), which means "claiming no ownership".

As explained in chapter 1, 有 is Tao One that is Mother of all things. It, nevertheless, claims no credit for what it does to grow the myriads of things. As a result, the myriads of things unknowingly assume they accomplish everything on their own and think nothing of Tao.

It loves and nourishes everything, yet seeks no possession

"Loves" is a translation of 爱 (*ai*4), and "nourishes" 养 (*yang*3). Tao loves, protects, nourishes and fosters the myriads of things. It feeds them with energy for growth. Even then, being formless and selfless, it seeks no possession of any of them. Neither does it attempt to dominate. It simply allows nature to take its course. This is the spirit of Tao and the superiority of Te.

Always without desires

Tao is constant and unchanging. It is perpetual and selfless, and "without desires" (无欲, *wu2yu*4)

It may be named "Small"

The word "small" (小, *xiao*3) here may be interpreted in two ways. Tao is everywhere. From the worldly perspective, it is so small we can find it in things as insignificant as an ant or a mosquito. Is it not small? From a spiritual perspective, Tao is small because a person of Tao has few desires. As Laozi says in Chapter 40, "Returning is how Tao works." A person of Tao is nonchalant. They are indifferent to bigger fame, larger houses, more money, and higher social status that people are after. They like it small. They care little about self-interests, have few desires, and don't contend with anyone. They are happy to be "small".

All things return to it, and yet it does not dominate. It may be named "Great"

Although Tao is where everything is derived from and where they return to, it claims no possession and never seeks to lord over them. The spirit is noble, and thus Tao may be named "Great (大, *da*4)".

At the same time, a person of Tao does the reverse of what most people do. Instead of wanting more, they want less. While most people go from one to two, then two to three, they return from three to two to one, then back to zero. "Zero", in this context, is the formless Tao. Nothing is bigger than formlessness. We may, therefore, name it "Great".

The first interpretation is about the spirit of greatness, and the second the formlessness of Tao. Both are Great.

By not claiming to be Great, it achieves greatness

Since the Sages don't see themselves as Great, they are humble and always find room for improvement and, paradoxically, become Great as a result. The greatness is incremental, and this is how they fully attain Tao in the long run. By the same token, it is because the Sages don't feel fully enlightened that they finally achieve complete enlightenment. This is what Laozi means when he says in Chapter 15, "Since they are never fully filled, they are able to wear out and renew."

Chapter 35
Hold Fast to Tao 执大象

Hold fast to Tao,
And wander the world.
Wander and suffer no harm,
Fill the heart with peace and calm.

Joy and bait,
Stop passers-by.
Words of Tao
bland and dull.
Look at it; we cannot see a thing,
Listen to it; we cannot hear a sound,

Yet putting it to use,
It is profuse and ever-flowing.

Hold fast to Tao, and wander the world

Laozi uses 大象 (*da4xiang4*) to symbolize Tao here. The pictograms mean "Great image", which implies the formlessness of Tao. When we hold fast to it, we see the greatness of Tao and use it to guide our life. "Wander" is a translation of 往 (*wang3*), which is made up of the radical 彳 and sub-character 主. 彳 implies "taking action", and 主 means "master". It implies that by adhering to Tao, we are in control of our life. In the current life, we live to a ripe old age and suffer no abrupt death or disaster. Beyond this life, because we are aware of the impact of karma, we do what is right and are thus in control of our destiny.

Wander and suffer no harm, fill the heart with peace and calm

By holding fast to Tao, we are masters of our current life and beyond. It allows us to wander the world and "suffer no harm" (不害, *bu4hai4*). "Peace" is a translation of 安 (*an1*). It is about non-being. Since we are in control of our destiny, we enjoy peace of mind and are in absolute stillness. "Calm" is a translation of 平泰 (*ping2tai4*). It is about being. We bask in the bliss of Tao and live a happy life.

Decoding Note: The preceding paragraphs depict what happens if we can attain the greatness of Tao. In the passages below, Laozi teaches us how we can make it a reality.

Joy and bait, stop passers-by

"Joy" (乐, *le4*) refers to the worldly pleasures. "Bait" (饵, *er3*) are external distractions like food, sights, sex, glory, and wealth. If we find ourselves longing for joy, like a fish we are hooked by the bait, we must regain control of ourselves and refocus our efforts back toward Tao cultivation. We must always remind ourselves: "Mastering our self is mighty".

We are all only "passers-by" (过客, *guo4ke4*) on the journey of life. Always remember that every form is illusory, even our body. Therefore, when we savor the "joy and bait" to pamper our temporal self, we must do it as a "passer-by" and know when to "stop" (止, *zhi3*). It is like a vacation. When it is over, think of it no more. Return to self-cultivation for the attainment of Tao.

Words of Tao, bland and dull

A person of Tao is indifferent to worldly pursuits. When they speak, chances are they would advise against fixation and encourage one to perform self-cultivation. To those who are not ready, "words of Tao" spoken by them can sound "bland and dull".

In a way, a lifestyle based on Tao can be "bland" (淡, *dan4*) and "dull" (无味, *wu2wei4*) as well. It is not as colorful as the pursuits of the ordinary folks. It can, however, be a true relish. Having deducted time for schooling, career, and reduced mobility during old-age, what is left for us, in terms of self-cultivation, is probably just thirty to forty years of our life. If we indulge in being a passer-by and fail to begin self-cultivation in time, we lose the opportunity to connect to the eternal Tao. The consequences can be grave. "Joy and bait" are temporal. Only Tao is eternal.

Look at it; we cannot see a thing. Listen to it; we cannot hear a sound. Yet putting it into use, it is profuse and ever-flowing

Tao is formless. It is elusive. We can neither see nor hear it. If we can relish and practice its wisdom, however, it is "profuse and ever-flowing" (不可既, *bu4ke3ji4*). Tao is inexhaustible. The sages, who have attained complete enlightenment, live alongside Heaven and Earth. They are forever happy without worries.

Chapter 36
Subtle Insight 微明

To shrink it,
Allow it to expand.
To weaken it,
Allow it to go strong.
To eliminate it,
Allow it to flourish.
To take,
We give.

This is a subtle insight.

The soft and yielding
Overcome the strong and hard.
Fish cannot survive out water,
A country's weaponry
Should not be displayed to anyone.

To shrink it, allow it to expand

We may call it the law of reversal: Things move in the reverse direction when it has gone to the extreme. When we bounce a ball off the wall, the more we want the ball to bounce, the harder we must throw it. Similarly, if we are going to jump higher, we must squat lower. The principle works everywhere. To "shrink" 歙 (*xi*1) it, allow it to "expand" 张 (*zhang*1).

This principle forms the basis of the Taijiquan applications. If we intend to turn to the left, we first turn to the right. To move forward, we must first step back. We will discuss it more in the Chapter: Apply the Wisdom To Taijiquan.

To weaken it, allow it to go strong

Applying the same principle, if we want to weaken (弱, *ruo*4) something, let it go strong (强, *qiang*2). If it is an army, inflate its ego, make it think that it is "strong" and invincible. Let it bully around and instigate conflicts. When it has drained its resources and made enough enemies, it is weakened and will lose its prowess.

To eliminate it, allow it to flourish

By the same token, if we want to eliminate (废, *fei*4) something, allow it to gain strength and "flourish" (兴, *xing*4). One of the stratagems seen in war is to feign a defeat and make a false retreat. Thinking it has the upper hand, the enemy may give chase and fall prey to an ambush.

To take, we give

To earn respect, we must first be respectful. To enjoy success, we must first put in the hard work. "Take" is a translation of 夺 (*duo*2), and "give" 与 (*yu*3). Unfortunately, this can be done in a negative way as well. Scammers give away sweeteners and prey on the unsuspecting. If we know the law of reversal, however, we will not be easily ensnared.

Decoding Note: This chapter leads some to comment that Laozi is crafty. This is not true. The Sage introduces to us a law of nature, which is a double-edged sword. Whether we are using it to do good or to hurt, it is all up to us.

This is a subtle insight

"Subtle insight" paraphrases 微明 (*wei*1*ming*2). "Subtle" refers to "wei", or the subtlety of Tao. As Laozi says in Chapter 14, "Grab it, yet it cannot be grasped; we name it *wei*." *Wei* or 微 (*wei*1) means "tiny". But embedded in it is the law of the universe. "Insight" refers to 明, which means "discerning". Although *wei* is tiny to the extent of formlessness, it is not Tao *per se*. It is its manifestation through the law of reversal, which has divides and in it the oscillation of Yin and Yang. Seeing the "subtle insight" is about technique. In itself it is insufficient to take us to the complete attainment of Tao.

The soft and yielding overcome the strong and hard

Trees yield to the wind to survive, and water softly washes away rock over time. Only kindness can end a war, not more violence. The power of softness allows an old Taiji exponent to control an opponent twice his weight and half his age.

Fish cannot survive out of water

A person cannot survive without Tao, just like a fish cannot "survive out of water" (脱于渊, *tuo*1*yu*2*yuan*1). Qi (炁) is Tao. If we cannot deviate from Tao, neither can we deviate from qi. The earliest mass of qi in the universe is the *taihe* qi. While we rely on oxygen to live, we tap into the *taihe* qi energy to return to our true nature.

A country's weaponry should not be displayed to anyone

"A country's weapons" (国之利器, *guo2zhi1li4qi4*) are destructive. They are forceful and hard and are meant for self-defense, not for showing off or to be "displayed to anyone" (示于人, *shi4yu2ren2*). A warlike, hostile temperament is a means to disaster! We must show off our softness through humility, modesty, gentleness, and kindness, not the harshness of weaponry.

Chapter 37
The World Finds its Peace
天下自定

*Tao does nothing
And leaves nothing undone.*

*If Lord and King can keep to it,
All things are transformed on their own.
Should they still want to act,
I will contain them with
Nothingness and pu.*

*With nothingness and pu
There is no desire.
No desiring is tranquility,
And the world under Heaven is in peace.*

Tao does nothing and leaves nothing undone

Tao is constant and eternal. When Laozi says that it does "nothing" (无, *wu2*), it means things behave like Tao, which is formless and "nothingness" in nature. When things flow with its nature, they "do nothing" (无为, *wu2wei2*) and "leave nothing undone" (无不为, *wu2bu4wei2*).

Tao is all-encompassing, and everything in the universe goes with the flow. If we, too, can do things naturally by adhering to Tao, we are more effective in the things we do. Although we cannot "do nothing and leaves nothing undone" immediately, we can definitely achieve a lot more with the same amount of effort.

If we can put non-doing into practice, we enjoy the instant benefit of having less worry. By observing the law of nature, our ego takes a backseat, and we don't control things that are beyond our control. This alone is enough to take a lot of stress away. Then, if we can improve our mastery of non-doing further through consistent practice, we become more and more effortless in things we do and bring ourselves closer to the proximity of Tao. One day, we will behave like a sage and "do nothing, and leave nothing undone".

To get started in non-doing, we practice the teachings of the *Tao Te Ching* and emulate what the sages do: "Create but possess not. Do but seek no glory. Grow but seek not to dominate. Accomplish but claim no credit"; "blunt the sharpness, untangle the knot, blend in with the light, merge with the dust". Of course, we can't do them in perfection. The practice, however, makes us a worthy person. If we persevere, we will fully attain Tao and become a sage one day.

If Lord and King can keep to it, all things are transformed on their own

"Lord" (侯, *hou2*) here means leaders. "King" (王, *wang2*) refers to a "Kingly" person, as explained in Chapter 25. They are accomplished in Tao and connected to both Heaven and Earth. If Lord and King can keep to non-doing, "all things are transformed on their own". "All things" here refers to their followers. They will emulate what Lord and King do and naturally transcend themselves (化, *hua*4). In other words, the Lord and King transform others by transforming themselves.

Should they still want to act, I will contain them with nothingness and *pu*

In the process of the transformation, emotions like greed and lust will continue to fight for our attention. The Sage will contain them with nothingness and *pu*. "Nothingness" (无, *wu*2) is the formless Tao. *Pu* is a translation of 名之朴 (*ming*2*zhi*1*pu*3), which is another name of Tao One. They are non-being and being, respectively. "Contain" paraphrases 镇 (*zhen*4), which means "suppression". In other words, the moment when undesirable thoughts emerge, the Sage will contain them with the non-being and being of Tao. We all need the containment now and then. Even a highly accomplished person of Tao needs to be regularly reminded of the teachings of Tao and the ephemeral nature of things. *Pu* is simple and pure; it is, however, not free of divides. We must guard it carefully so that it will not be contaminated by selfishness, bigotry, and other distractions.

With nothingness and *pu*, there is no desire. No desire is tranquility, and the world under Heaven is in peace

With nothingness and *pu*, the undesirable thoughts are stopped from arising. As a result, "there is no desire" (不欲, *bu*4*yu*4). If we can do it consistently, we are in "tranquility" (静, *jing*4), and the ultimate tranquility connects us back to the nothingness of our true nature. It allows us to integrate with the *taihe* qi energy and, subsequently, the Primordial Yang. In this way, we bask in the radiance of Tao, and the world under Heaven "is in peace" (自定, *zi*4*ding*4). We are now in the proximity of Tao Core. In deep stillness, we no longer generate desires. It allows us to witness Tao Core and realize our very true nature. We are in One with Heaven and Earth.

The journey of Tao attainment is long and arduous. Before we arrive at the state where "the world of Heaven is in peace", we need to be in the ultimate tranquility. Only then are we able to integrate with the Large Taiji. Most of us are still far from it. The *taihe* energy that we can connect to is that of the Small Taiji. It is meager in comparison to the energy of the Large Taiji. It is many, many times bigger, which can light up thousands of universes. This explains why, when a Sage attains complete enlightenment, it is accompanied by phenomenal changes in Heaven and Earth. It is a moment when Heaven unites with Earth to usher in the Sage!

Chapter 38

Stay with the Thick and Solid 处厚处实

A person of the highest Te
Does not think of Te
But lives naturally with Te.
A person who is weak in Te
Is fixated on Te
But lives with no Te.
A person of the highest Te
Thinks and acts non-doing.
A person who is weak in Te
Thinks non-doing
But acts "doing".

The benevolent acts "doing" but think non-doing.
The self-righteous thinks and acts "doing".
Those with propriety acts "doing",
And if they see no response,
They grab one's arms to throw one out.

Therefore,
When Tao is lost, Te follows.
When Te is lost, benevolence follows.
When benevolence is lost, self-righteousness follows.
When self-righteousness is lost, propriety follows.

> *Propriety is the flimsiness of faith,*
> *And the precursor of chaos.*
> *Mentioned earlier*
> *Are an embellishment of Tao*
> *And the beginning of foolhardiness.*
> *Thus the Gentle-person*
> *Stays with the solid, not flimsy;*
> *Stays with the substance, not the embellishment.*
> *They discard the outer for the inner.*

A person of the highest Te does not think of Te but lives naturally with Te

"A person of the highest Te" (上德, *shang4de2*) "does not think of Te" (无德, *wu2de2*). This is consistent with the behavior of the formless Tao, which "creates but possesses not, does but seeks no glory, grows but seeks not to dominate, accomplishes but claims no credit". They flow with Tao, and live naturally with Te" (有德, *you3de2*).

A person who is weak in Te is fixated on Te but lives with no Te

"A person who is weak in Te" (下德, *xia4de2*), on the other hand, is "fixated on Te" (有德, *you3de2*). They are eager for credit and praise. This is inconsistent with the behavior of Tao. They, therefore, live with no Te" (无德, *wu2de2*).

A person of the highest Te thinks and acts non-doing

A person of the highest Te is consistent with Tao. They "think and act non-doing" (无以为, *wu2yi3wei2*). In fact, the notion of non-doing doesn't even cross their minds. What they think and what they do is consistent with Tao. They allow things to happen naturally.

A person who is weak in Te thinks non-doing but acts "doing"

A person who is weak in Te is aware of non-doing. They, however, "think non-doing" (无为, *wu2wei2*) and "act doing" (有以为, *you3yi3wei2*). They think of no reward in the things they do. Having done it, however, their ego gets the better of them, and they begin to long for credit. "Friend, I've helped you! You better don't forget what I've done for you!" What begins as "non-doing" now becomes "doing".

A person of the highest Te conforms to Tao both in thoughts and in acts. A person who is weak in Tao is inconsistent. They are non-doing in thoughts, but "doing" in their actions. Even then, they still perform Te and are rewarded with good fortune in life.

The benevolent acts "doing" but think non-doing

"The benevolent" is a translation of 上仁 (*shang4ren2*). Here, it refers to people who are compassionate but confine their benevolence to a specific group of people. Although not without divides, they think non-doing (无以为, *wu2yi3wei2*). Their actions, however, is that of "doing" (有以为, *you3yi3wei2*).

The self-righteous thinks and acts doing

'The self-righteous" is a translation of 上义 (*shang4yi4*). They are people who begin with "doing" and end with "doing". They are loyal, but the loyalty is blind. For the sake of camaraderie or kindness, they can turn a blind eye to Tao and commit misdeeds. They can, for example, go against their conscience and cover up a murder for the sake of a friend. The attitude is prevalent in secret societies. Both their thoughts and acts deviate from Tao.

Those with propriety acts "doing". And if they see no response, they grab one's arms to throw one out

"Those with propriety" is a translation of 上礼 (*shang4li3*). Laozi describes what they do as "the precursor of chaos". These are certainly not what a person of Tao does. Like the self-righteous, they lay down strict protocols, something like the dos and don'ts of a secret society. What if they see someone who doesn't respond to their rules? They become angry and resort to corporal punishment. They rule by protocols, not reason.

Therefore, when Tao is lost, Te follows. When Te is lost, benevolence follows. When benevolence is lost, self-righteousness follows. When self-righteousness is lost, propriety follows.

Tao, Te, benevolence, self-righteousness, and propriety illustrate the order of the ways where Tao is observed. The ultimate is Tao, followed by the highest Te, which is in the proximity of Tao. After that are behaviors of divides, including benevolence, self-righteousness, and propriety. Each level down the order takes us further away from Tao.

Propriety makes faith flimsy, and is the precursor of chaos

"Faith" is a translation of 忠信 (*zhong*1*xin*4). 忠 is usually interpreted as "loyalty", but it has a particular connotation here, and differ from the interpretation of Confucianism. The pictogram consists of two sub-characters: 中 and 心. The first means "middle"; and the second "heart". "Heart" is the heart of Tao, so the word implies faith and thus "keeping to the center". The second pictogram, 信 means "trust". It is fundamental to Tao practice. "propriety makes faith flimsy (薄, *bo*2)." It dilutes the devotion to Tao and leads us further and further away from Tao. When this happens, troubles begin. So, it is "the precursor (首, *shou*3) of chaos (乱, *luan*4)"!

A country plunges into chaos because it can no longer maintain the high order of Tao and Te. When self-righteousness and propriety take over control, people are very selfish. They disregard the interests of others and are not hesitant to cause harm to protect their own interests. When things are not done in the spirit of win-win, we usher in the "precursor of chaos".

Mentioned earlier are an embellishment of Tao and the beginning of foolhardiness

"Embellishment" paraphrases 华 (*hua*2), which means "resplendence". The word used to be a description of "flower" in ancient Chinese. Since the flower is situated at the tip of a plant, it can be blown away at any moment. It is the "beginning (始, *shi*3) of foolhardiness (愚, *yu*2)". This is in contrast to the root that is firm and can't be blown away.

Thus the Gentle-person stays with the solid, not flimsy

The "Gentle-person" (大丈夫, *da*4*zhang*4*fu*1) is a person of Tao. They stay with the "solid" (厚, *hou*4), as opposed to the "flimsiness" (薄, *bo*2) that we mentioned earlier. It is the quality of "the highest Te", and the virtue that we aspire. If we don't stay with the "flimsy", we are not in the constraints of the propriety.

    Decoding Note: "Gentle-person" is a translation of 大丈夫. The first pictogram 大 means "big". In this context, it is the Tao Core that is formless and immeasurably big. The second pictogram 丈 is made up of the sub-characters 一 and 乂. 一 means "one", and refers to Tao One. It means nothing should bother us except Tao One. The third pictogram 夫 is made up of the sub-characters 一 and 大, implying Tao One and Tao Core. Each of the three pictograms is related to either Tao Core or Tao One or both. The word is, therefore, a description of a person who knows Tao.

Stays with the substance, not the embellishment. They discard the outer for the inner

"Substance" (实, *shi*2) is about Tao Core and "the highest Te". "Embellishment" is about propriety. So, the sentence means we want "the highest Te", not "propriety". "Discard the outer" is to discard propriety. "For the inner" is to retain "the highest Te".

Chapter 39
One with Tao 得一

*According to the ancients
Who were One with Tao:
Heaven with One is clear,
Earth with One is peaceful,
Spirit with One is divine,
Valley with One is fulfilled,
All things with One are vibrant.
When Lord and King are with One
The world integrates.*

*In extreme, things depart from One.
Heaven that is not clear splits asunder,
Earth that is not at peace is useless,
Spirit that is not divine fades away,
Valley that is not fulfilled dries up fast,
Things that are not vibrant perish and die,
Lord and King who earn no integrity and dignity fall apart.*

*Thus the noble finds its root in the unworthy,
The high up relies on the low to form its base.
When Lord and King call themselves
'Orphan', 'widowed' and 'improper',
Is this not seeing the unworthy as their root?
Is this not so?
The highest honor is no honor,
Aim neither to be glistening jade
Nor humble pebbles.*

From this chapter, we see the order of how things are generated: Beginning from the Source, i.e., the formless Tao Core, Tao One, and Heaven and Earth emerged, followed by spirits, valleys, the myriads of things and the Lord and King. Among them, only the truly enlightened — exemplified by the Lord and King— are capable of returning to the Source upon complete attainment.

According to the ancients who were One with Tao:

"The ancients" are people of the past (昔, *xi*1). One (一, *yi*1) is Tao One, i.e., the use of Tao. The formless Tao Core has no effect on things, only Tao One has. By conforming to Tao One, things thrive. As we mentioned in Chapter 1, it is "Mother of all things".

Heaven with One is clear

Heaven (天, *tian*1) emerged upon the convergence of *taihe* qi and *Yuanyang* — the Primordial Yang. With the blessings of Tao One, the universe is in harmony. The weather is fine, and the sky is clear (清, *qing*1).

Earth with One is peaceful

Earth (地, *di*4) was born upon the emergence of Heaven. When Earth holds to the Oneness, it is "peaceful" (宁, *ning*2). Everything takes its bestowed position. A mountain towers in stillness, and a river runs. They do what their nature dictates. When a river is overflown with water, it calmly discharges the excess to prevent a flood. When everything is in its proper place, nothing goes amiss. Disasters like earthquakes are unheard of. Earth is peaceful.

Spirit with One is divine

The ancients believe that all things have a spirit (神, *shen*2). It is known as the "good energy" when given a modern twist. When the spirit holds to the Oneness, it is divine (灵, *ling*2) and able to release energy to help the sentient beings who seek its blessings.

Decoding Note: Of the myriads of things mentioned in this chapter, only Heaven, Earth, and spirits are directly connected to Tao One, and thus naturally with One. The remaining, beginning from valleys, are derived from the union of Yin and Yang. They are, therefore, divisive and do not always hold on to the Oneness. Only when they conform to Tao do they not drift further away and are able to be back with One.

Valley with One is fulfilled. All things with One are vibrant

A valley (谷, *gu*3) is "fulfilled" (盈, *ying*2) when it is alive and vibrant. The Yin energy of water at the bottom of the empty valley evaporates upward, while the Yang energy of the Sun descends downward. When they mingle, the valley is with One that generates the abundance, allowing all things to be blessed and flourish.

Decoding Note: Valleys are echoic and thus responsive. It is a translation of 谷 (*gu*3). The pictogram consists of two sub-characters 人, which means "people"; and the sub-character 口, which means "the mouth". It symbolizes two people talking to each other; implying interaction. "Valley with One is fulfilled." A responsive valley can thrive because it responses to the blessings of Tao One and basks itself in the divine light of Tao. Similarly, the myriads of things (万物, *wan*4*wu*4) are vibrant (生, *sheng*1) only when they are like a "valley with One". They enjoy the abundance when they react positively to Tao. Otherwise, they go into decline. It exemplifies the theory of evolution.

When Lord and King are with One, the world integrates

Throughout this book, as previously mentioned, "Lord" (侯, *hou*2) and "King" (王, *wang*2) refer to those who are accomplished in Tao. They are "with One" for their impartiality and selflessness. They govern with honesty, and so "the world integrates" (天下正, *tian1xia4zheng4*). Under them, the wayward and wicked cannot wreak havoc, and the people live happily together.

In extreme, things depart from One

Governed by the law of reversal, things take a reverse path upon reaching an extreme (致之, *zhi4zhi1*). When One is lost, the world becomes divisive and is driven by selfishness. Tao One is eclipsed.

Heaven that is not clear splits asunder

When Heaven loses Tao One, so goes the blessings of *Yuanyang* and the divine light of Tao. The wicked rise to dominance to devour the world with greed. How can Heaven ever be clear when this happens? The order of nature is disrupted. The weather is unpredictable, and the Sun and Moon pale. Winter is no longer like winter nor summer like summer. Frequent outbreaks of drought, floods, and diseases devastate the world. Not only is "Heaven not clear", but it is about to break into pieces or "split asunder" (裂, *lie4*).

Earth that is not at peace is useless

Tao One and *Yuanyang* are life-giving, and they loathe killing. When Earth loses Tao One, the wicked takeover. They compete for the control of resources, resulting in rampant damage to nature. Calamities like earthquakes and tsunami become commonplace. Not only is Earth no longer peaceful, but it also runs the risk of becoming useless (废, *fei4*).

Spirit that is not divine fades away

The spirit that loses blessings of Tao One and the divine light is feeble and too weak to perform its divine duties. Like a battery about to deplete, its energy "fades away" (歇, *xie1*).

Valley that is not fulfilled dries up fast

The valley relies on the energy of Heaven and Earth to survive. Now that the valley is no longer responsive, the sunshine can no longer mingle with its water, and the vitality is lost. The valley is deprived of the abundance and "is not fulfilled". Sadly, "it dries up" (竭, *jie*2) fast.

Things that are not vibrant perish and die

If *Yuanyang* and the divine light do not bless Heaven and Earth, there is insufficient energy to sustain the vitality of the myriads of things, and they will soon "perish and die" (灭, *mie*4). The universe is on the verge of depletion and moving toward extinction.

Lord and King who earn no integrity and dignity fall apart

"Fall apart" paraphrases 蹶 (*jue*2), which means "running into difficulty and failing". Lord and King can effectively lead because of the "integrity" (贞正, *zhen*1*zheng*4) and "dignity" (贵高, *gui*4*gao*1) that they have earned. Now that the world is in chaos and the wicked are rampant, they are no longer in control and cannot rule with love and respect. Sadly, they are about to "fall apart".

Thus the noble finds its root in the unworthy. The high up relies on the low to form its base

The Lord and King can lead with "dignity" (贵, *gui*4) from above because of support from the "unworthy" (贱, *jian*4) people below. Without the support, there is no dignity to speak of, and Lord and King can no longer lead from above. The relationship between the high and the low is similar. A building cannot stand tall without the foundation of solid rocks below. We must not forget the root when we enjoy high positions. Whether we are the king of a country or boss of a company, we are what we are only with support from the people. The "high up" (高, *gao*1) "relies on" (以, *yi*3) the "low" (下, *xia*4) to "form its base" (为基, *wei*2*ji*1).

When Lord and King call themselves "orphan", "widowed" and "improper", is it not seeing the unworthy as their root? Is this not so?

Knowing that their nobility and high positions are possible only with the support of their people below, the Lord and King "call themselves orphan, widowed, and improper". Being self-deprecating reminds them of their roots.

Traditionally, rulers in ancient China described themselves as 孤寡不谷 (*gu*1*gua*3*bu*4*gu*3). 孤寡 means "orphaned and widowed", implying ignorance. 不谷 literally means "not behaving like a valley", so they are apologetic for not being responsive or accommodating. It is as if the ancient rulers were saying, "Please bear with me. I'm sure there is room for improvement." So, the self-bestowed titles signal humility and modesty. They are adhering to the principle of "the high up relies on the low to form its base"! Are they not?

The highest honor is no honor

While the "highest honor" (致誉, *zhi*4*yu*4) is "the complete attainment of Tao", "no honor" does not mean "no attainment of Tao". The latter paraphrases 无誉 (*wu*2*yu*4). 无 is *wu* or non-being of Tao. So it refers to Tao Core. 誉 is an honor. In this context, the "highest honor" is the honor of nothingness or Tao, because it is eternal. Whether we are a big boss of a company or president of a country, the honor we carry can never be as high as that of Tao. The eternal honor only befits sages such as Laozi.

Aim neither to be glistening jade nor humble pebbles

What is the difference between a piece of "jade" (玉, *yu*4) and a "pebble" (石, *shi*2)? People dignify jade and look down on a pebble because of their entrenched mindsets. In the eyes of Tao, a string of pebbles is no different from a necklace of jade. The same applies to other things in the world. By giving the highest honor to Tao, we have no divides and see no difference between jade and stone.

Chapter 40
Being and Non-being 有无

Returning is how Tao works,
Softness is how Tao moves.

All things are born of being,
And being is born of non-being.

Returning is how Tao works

"Returning" is a translation of 反 (*fan3*), and "works" 用 (*yong4*). The sentence can be interpreted in two ways: Being and non-being.

First, let's look at it from the perspective of being. It refers to the returning of a cycle. Everything in the universe follows a cyclical movement. The cycle of seasons is a good example. It repeats itself, again and again. It also refers to the law of reversal: Anything that reaches the extreme travels back in a reverse direction. "To shrink it, allow it to expand," says Laozi in Chapter 36. In order to jump high, we squat low.

Now, let's look at it from the non-being perspective. In Tao cultivation, "returning" refers to a reverse mindset. To attain Tao, we do what most people don't. Most people want more; we are happy to have less. Most people are driven by endless desires, and we are happy to have only few. Most people don't know when to stop; we know our limit. It is only with "returning" — doing the reverse — that we are able to attain Tao.

Softness is how Tao moves

"Softness" is a translation of 弱 (*ruo4*), and "moves" 动 (*dong4*). Every life begins soft. Once it is hardened, it begins its decline. A person begins their life-cycle soft and weak. As a baby, softness conditions rapid growth. As a person gets older, however, they harden. At the point of death, they are stiff. So is a plant. It is soft and weak when it is a new seedling. Pull it gently, and it is uprooted. The softness aids its growth into a big tree. Then, it cannot be easily uprooted anymore. Similarly, as it gets older, it hardens. At death, it is brittle and dry.

Softness is a movement of gradual and incremental changes. In Taiji, the martial arts, when the opponent presses hard, we yield and reverse the force instantaneously back to his heels to tilt his balance, and turn our softness into strength. In Taiji, yielding leads to calmness, which overcomes movements.

This is evident in other changes as well. In spring, the Yang energy is small and weak. Slowly, it grows in intensity. It gets stronger and, by summer, reaches its peak. Then, the Yang energy gives way to the Yin and allows the Yin energy to grow from weak to strong. In autumn, the Yin energy grows in intensity, lowering the temperature in the process. Summer does not skip autumn to jump into winter, nor winter skip spring to jump into summer. The Yang energy goes from weak to strong, so does the Yin. This is how nature works. It is unhurried, allowing changes to take place gradually.

This explains why we must stay modest, humble at all times, patiently allowing space for changes to arise. This is how "Tao moves" (道之动, *dao4zhi1dong4*), and how we attain Tao.

All things are born of being, and being is born of non-being

As Laozi mentions in the first chapter, "Being, Mother of all things". Being is Tao One, from which all things are derived. It is the One Source of the myriads of things.

"Non-being, the beginning of Heaven and Earth." Non-being is Tao Core, also known as Tao Zero. It is *wuji* and infinite. "Being", on the other hand, is One. It is Taiji, finite, and is derived from non-being. Only when there is Zero, can there be One.

Chapter 41
Hear of Tao 闻道

When the wise hear of Tao,
They diligently practice it.
When the average people hear of Tao,
Now they believe, and now they don't.
When the ignorant hear of Tao,
They roar into laughter.
Without the laughter,
There is no substance in Tao.

So goes the established wisdom:
Enlightenment looks insipid,
The advance of Tao looks regressive,
The level path of Tao looks bumpy.

The highest Te looks like a valley,
The purest white looks grubby (dark).
The richness of Te looks inadequate,
The constructive Te looks stealthy.
The most real seems wavering.

Great squares have no angle,
Great pieces of art take time to complete,
Great sounds are hardly heard,
Great images show no form.

Tao is hidden and did not have a name.
It is Tao,
that gives and accomplishes.

When the wise hear of Tao, they diligently practice it

"The wise" paraphrases 上士 (*shang4shi4*). They are people who have a natural inclination for Tao. Not everybody reacts to Tao in the same way. Some people are quick to accept it; others are slow. The wise are those who are quick. Upon hearing of Tao, they "diligently" (勤而, *qin2er2*) practice it" (行之, *xing2zhi1*). For the fact that you are reading the *Tao Te Ching*, I do not doubt that you are among "the wise".

When the average people hear of Tao, now they believe, and now they don't

"The average people" (中士, *zhong1shi4*) are slower. Upon hearing of Tao, "now they believe, and now they don't" (或存或亡, *huo4cun2huo4wang2*). Even if they do practice it, they are inconsistent. Why is this so? It all boils down to belief. They are half-hearted and choose to hear only what they like to hear. It is just a matter of time. When the time is right, they will grow in their belief and walk the path of Tao as the wise.

When the ignorant hear of Tao, they roar into laughter

The ignorant (下士, *xia4shi4*) are apathetic to Tao and regard it as silly. To them, pursuit of worldly pleasures is the only way. They fail to understand why we must have fewer desires. Because they do not understand the idea, they push it aside by making fun and laughing at it.

Without the laughter, there is no substance in Tao

"Without the laughter" (不笑, *bu4xiao4*), we cannot tell what the ignorant have missed and what the wise have enjoyed. We cannot see the "substance" (足, *zu2*) in Tao. Tao follows what naturally is. This is beyond the ignorant, so it is natural for them to roar into laughter. The ignorant need our empathy. They may have missed the opportunities to learn Tao or are experiencing a stumbling block. We must feel happy for them that at least they do hear it now, even though Tao sounds foolish to them.

As mentioned in Chapter 17, "Those who do not trust enough will not be trusted." The ignorant are worse: They simply have no trust. They need to be guided and given access to Tao. However, we must be patient. It is quite an achievement if we can help them progress to become an average. When introducing the *Tao Te Ching*, do not make it overly complicated. It is a beautiful thing to hold their hands as if they are kindergarten children and help them take it one step at a time. Slowly, we explain to them what being natural means, and how we can learn the law that governs the universe by understanding the seasons and the relationship between what we sow and what we reap.

Milieu or the environment is important. The ignorant may not have the environment, and to change their current one may not be easy. We must exercise patience. A common misunderstanding among the ignorant is that Tao is anti-science. Let them know that many modern scientists find a surprising similarity between their discoveries and Laozi's teachings written more than two millennia ago. For example, modern quantum physicists have discovered that physical things ultimately do not have a physical structure; that all things are merely matter vibrating at different frequencies. This echoes what Laozi describes as non-being or nothingness thousands of years earlier.

Decoding Note: "The wise" are likely to be fast learners of Taijigong. Since they are devoted to Tao and diligent in its practice, they are sensitive to the qi energy. Tao is, after all, qi. When the wise find harmony between their true self and qi, they can easily permeate their entire body with the small *taihe* qi (炁) energy, setting the stage for the integration with Heaven and accomplishment in Taijigong.

So goes the established wisdom

The "established wisdom" (建言, *jian4yan2*) refers to views that add to the appreciation of Tao. They include the advice given in the following passages.

You may wonder why Laozi uses expressions of uncertainty, such as "look" and "like", time and again. It is not that he is uncertain. Since we can only remotely describe what Tao is, it is only natural that he sounds hesitant when talking about it.

Enlightenment looks insipid

"Insipid" is a translation of 昧 (*mei*4), which means "dull" or "ignorant". "Enlightenment" (明道, *ming2dao*4) may look insipid but not necessarily dull. It is difficult to describe Tao. Although the enlightened live the philosophy, it is hard to explain and put it into words. Tao can only be relished. The more we are immersed in it, the more that we are aware of the nuances. It is, however, very difficult to relate the experience.

Although insipid in appearance, the enlightened are exceptionally wise. They do not try to sound smart. Tao is "what is", and to the enlightened, there is so much more to say about it. Because it is difficult to speak of Tao, the enlightened inspire only those who have the quality to be inspired. Laozi uses 昧 to describe the enlightened, and this is very apt because it means "dimness". The pictogram is made up of two words: 日 and 未. 日 means "the sun", and 未 means "yet to happen". Literally, it means "yet to have sunshine", or "appears gloomy". The enlightened can be so humble they even appear silly.

Many excellent Taoists are known to be insipid. Master Zhang Sanfeng, the legendary Taoist to whom some attribute the invention of Taijiquan, was also known as Scruffy Zhang. The legendary monk Jigong, who trudged frivolously in a pair of broken shoes wherever he went, was also insipid.

The advance of Tao looks regressive

This sentence can be interpreted in two ways. First, advance (进, *jin*4) in the attainment of Tao can appear to be regressive (退, *tui*4). "Richness in Te looks inadequate." It is a long and arduous journey. When we have reached a milestone, there is another in front of us.

We feel inadequate wherever we are. The journey is like rowing a boat against the current. If we do not forge ahead, the water pushes us back. So, we must always be aware of regression and cannot afford to stay at a standstill. The moment we feel that we are good enough, we stop progressing.

Second, attaining Tao is a regression in the eyes of the world. Progress in the learning of Tao weakens our worldly desires. Instead of wanting more, we choose to have just enough. We are no longer greedy and stop chasing glory and wealth once our goal is met. To ordinary folks, it may appear that we are not progressing. Therefore, the advance of Tao can look regressive.

The level path of Tao looks bumpy

Although the path of Tao is "level" (夷, *yi*3), it can appear "bumpy" (纇, *lei*4) because it is riddled with many challenges. To align ourselves with Tao, we must practice great self-discipline in order to remain peaceful, kind, and compassionate at all times and under all circumstances. This requires us to extricate ourselves from greed, selfishness, and earthly pleasures. Otherwise, we may mistake small achievements along the way as realizations of our true nature. This is misleading and dangerous. It makes the path to the attainment of Tao bumpy, because we may go wayward as a result.

The highest Te looks like a valley

Those with "the highest Te" (上德, *shang*4*de*2) are the Tao adepts who practice non-doing. They "do nothing, and leave nothing undone". They are highly enlightened and in the proximity of Tao Core and Tao Use. So wise and profound, they are "like a valley". The word "valley" is a translation of 谷 (*gu*3). It first appears in Chapter 6 and is used in various chapters of the *Tao Te Ching*. It implies being echoic and interactive. Although those of "the highest Te" are as profound as a valley, they do not see themselves as being superior. Instead, they are solidly grounded and are as humble as a valley. Being responsive, they are always ready to help when approached for assistance.

The purest white looks grubby (dark)

"The purest white" is a translation of 大白 (*da4bai2*). 大 means "big" and implies the invisible Tao. 白 means "white" and implies purity. "Grubby" is a translation of 辱 (*ru3*), which means "humiliation". The enlightened are white and pure even when there is no one watching. "The purest white" may also be interpreted as the people of great wisdom. They are near those with the highest Te. Taking humiliation in stride, they "know the honor, and shun not the humiliation". No matter how grave the insult is, they are unruffled.

Monk Han Shan asked his fellow monk, "There are people who slander me, bully me, humiliate me, laugh at me, look down on me, demean me, sully me, lie to me. How should I react?" His fellow monk, Shide, replied, "Just bear with them, let them, allow them, avoid them, be patient with them, respect them, ignore them. Then, look at them again a few years later." It is an excellent example of "the purest white looks grubby (dark)".

The richness of Te looks inadequate

People with "richness of Te" (广德, *guang3de2*) always feel that they are "inadequate" (不足, *bu4zu2*), so they never stop performing good deeds. It is precisely the feeling of inadequacy that prompts them to improve continuously, making their virtue even richer.

The constructive Te looks stealthy

People of "constructive Te" (建德, *jian4de2*) never blow their own horn. They quietly perform, almost stealthily (偷, *tou1*). They are the stark opposite of those who cannot wait to announce what they have done or the money they have donated. The two types of people are worlds apart.

The most real seems wavering

"The most real" is a translation of 质贞 (*zhi4zhen*1). 质 means "quality" or "essence". 贞 means "true nature". Together they mean "unchanging nature". "Seems wavering" is a translation of 若渝 (*ruo4yu2*). 若 means "as if", and 渝 means "changes". We may, therefore, interpret the phrase as saying "as if changing". This makes the entire sentence a paradox: "The unchanging nature is as if changing". How is this possible? The unchanging nature is our true nature, so it is the Tao in us. It is constant and does not change. Things in the world, however, change all the time. When things change, the Tao within them does not change. Recognizing this, it reminds us not to be bigoted about things. Putting on a warm jacket is appropriate in the winter but not in summer. We change with the time, but do not forget the constant: The proper body temperature to maintain a healthy body.

We can also interpret the sentence from the perspective of being and non-being. "The most real" is non-being. It is unchanging. It is in the proximity of Tao Core. "Wavering" is being. In non-being, the Sage connects to the Tao Core and witnesses their "unchanging nature". When they go about helping people, they are going with the flow of changes. As such, they are principled and flexible. They change in consideration of the appropriateness of time, place, and nature of things but keep "the most real" constant.

Great squares have no angle

"Great" (大, *da4*) implies the formless Tao. "Square" (方, *fang1*) implies uprightness. While Tao is upright, it is not angular. Squarish objects cut because they have sharp "angles" (隅, *yu3*). Tao is formless and has no divides, so it is square with no sharp corners and thus does not cut. It benefits without hurting.

Great pieces of art take time to complete

"Great pieces of art" (大器, *da4qi4*) are art pieces crafted with Tao in mind. This is what we do to our self for the attainment of Tao. We craft our self into an art piece of excellence. It "takes time to complete" (晚成, *wan3cheng2*). If the Buddha, as we mentioned earlier, had to be reborn 500 times before he attained complete enlightenment, it is not a surprise that we will take longer. How long it takes does not matter. Every improvement is a refinement of the piece of art and a cause for celebration.

Great sounds are hardly heard.
Great images show no form

"Great sounds" (大音, *da4yin1*) are the sound of Tao. It is "inaudible" (希声, *xi1sheng1*) to the uninitiated. "Great images" (大象, *da4xiang4*) are images of Tao. They are "invisible" (无形, *wu2xing2*) to most people.

Although Tao is invisible to most people, the enlightened are able to discern it. In fact, even people new to cultivation can hear it and see its existence, if they are truly calm.

One day, my Master, Wu Tunan, suddenly said to me, "Serve Master Sanfeng tea." I was stunned as Master Zhang Sanfeng was a Master who had passed away centuries ago. Was he around in the house? Apparently, he was. Not only did my Master see him, he knew precisely the spot where the ancestor was and asked me to serve him tea as a form of respect. My Master was then yet to attain complete attainment, and yet he was already able to see Master Sanfeng's spirit.

Tao is hidden and did not have a name

"The Great Tao flows everywhere, both to the left and to the right," says Laozi in Chapter 34. Although Tao is invisible, it is everywhere and all around us. It "did not have a name" (无名, *wu2ming2*), and

Laozi calls it "Tao" out of necessity. While "hidden" (隐, *yin*3), Tao is incredibly big on the one hand and incredibly small on the other. It is so big that it is formless and so small that it escapes the perception of the naked eye. It is Taiji, i.e., the ultimate extremity.

It is Tao that gives and accomplishes

"Gives" is a translation of 贷 (*dai*4), which means "giving a loan", although in this case, the giver expects no repayments. A person of Tao gives unconditionally and wholeheartedly, expecting nothing in return when they "accomplish" (成, *cheng*2) what they do. They are always ready to give, be it in the form of sharing knowledge or wealth.

In Taijigong, we are always ready to give. In sparring, we give way to the attacking force of the opponent. When they push us to the left, we follow them to the left and vice versa. We do not resist. Taijigong is thus an art of Tao, and giving is in its heart. If we are good at giving, we are good at fulfilling the spirit of Tao. Laozi, therefore, says, "It is Tao that gives and accomplishes."

Chapter 42
Blending Yin Yang 冲和

Tao generates One,
One generates Two,
Two generates Three
And Three generates the myriads of things.

All things turn their back to Yin
And embrace Yang.
By blending the Yin and Yang,
they produce harmony.

What people loathe,
Are being orphaned and widowed,
And unable to respond like a valley.
Yet they are what the Kingly calls themselves.

For sometimes things gain by losing,
Or lose by gaining.

Tao generates One. One generates Two. Two generates Three, and Three generates the myriads of things

Tao is formless, how does it "generate" (生, *sheng*1) "One (一, *yi*1)"? Before the universe was born, there was only a mass of energy that consisted of *taihe* qi. When the energy converged with *Yuanyang*, the Primordial Yang, it sparked off the light of Tao that traversed countless miles and lit up the newly-formed universe. So "Tao generates One".

Derived directly from *Yuanyang*, One, also known as Tao One, was full of Yang energy and was life-giving. It created Heaven, followed by Earth, and Yin and Yang came into being. Now, One generates "Two" (二, *er*4). With Yin and Yang, things were born, and they continued to procreate. Soon Two generates "Three" (三, *san*1), and "Three" produces the myriads of things.

So Heaven and Earth are born of "One", and the human being "Two". Unlike other beings, the human is blessed with the intelligence that has the capacity of taking us back to Tao One and Tao Core. We are able to integrate ourselves with the energy and Te of Heaven and Earth, *Yuanyang*, and the divine light of Tao. Other beings cannot. They have to be reborn as a human first to do just that. This is why Heaven, Earth, and the human being are described as the "Three Talents" of the universe.

We should, therefore, treasure the privilege of being a human being. If we are consistent in our cultivation, we will eventually return to Tao Core. The journey, however, is long and arduous and can take many lifetimes and thousands and millions of years to complete. As Laozi says in Chapter 64, "A journey of a thousand miles begins with a single step." So long as the direction is right, we will arrive.

All things turn their back to Yin and embrace Yang

Yin (阴, *yin*1), in this context, may be seen as "negativity" or "what people dislike". Of the four seasons, autumn and winter are primarily Yin. Bleak and harsh, they have the tendency to eliminate and destroy. They are things people "turn their back" (负, *fu*4) on.

People "embrace" (抱, *bao*4) Yang (阳, *yang*2), exemplified by the energy of spring and summer, which is bright and warm and conducive to growth.

By blending the Yin and Yang, they produce harmony

"Blending" is a translation of 冲 (*chong*1). The pictogram is made up of radical 冫 and the sub-character 中, which means "middle". The radical, consists of a dot and a tick, implies Yin and Yang, respectively. The sub-character implies neutralization of the energies of Yin and Yang, which is a vitally important process that stabilizes the universe. We see it in the transition of seasons, which takes place gradually. Thanks to the "blending" of the Yin and Yang. It helps the myriads of things to adapt to changes, and the universe to continuously renew itself.

What people loathe, are being orphaned and widowed and unable to respond like a valley. Yet they are what the Kingly call themselves

"Being orphaned and widowed" is a translation of 孤寡 (*gu*1*gua*3). It has two implications. First, ignorance, and second, solitude and loneliness. People loathe being in these states. "Unable to respond like a valley" is a translation of 不谷 (*bu*4*gu*3). We cannot respond to people's calls for help and keep relationships going. We are lonely. While these are unpleasant qualities, "they are what the Kingly call themselves", because the Kingly is modest and humble. It reflects the richness of their Te.

For sometimes things gain by losing, or lose by gaining

Whenever a choice is made in life, we gain something and lose something — all at the same time. A jacket we buy could be at the expense of an exquisite dinner. While losing a job is unfortunate, it could set us free to pursue a more rewarding interest. "As one door closes, another opens," as the saying goes. So, to lose is to gain, and to gain is to lose. Besides, there are occasions when the best gain is to lose. In order to gain, we must be prepared to lose. The secret is to blend the Yin and Yang to strike a balance between them.

There is, however, a difference between gaining at the expense of those above and those below. This is explained in detail in the two hexagrams of the *Yijing*: Loss (损) and Benefit (益).

If we cause a loss to the people who are in need, so as to bring gains to the people who have excess, this is a "true loss". It is like a boss sacrificing the interests of his employees to bring in more profit for himself. The boss becomes richer, and his employees poorer. The little gain the boss gets is insignificant when compared to the Te he drains away. On the other hand, when we cause a loss to the people who have excess so as to bring gains for those in need, then it is a "true gain". When the boss takes care of the employees, he earns his employees' loyalty. More importantly, he moves himself closer to Tao! He gains in his Tao attainment.

Chapter 43

The Soft Overcomes the Hard 柔克刚(至柔)

The softest of all things
Can overcome the hardest.
That without form
Penetrates that without space.
Through which I find out
The value of non-doing.

Teachings of no words,
Benefits of non-doing,
Few in the world can truly achieve it.

The softest of all things can overcome the hardest

"Overcome" paraphrases 驰骋 (*chi2cheng3*), which is often used to describe the galloping of a horse. In this context, it implies "taking control".

Although the "softest" (至柔, *zhi4rou2*) of all things can potentially overcome the hardest (至坚, *zhi4jian1*), it is not a matter of course. For it to happen, at least a pair of conditions must be met. The first is consistency. Water, for example, cannot drill a hole in the ground unless it consistently drips from the roof. The second is yielding. When water crashes upon a rock, because water is yielding, neither the water nor the rock is hurt. In this way, water can come back, again and again, to erode the rock over time.

It is because of softness that an old and seemingly frail Taijiquan master is able to fight off an opponent twice his size and half his age. With the softness, he has the room to listen and deflect the force back to the opponent. Softness has other benefits as well. Chief among them is health. This is how my Master Wu Tunan was able to perform the Golden Rooster Stance at age 102. The posture is challenging even for people who are much younger. It is like the tree pose of yoga and requires the practitioner to stand on a single leg with the other three limbs posing in alignment in the air.

That without form penetrates that without space

"That without form" paraphrases 无有 (*wu2you3*), which literally means "having nothing", and refers to non-being or the nature of Tao Core. "That without space" (无间, *wu2jian1*), on the other hand, refers to "something" and refers to being. No matter how solid an object, or being, is, non-being is always able to penetrate (入, *ru4*) it.

Through which I find out the value of non-doing

By observing how the soft overcomes the hard, the Sage marvels at the power of non-doing. The "non" of non-doing is a noun, not an adjective. It refers to non-being, i.e., nothingnesses, of the invisible Tao Core. Putting the virtue of nothingness to work, the Sage "creates but possesses not, does but seeks no glory, grows but seeks not to dominate, accomplishes but claims no credit".

"The value" is a translation of 有益 ($you3yi4$). 有 means "substance", and 益 means "value". 有益 thus means the "value of being". Through softness, the Sage sees the power of non-being via its impact on being. "The value" is derived from the formless Tao.

Teachings of no words, benefits of non-doing. Few in the world can truly achieve it

Since Tao is formless, we cannot describe it precisely in words. Teachings of "no word" (无言, $wu2yan2$), therefore, are the teachings of Tao that guide not through words but examples. We can only, like the old Chinese saying goes, "learn it by knowing it in the heart and realize it through practice". When we "know it in the heart", we internalize the teachings. When we "realize it through practice", we verify our understanding through taking action. By tapping into "the teachings of no words", we learn to work with non-being and truly benefit from Tao. Unfortunately, "few" (希, $xi1$) in the world can "truly achieve it" (及之, $ji2zhi1$).

Decoding Note: The Buddhist scripture, the *Diamond Sutra* says sages have different levels of achievement due to different levels of mastery in non-doing. So, the value of non-doing can well be a measure of one's attainment of sageness.

Chapter 44

Knowing Enough and When to Stop 知足知止

Fame or self:
Which is dearer?
Self or wealth:
Which is more valuable?
Loss of gain or loss of life:
Which is more miserable?
Thus extreme love is draining,
Hoarding inflicts heavy loss.

Those who are content suffer no disgrace,
Those who know when to stop suffer no peril.
They are enduring.

Fame or self: Which is dearer?

Between "fame" (名, *ming*2) and "self" (身, *shen*1), which is "dearer" (亲, *qin*1)? The answer is obvious: The self. What is fame for, when our self is lost and we are no longer alive? Even though the physical body is temporal, it is indispensable to self-cultivation. Without cultivation, we cannot refine our perpetual self.

Self or wealth: Which is more valuable?

Between "self" and "wealth" (货, *huo*4), which is more "valuable" (paraphrases 多, *duo*1)? Again, the answer is clear. If we are threatened at knife-point for our money, do we prefer the money to our life? Even if we retain wealth, what is the point if life is lost. We can bring the money back, not life. Furthermore, we cannot conduct self-cultivation as a result, putting our perpetual self in peril. We must not let our physical body perish for no good reason.

Loss of gain or loss of life: Which is more miserable?

Between the loss of "gain" (得, *de*2) and loss of "life" (亡, *wang*2), which is more "miserable" (病, *bing*4)? In the final analysis, it is still the self that is more important. There are ways to bring back the money, fame, and other possessions; not life.

Thus extreme love is draining

"Extreme love" is a translation of 甚爱 (*shen*4*ai*4). Whether it is money or fame, too much attachment to it is draining (大费, *da*4*fei*4). It deprives us of our energy for self-cultivation. If we want to refine our true selves, we cannot drain our energy in other pursuits.

Hoarding inflicts heavy loss

"Hoarding" is a translation of 多藏 (*duo1cang2*), which means "stocking up". "Heavy loss" paraphrases 厚亡 (*hou4wang2*), which implies "miserable death". If we are fixated on hoarding wealth, it inflicts harm on our body, leading to heavy loss of self. "Hoarding" is, in itself, already against Tao. Now that the physical body is harmed, we suffer a double setback. We must stop when we have enough.

Those who are content suffer no disgrace. Those who know when to stop suffer no peril. They are enduring

Those who are "content" (知足, *zhi1zu2*) are not greedy. They "know when to stop". "Enduring" paraphrases 长久 (*chang2jiu3*), which means "forever". They are enduring, because whatever they do conform to Tao, which is eternal.

If we can be content and happy with just enough to get by and focus our attention on the cultivation of Tao, we will "suffer no disgrace" (不辱, *bu4ru3*).

If we can stop anything that hampers our pursuit of Tao, we will "suffer no peril (殆, *dai4*) in our cultivation. To do that, we must be "content" and "know when to stop". It makes our virtue of Tao "enduring" and makes our attainment of Tao more complete.

Laozi is kind. He wants us to be "content" and "know when to stop", rather than giving up everything. He wants us to have "fewer thoughts and little desires", rather than having no thoughts and no desires. If we can do what he teaches, we will make a good advance in our journey of Tao attainment.

Chapter 45

Stay Serene and the World is in Peace

清静为天下正

Great attainment seems flawed,
Yet its use is unfaltering.
Great fulfillment seems fluid,
Yet its use is inexhaustible.

Great straightness looks crooked,
Great dexterity looks awkward.
Great eloquence sounds halting.

Movement beats the cold.
Stillness generates heat.
Stay calm and serene,
And the world is in peace.

Just as he did in Chapter 41, Laozi uses the word "Great" repeatedly in this chapter. Similarly, it is another name of Tao.

Great attainment seems flawed, yet its use is unfaltering

Since "Great" implies Tao, the "Great attainment" (大成, *da*4*cheng*2) refers to the attainment of Tao. No matter how good we are, our attainment seems "flawed" (缺, *que*1). Tao is infinitely big, so there is no way that we can know it all. The sense of inadequacy keeps complacency in check. We are always humble and find room for improvement. The more that we find ourselves lacking, the more we find ways to do things better and the less mistake we make. Its use is thus "unfaltering" (不弊, *bu*4*bi*4).

If the "Great attainment" signals success in life, then applying the principle reminds us not to rest on our laurels. If we are running a business, we save for the rainy days, rather than becoming wasteful in the use of the resources just because there is a profit. We continuously look for ways to serve the customers better. Every achievement takes us a step nearer to our goals. The business continues to thrive, and we are unlikely to fail.

Great fulfillment seems fluid, yet its use is inexhaustible

"Great" is Tao. "Fulfillment" paraphrases 盈 (*ying*2), which means "fullness". So, the sentence is about the fulfillment of Tao. It has to stay "fluid" (冲, *chong*1) so that it will not get stagnant. Upon completion of a cycle, we seek renewal for a new cycle to begin. One cycle moves on to another, continuously unabated. This is how the universe works.

The pictogram of "fluid" 冲 is made up of a radical that consists of a dot and a tick and symbolizes Yin and Yang, respectively. It is the same pictogram that we encountered in Chapter 42. Take note that we translate the pictogram as "blending" there, but as "fluid" here, because of a slight difference in emphasis. The sub-character 中, meaning "middle", illustrates the fluid movement that fuses the Yin and Yang energy. The process is gradual and steady. When the heat of summer reaches its peak, the fusion of Yin Yang brings the temperature down, and usher in the crisp autumn. Similarly, before winter becomes too cold, the fusion brings the temperature up as a herald of spring. The fluidity keeps the universe lively. As long as the "Great fulfillment seems fluid", the vitality continues, and its use is "inexhaustible" (不穷, bu4qiong2).

In an unlikely scenario, if Great fulfillment is not fluid, then there is no fusion of Yin Yang. A hot summer can only get hotter and winter colder. It spells calamities, as living things will either be burned or frozen to death. When the universe is lifeless, Great fulfillment is no longer inexhaustible.

Great straightness looks crooked

"Straightness" is a translation of 直 (zhi2). "Great" is Tao. So the "Great straightness" here refers to direct access to Tao. While the path of Tao is supposed to be straightforward, it is not always the case in reality. "Looks crooked" is a translation of 若曲 (ruo4qu1). Along the way, there is no lack of trials that test our mettle and humiliations that sap our endurance. The experiences make the straightness of the path appear crooked. They, however, do not change the directness of the path. It remains straight.

Great dexterity looks awkward

"Dexterity" is a translation of 巧 (qiao3). Since "Great" is Tao, "Great dexterity" is the use of Tao. Although it is supposed to be spontaneous, natural, and effective, the skill may look "awkward". "Awkward" is a translation of 拙 (zhuo2). The pictogram consists of radical 扌, which implies "hands" and thus "skills" or "dexterity"; and the sub-character 出. The sub-character is made up of two 山, which means "mountain", one on top of the other. In the *Yijing*, the hexagram of Mountains (艮, *gen*4) implies "stillness" and "quietude". Here, we may interpret the "mountain" above as a nothingness of self, and the one below as calmness of the present. So, although we are skillful, we are at the same time demure and inward-looking. There is no pretense, and it is thus not always impressive.

Great eloquence sounds halting

"Eloquence" paraphrases 辩 (*bian*4), which means "debate". "Halting" paraphrases 讷 (*ne*4), which means "awkwardness in speech". Structurally, the pictogram consists of radical 言, which means "speech", and the sub-character 内, which means "inner". So, the sentence is about the inner speech. "Great eloquence" is a debate or narrative on Tao, which is truthful but with no intention to impress. "The Tao that can be described is not the eternal Tao." It is awkward when we talk about its truthfulness.

Movement beats the cold. Stillness generates heat

"Movement" paraphrases 躁 (*zao*4), which literally means "agitation". "Cold" is a translation of 寒 (*han*2). When the weather is cold, intensive movements helps attenuate the cold. I still remember an experience in Chile. I was conducting a martial arts examination in the winter when the temperature was about 7 or 8 degrees Celsius. The hall was big, and I was wearing only a thin uniform. The cold was getting too much for me to endure, especially when I was seated. Then, it struck me that I should try overcoming the cold with the "Earth Gate" exercise, where I could draw the qi energy from the earth by trembling my body. I found a secluded spot to relax my body and began the exercise. The qi energy gushed through my feet and went around my entire body. Soon, it warmed up my body. Within three minutes, I was sweating.

"Stillness" is a translation of 静 (*jing*4), which means "serenity". "Heat" is a translation of 热 (*re*4). If we can relax our bodies, we will be able to draw heat from the surrounding environment. Following the "Earth Gate" exercise I mentioned above, I quieted down and allowed myself to go into stillness. My body was totally relaxed, and I drew in energy from around me to beef up the qi energy within me. The warmth was enough to sustain me for the next whole hour. This is a vivid example of "movement beats the cold" and "stillness generates heat".

Stay calm and serene, and the world is in peace

Taoist Master Li Daozi describes the state of tranquility as: "The spring is clear and the river calm." When the spring is clear, we get to see our innate self 性心 (*xing*4*xin*1). We are in the nothingness of non-being. When the river is serene, there is a calmness of mind, and we are keenly in the present. We attain the "clear spring" when we realize the fleeting nature of things, and access the "calm river" when we refuse to be swayed by all forms of distractions. It sets us the stage for the assimilation of the powerful energy derived from the world under Heaven, bringing us closer to Tao Core, and "the world is in peace" (天下正, *tian*1*xia*4*zheng*4).

Chapter 46
Always Have Enough 常足

When the world is
In harmony with Tao,
Warhorses plow the land.
When the world
Has departed from Tao,
Foals are bred

In the open field.
There is no greater crime
Than condoning selfish desires;
No greater disaster
Than discontent;
No greater misery
Than wanting more and more.

So those who know when enough is enough,
Always have enough.

When the world is in harmony with Tao, warhorses plow the farmland

When the world is "in harmony with Tao" (有道, *you3dao4*), there are no divides, and people live in peace. Since there are no wars, the warhorses have nothing to do. To keep them occupied, "warhorses plow the farmland" (走马以粪, *zou3ma3yi3fen4*).

When the world has departed from Tao, foals are bred in the open field

When the world has "departed from Tao" (无道, *wu2dao4*), there are divides, and people are selfish, greedy, and combative. They engage in frequent and prolonged fights. When battles are frequent, mares are sent to the battlefields when there are not enough warhorses. Even the pregnant ones are not spared. As a result, they have to give birth to foals in "the open field" (郊, *jiao1*) because they cannot go back in time to the stable for delivery. When the foals are born, the mares must return to battle. So, when countries are in conflict, even horses suffer.

There is no greater crime than condoning selfish desires

"Selfish desires" is a translation of 可欲 (*ke3yu4*), which means "keep wanting more". When we condone selfish desires, we allow the insatiable greed to prevail. We want more and more of everything, from power and wealth to lust. When others do the same, we fight for the limited resources, and there are endless conflict in the world. "Crime" is a translation of 罪 (*zui4*), which means "guilt" or "sin". "Selfish desires" lead to contentions. In addition to fights, there are those in power who do not hesitate to steal and inflict harm. This explains why there is no greater crime than "condoning selfish desires" (欲得, *yu4de2*).

No greater disaster than discontent; no greater misery than wanting more and more

"Disaster" is a translation of 祸 (*huo*4). When there are "selfish desires", there are conflicts. People are discontent and keep fighting for all sorts of reasons. Having conquered a village, they want another. And then, yet another. There is no end to it. "Discontent" (不知足, *bu*4*zhi*1*zu*2) itself is disastrous, and the damage it can cause is beyond imagination. "Misery" is a translation of 咎 (*jiu*4). It is the result of a lack of repentance for wanting more.

So those who know when enough is enough, always have enough

In summary, contentment is bliss. It is when we are content that we are truly rich. Without contentment, we always feel deprived. "Knowing enough is enough" is a translation of "知足之足" (*zhi*1*zu*2*zhi*1*zu*2), which means "the contentment of knowing contentment". We are happy with whatever we have and expect nothing more than that. We let go entirely. Consequently, the previously-mentioned misery and disaster won't affect us. It is a type of contentment that endures and makes us forever rich. We always have enough (常足矣, *chang*2*zu*2*yi*3) and enjoy lasting peace, allowing our temporal body to focus on cultivation and the refinement of our soul. There is no disaster for both our temporal or real self.

Chapter 47

Wander Not and Yet They Know 知见

Without stepping out the door,
They know the world.
Without gazing through the window,
They know Tao of Heaven.

The farther they wander,
the less they know.

The Sage wander not, and yet they know;
See not, and yet they see the light;
Do nothing, and yet get everything done.

Without stepping out the door, they know the world

The Sage, having witnessed One Source, is able to do nothing and leave nothing undone. They "know the world" (知天下, *zhi1tian-1xia4*) without having to "step out the door" (出户, *chu1hu4*). "Door" is a translation of 户. Everything in the universe is derived from One Source. When the Sage has witnessed the One Source where all things originated, nothing is unknowable to them.

Without gazing through the window, they know Tao of Heaven

"Gazing" is a translation of 窥 (*kui1*), and "window" 牖 (*yong1*). There is no need for the Sage to gaze through the window to find out every detail of the "Tao of Heaven" (天道, *tian1dao4*). Although we are not a sage, we can do those mentioned above in a limited way. In stillness, we bring ourselves close to Tao to witness the unfolding of the mystery of the universe. Even when we don't "step out the door" or "gaze through the window", we get to know more and more about the world.

The farther they wander, the less they know

"When the wise hear of Tao, they begin to practice it diligently," says Laozi in Chapter 41. There is no need for them to travel far and wide in search of wisdom; they can find it right in their heart. In fact, "the further they wander" (其出弥远, *qi2chu1mi2yuan3*), the more that they are distracted, and "the less they learn" (其知弥少, *qi2zhi1mi2shao3*).

Some people like to travel to divine sites in remote places to pay pilgrimage. More often than not, they waste time on traveling and pleasures along the way, leaving little for spiritual activities. For Tao cultivation, all places are divine sites. What they need is nothing more than a calmness of mind and a state of the present. The pilgrimage is here and now. In fact, if we cannot stay calm and be in the present, it makes no difference even if we are in the most renowned temple. The farther we wander away, the more distracted and less enlightened we are.

The Sage wander not, and yet they know; see not, and yet they see the light; do nothing, and yet get everything done

There is no need for the Sage to wander thousands of miles to learn the world. They "wander not" (不行, *bu4xing2*), yet "they know" (知, *zhi1*) and are aware of the changes within. They "see not" (不见, *bu4jian4*), yet they "see the light" (明, *ming2*). They can even pierce through the surface and read the thoughts and destiny of people. By going with the flow of Tao, they "do nothing" (不为, *bu4wei2*) and yet are able to "get everything done" (成, *cheng2*).

Chapter 48
Let Go and Let Go
损之又损

Learning knowledge,
We add something every day.
Assimilating Tao,
We let go of something every day.
Let go and let go,
Till we do nothing.
Do nothing,
And nothing is left undone.

We can rule the world
By doing nothing.
Once we start to force our will,
We cannot rule the world.

Learning knowledge, we add something every day

"Learning knowledge" (为学, *wei2xue2*) helps us navigate through the world of divides and prejudices to meet the demands of life. The more knowledgeable and skillful we are, the better we are equipped to cope. It explains why the universities are packed with new and more areas of study, which grow more complex as time passes.

Although knowledge improves competence, it doesn't always deepen the appreciation of Tao. The advent of technology, such as the application of artificial intelligence, replaces many of the tasks we perform by machines. However, we are getting more comfortable but not always wiser as a result. Knowledge cannot replace the cultivation of Tao.

Assimilating Tao, we let go of something every day

"Assimilating" paraphrases 闻 (*wen2*), which means "to hear" or "to smell". The pictogram is made up of two sub-characters: 门 and 耳, which mean "door" and "ear", respectively, implying that we must keep our ear indoors, and listen to the teachings of Tao attentively. At the same time, we must also be ready to "let go of something every day". "Let go" paraphrases 损 (*sun3*), which means "to lose". We must stay modest, soft, and weak. Many people find it difficult to let go because they are afraid to lose. It is, nevertheless, imperative that a person of Tao let go of something every day, to the extent of non-doing.

Let go and let go till we do nothing. Do nothing, and nothing is left undone

We make it a point to let go of something on a daily basis until there is nothing for us to cling on to. By letting go, the Sage arrives at nothing and in the state of non-doing. They act with the power of non-being, and this empowers them to accomplish everything they do.

We can rule the world by doing nothing

"Nothing" is a translation of 无事 (*wu2shi4*), and "doing nothing" means non-being. If we want to rule the world, we, too, must constantly reach for the power of non-being.

Once we start to force our will, we cannot rule the world

"To force our will" is a translation of 有事 (*you3shi4*), which means "having something". It means that, instead of doing *nothing*, we do *something* and allow divides to become dominant as a result. By so doing, we no longer conform to the formlessness of Tao Core and will not be able to "rule the world" (取天下, *qu3tian1xia4*).

Chapter 49
Goodness of Te 德善

The Sage thinks nothing,
They think what people think.

Those who are good, they are good to them.
Those who are not good, they are also good to them.
This is the goodness of Te.

Those who have faith they have faith in them.
Those who have no faith, they also have faith in them.
This is the faith of Te.

Being part of the world,
The Sage is fully devoted to the world,
And stay truthful to their nature.
People are all eyes and ears,
The Sage guides them as if they are children.

The Sage thinks nothing. They think what people think

"Think nothing" is a translation of 无心 (*wu2xin*1), which literally means "having no heart". In this context, it is the "nothingness" of Tao that the Sage thinks. When "the Sage thinks nothing", they think with the formless Tao in mind and the interests of the people at heart. They think what "the people think" (百姓心, *bai3xing4xin*1), instead of what they want, and see it as their mission to help the people in their redemption.

Those who are good, they are good to them. Those who are not good, they are also good to them. This is the goodness of Te

"Good" is a translation of 善 (*shan*4). It is the highest Te, and not just being good in a normal sense. It is as virtuous as water, which shuns not the filthiest spot if it has to be there. It serves without thinking of getting anything in return. Laozi calls this "the goodness of Te" (德善, *de2shan*4).

Tao Core is formless. Te is its manifestation. We get to see Tao through Te. The "good", being the highest Te, means more than casual kindness. We are kind to people who are kind to us. But the goodness here refers to the extraordinary kindness. It means we are "good" to even people who have inflicted harm on us. Such kindness is formless and without divides. We can do it only when we are like the sages who have "the "goodness of Te".

Those who have faith, they have faith in them. Those who have no faith, they also have faith in them. This is the faith of Te

"Faith" (信, *xin*4) or trust is the foundation of Te and the basic ingredient of self-cultivation. "Those who have faith" is reminiscent of what Laozi says in Chapter 41. They are "the wise" who diligently put Tao into practice. The Sage, understandably, has faith in them. "Those who have no faith" are "the ignorant" who roar into laughter upon hearing of Tao. The Sage, nevertheless, has faith in them as well. Why? Because they see the spirit of kindness in everybody's heart, including the ignorant. The Sage has faith in kindness, which is the nature of Tao in every human being.

The Sage discards no one. To them, every person is a precious gem. The only difference is only in the thickness of dust that covers them. The dust on "the wise" is slight and easy to remove. The dust that covers the "average people" requires more effort to remove. "The ignorant", in comparison, are wrapped up in ugly darkness. Can the dust be removed? Yes, and it should. They are, after all, a precious gem! The Sage can see the inner shine despite the dark surface. It, however, takes time, patience, and effort to do the job.

There is a story about Culapanthaka, who was a disciple of the Buddha. Fellow disciples thought he was so dull that he could never be enlightened. The Buddha, however, did not doubt him because of his "faith of Te". In the end, Culapanthaka proved the Buddha correct and became an Arhat. It is not easy to be as broad-minded as the Buddha. Giving up on the ignorant, however, shows that we are yet to have the quality of a sage. We are walking the path, but the destination is still far, far away.

Being part of the world, the Sage is fully devoted to the world, and stay truthful to their nature

The Sage's mission in the world is to support and help sentient beings with their redemption. "Fully devoted" paraphrases 惵惵 (*die2die2*), which literally means "fearful". The radical of the pictogram 惵 is 忄, which means "heart". The word thus implies love and devotion. "Truthful to their nature" paraphrases 浑其心 (*hun-4qi2xin1*), which means "mingle the hearts". 浑 may be seen as the state of chaos before the universe was formed, which was basically a mass of *taihe* qi energy and some unknown elements. So "nature" has a special connotation here. It is in the state of the mingle, or the Oneness, that a person is capable of returning to. In it, there is no difference between you, me, and others. Neither is there a difference between good and evil. We hold to Oneness.

People are all eyes and ears. The Sage guides them as if they are children

"People" here refers to followers of the Sage. They are "all eyes and ears" (注其耳目, *zhu4qi2er3mu4*); watching what the Sage do and reflecting on what Tao means to them. The Sage "guides them as if they are children" (皆孩之, *jie1hai2zhi1*). The Sage is like a parent keeping a watchful eye to ensure their children don't go astray and lose their perpetual selves. They take great pains to guide them slowly back to Oneness. They bring "the children" home!

Chapter 50

Where Death Cannot Enter 无死地

Between birth and death.
Three in ten live a full life,
Three in ten die tragically.

Also, three in ten court death,
Although given a life to live.
Why is this so?
It is because of their
Excessive concerns about living.

It is said that those who know truly how to live,
Meet no rhinoceros or tigers
When walking through the jungle,
Avoid no armored soldiers
When walking across a battlefield

Rhinoceros cannot stick their horns in them,
Tigers cannot sink their claws in them,
Soldiers cannot stab them with their blades.

Why is this so?
Because they stay at the place
Where death cannot enter.

Between birth and death

"Birth" (出生, *chu1sheng1*) refers to a person's arrival in this world through their mother's womb. "Death" (入死, *ru4si3*) refers to their passing. They happen to everybody. Although we are all born similarly, the way we die, however, can be quite different. Laozi outlines here four types of death.

Three in ten live a full life

"Live a full life" paraphrases 生之徒 (*sheng1zhi1tu2*). One-third of the people live fully and die at a ripe old age. So long as they conform to Tao and go with the flow, they optimize their innate potential to live the destined number of years peacefully with no mishaps. It is a blessing. While Tao cultivation can enhance the quality of their life, it is not a must. In all cases, this type of death is better than the other two mentioned below.

Three in ten die tragically

"Die tragically" paraphrases 死之徒 (*si3zhi1tu2*). Another one-third of people don't die in peace as a consequence of bad karma they inherit. They die in natural or human-caused mishaps. Even if they do pass away on a bed, which is a relative blessing, it is not quite like passing away having lived "a full life".

Also, three in ten court death, although given a life to live

"Court death" paraphrases 动之死地 (*dong4zhi1si3di4*). Another one-third of people could have lived to a ripe old age, but ruin their good fortune by committing evil and end up dying tragically. They bring bad karma upon themselves.

Why is this so? It is because of their excessive concerns about living

"Excessive concern for living" paraphrases 生生之厚 (*sheng1sheng-1zhi1hou4*), which means "the eagerness to live a comfortable life". It refers to the last thirty percent of the people. It is all right to live a good life, but to commit evil for the sake of it is a different matter. It happens when they don't know when to stop and are sucked into the whirlpool of insatiable desires. They are not necessarily impoverished, but just being greedy. It is a miserably bad deal. Just imagine! They give up a full life for a tragic death!

It is said that those who know truly how to live

Having covered 90 percent of the people, we are now at the final ten percent. "Know truly how …" paraphrases 闻善 (*wen2shan4*). 闻 is "to hear, accept, and to be enlightened". 善 is the highest Te and is almost as good as Tao. The sentence describes the group of people who know "truly how to live" (摄生者, *she4sheng1zhe3*). They are the enlightened referenced in Chapter 48.

Meet no rhinoceros or tigers when walking through the jungle, avoid no armored soldiers when walking across a battlefield

The people who "know truly how to live" are not confronted with the ferocity of "rhinoceros or tigers" (兕虎, *si4hu3*) when "walking through the jungle" (陆行, *lu4xing2*). Neither do they have to deal with the assaults of "armored soldiers" (甲兵, *jia3bing1*) when "walking across a battlefield" (入军, *ru4jun1*). They will not fall victim to conflicts or disasters.

Rhinoceros cannot stick their horns in them. Tigers cannot sink their claws in them. Soldiers cannot stab them with their blades

Why? First, conformance with Tao enables them to enjoy the blessings of Heaven. Second, they understand the importance of self-defense. These protect them from disaster. Furthermore, because they don't have a harmful intention, they don't provoke an attack.

Why is this so? Because they stay at the place where death cannot enter

"The place where death cannot enter" paraphrases 无死地 (*wu2si3di4*), which means "no place for death". This category of people understands the consequence of karma. If they owe the rhinoceros, tigers, or soldiers their life, they are ready for the repayment. As they are integrated with Heaven, even if they die, the passing of their temporal body allows the perpetual self to ascend to a higher order and clear them of their bad karma. They, thereby, enter the place "where death cannot enter".

Chapter 51

Revere Tao and Value Te
道尊德贵

All things arise from Tao,
Nurtured by Te,
Formed by matter,
Fulfilled by the flow.

Thus without exception,
All things revere Tao and value Te.
Revering Tao, valuing Te,
Alas, no one gives the command,
Yet the actions arise all naturally.

So Tao gives rise to them;
Nurtures, grows,
Fosters, actualizes,
Matures, conserves, and
Seeds them.

Creates but possesses not,
Does but seeks no glory,
Grows but never seeks to dominate,
This is the Mystery of Te.

All things arise from Tao, nurtured by Te, formed by matter, fulfilled by the flow

This chapter depicts the cycle of changes inherent in everything, be it the change of seasons or making of tea. Knowing the cycle sheds light on the ways things behave and helps us tackle changes with ease.

A cycle of change is divided into four phases: Birth, nurture, formation, and fulfillment. It begins with birth, where Tao "gives rise" (生, *sheng*1) to things. Tao Core is the origin of all existence, so everything is generated from it. It is, however, formless, and has to rely on Te, its manifestation, to make things happen. As previously discussed, Te is Tao Core in action. In this sense, all things are "nurtured" (畜, *xu*4) by Te. It conditions their creation. Before the emergence of the universe, for example, the *taihe* energy, *Yuanyang*, divine light of Tao, and the various dark matter were put together by Te to condition its formation, as mentioned in Chapters 1 and 25.

With the nourishment, things begin to take shape. Now, things are "formed" (形, *xing*2) by "matter" (物, *wu*4). With the forms, momentum picks up, and they grow to have them "fulfilled" (成, *cheng*2) their destiny. The momentum is made possible by "the flow" (势, *shi*4). With the fulfillment, the cycle comes to an end, before a new one begins.

This is how things in the universe function. It happens to everything and takes place everywhere. We may call it Taiji. As referenced in Chapter 14, the "Taiji" here is not the same as Taijiquan, the exercise we practice for health. Literally meaning "the supreme ultimate", it is a state of Tao where various realms of existence reside. We may, say, see small Taiji on a personal level, Middle Taiji on a national level, and Large Taiji on the universe level.

Let's begin with the Small Taiji. As an individual, we are in this world for a reason. Tao gives birth to us. However, Tao provides only a seed, and we need a physical body to fulfill our destiny. This is what Te does. A mother goes through a union of spirit and body during pregnancy. This is the time when the baby is being "nurtured" by Te. When the baby is born, they have a body. Scientifically speaking, they are "formed" by matter. Te gives the baby their soul, and the matter give the baby their form. As a human, when the baby goes with "the flow" of nature, they grow into an adult. Then, there are death and rebirth. When they have fulfilled their destiny, a new cycle begins.

As for Medium Taiji, we may use it to describe the development of a country. Let's use the rebirth of China as an example. The country had been a leading power of the world, both politically and economically, for 2,800 years, but took a nosedive 200 years ago when the Qing Dynasty began its decline. It plunged the country into the darkest moments of its history. Fortunately, going with the law of reversal, China took a rebound. "Tao gives rise to it." The country had since departed from its darkest days and resumed the glory reminiscent of its heydays. Upon its rebirth, the world environment was favorable to China's development and supported its growth. It soon became an integral part of the international community. It was nurtured by Te.

This brings it to the phrase "Formed by matter." "Form", in this case, may be seen as things that facilitate the country's growth. In terms of building a nation, it includes infrastructure such as transportation and electrical systems and more. After China regained its foothold in the global economy, these things were rapidly improved or built in just a couple of decades.

As the development gains momentum, China leverages its rich cultural heritage to bring it to a new level. By going with the flow, the country is expected to continue its growth in the next decade. In the process, traditional Chinese culture is going to flourish further.

Now, let's take a look at the Large Taiji. "All things arise from Tao, nurtured by Te" is an illustration of One Source. "Formed by matter" sees the generation of the myriads of things from One Source. "Fulfilled by the flow" is to allow the cycle of life to run its course. It goes unabated like the unfolding of the seasons. Spring sprouts, summer grows, autumn harvests, winter conserves. The cycles go on and on, and they are unstoppable. It is the "flow" that ensures the vibrancy is maintained, and the lives of the universe are fulfilled.

Thus without exception, all things revere Tao and value Te

Everything in the universe — be it in the Big, Medium, or Small Taiji — is governed by Tao. Tao is truthful, selfless, impartial, and always ready to serve. Since everything goes with the flow of Tao as "the way" (Te) to live and grow, it is no wonder that, without exception, they "revere" (尊, *zun*1) Tao and "value" (贵, *gui*4) Te.

Revering Tao, valuing Te. Alas, no one gives the command, yet the actions arise all naturally

Tao is revered, and Te valued because of their selflessness. They grow and nurture the myriads of things by non-doing. Although "no one gives the command" (莫之命, *mo4zhi1ming4*), yet the actions "arise all naturally" (常自然, *chang2zi4ran2*). They are constant, eternal, spontaneous, and continuous.

So Tao gives rise to them, nurtures, grows, fosters, actualizes, matures, conserves, and seeds them

Here, we look at the cycles of changes and the role of One Source again. We may group them into four phases.

"So Tao gives rise to them". It is about the role of One Source, which "nurtures" with Te. "Grows" is a translation of 长 (*zhang*3), which is about development. Seeing it from the perspective of a person's life cycle, it is the early years where we are like plants flourishing in spring.

"Fosters" is a translation of 育 (*yu*4), which is about raising. "Actualizes" is a translation of 成 (*cheng*2), which is about the shaping of beings. In this phase, a person receives education and matures into an adult. We are as if plants thriving in summer.

"Matures" is a translation of 熟 (*shu*2), which means "coming into fruition". "Conserves" is a translation of 养 (*yang*3), which implies to "conserve for revitalization". The description "seeds them" is a translation of 覆 (*fu*4), which literally means to "cover", and implies covering the land with seeds. So this line is a phase of harvest, conservation, and revitalization. It depicts the part of life where we live the ripe old age, demise, and rebirth. The cycle goes on.

Creates but possesses not, does but seeks no glory, grows but never seeks to dominate. This is the Mystery of Te

Tao creates everything but thinks nothing about it. "No one gives the command, yet the actions arise all naturally". This is why we revere Tao and value Te. A person who manifests these virtues is selfless and magnanimous. They don't discriminate, they don't seek glory, and they have no desire to dominate.

This line sums up the "Mystery of Te". "Mystery" is a translation of 玄 (*xuan*2), which is explained in Chapter 1. "One mystery after another, the gate to all wonders." "Mystery", therefore, is about Tao Core and Tao Use. As previously explained, Te is a manifestation of Tao. "The Mystery of Te", therefore, is the virtue of Tao.

Chapter 52
Inheriting Constancy 襲常

The beginning of the universe
Is Mother of all things.
From the Mother,
We know the child.
Knowing the child,
We return and keep to the Mother,
And preserve the self from harm.

Guard the desires,
Shut the doors,
Exert only sparingly.
Set the desires free,
Meddle with things,
and we are beyond salvation.

Seeing small is clarity,
Staying soft is a strength.
Use her light,
Radiate her wisdom,
There is no regret and misery.
This is inheriting the constancy.

The beginning of the universe is Mother of all things

"Beginning" paraphrases 有始. The first pictogram 有 (*you*3) usually means "having", but here it refers to "being" or Tao One. 始 (*shi*3) means "the origin". The beginning of the universe of being, i.e., Tao One. Like Laozi says in Chapter 42, "One gives birth to Two, Two to Three, and Three to the myriads of things." One is "Mother of all things".

From the Mother, we know the child

All things in the universe, from the seas and the mountains to you and I, are children of Tao One, i.e., the Mother (母, *mu*3). Every one of her children is so intimately connected to her that a "quantum entanglement" exists between them. Therefore, by knowing the Mother, we know how the "child" (子, *zi*3) behaves.

Knowing the child, we return and keep to the Mother, and preserve the self from harm

As children of Tao One, we must "return" (复, *fu*4) to the source and become who we truly are. This is what self-cultivation does. We "keep to" (守, *shou*3) the Mother, so that we will not drift away from her. Otherwise, we may one day find ourselves unable to go back. Although it is fine to go astray for a while, we must know how to stop in time. With cultivation, we keep to the Mother. We refine our "perpetual selves" (没身, *mo*4*shen*1) so that we can "preserve the self from harm" (不殆, *bu*4*dai*4) when the temporal self vanishes.

In the following passage, Laozi outlines what we should do during self-cultivation.

Guard the desires, shut the doors, exert only sparingly

"Guard" paraphrases 塞 (*sai*1). The pictogram originally means "a plug", implying preventing liquid from flowing out. "Desires" paraphrases 兌 (*dui*3), which implies "pleasure". "Guard the desires", therefore, may be interpreted as guarding our energy, so that it will not be squandered on worldly pleasures.

兌 is one of the eight trigrams in the *Yijing*, sometimes translated as "Joyous". It is portrayed as ☱ and made up of two solid lines below and a broken line on top. Visually it looks like a mouth or the opening of a channel. It is sometimes used as a metaphor for sexual pleasures, although it is not the only indulgence it refers to. As the broken line looks like a mouth, the trigram also implies bad mouthing others or sowing discord. In a nutshell, "Guard the desires" implies restraint and to snub such unhealthy desires whenever it arises to keep our principles — essence, qi, and spirit — intact.

While "guard the desires" is about preventing an outflow of energy, "shut the doors" is about blocking the inflow of disruptions. "Shut" is a translation of 閉 (*bi*4); and "doors" 門 (*men*2). The external allure enters our minds through the senses, so they are the doors. If we can "shut the doors", we minimize disruptions to our inner peace needed for self-cultivation.

Having desires and indulging in pleasures are not wrong. As long as we exercise restraints, we can "exert only sparingly" (不勤, *bu*4*qin*2). We should direct energy to things that are fundamentally important. Laozi doesn't promote total abstinence; he only wants us to impose restraint by moderating the senses. Savoring the taste of food is good, but overeating and gluttony are harmful. We must avoid excess.

Set the desires free, meddle with things, and we are beyond salvation

On the other hand, if we "set the desires free" (开其兌, *kai*1*qi*2*dui*4), and "meddle with things" (济其事, *ji*4*qi*2*shi*4), the insatiable desires and allure drain our energy. The consequence is grave. We spend too much time and energy indulging in pleasures, socializing, or bad-mouthing others, and neglect the primary goal of life: To cultivate the temporal body to refine the real body. If we don't cultivate, we may not be able to refine our real self in time when our temporal body perishes, making the real self "beyond salvation" (不救, *bu4jiu4*). What a pity!

Seeing small is clarity

By guarding the desires and shutting the doors, we get to "see small" (见小, *jian4xiao3*) to gain "clarity" (明, *ming2*). 明 is made up of two words: 日 and 月, meaning "sun" and "moon", respectively. It implies that whether it is day or night, every activity, however micro, is discernible. The sages are keenly aware of the "small" matters around them. Even dialogues of insects are audible. If we can be like the sages and "see small", our perception of the universe tremendously changes.

Staying soft is a strength

As mentioned in Chapters 36 and 43, softness is so powerful it can overcome the strongest things in the world. It is a wonder.

During Taiji sparring, if we can soften the contact point to make it as yielding as water, we can nullify the attacking force of the opponent. If we can, at the same time, deflect the attacking energy by maneuvering it with softness, we will be able to return the force to the opponent. In Taiji, we call it "beat a thousand-pound by lifting a finger" (四两拨千斤).

Spiritually, when we "stay soft", we are modest, humble, and yielding. Most people want to be "strong", but we do exactly the opposite by "staying soft". It helps open us to possibilities and receive intelligence from the universe. This is why being soft is the first thing we must do in order to attain Tao.

Use her light, radiate her wisdom

"Use her light" means not only to bask in the divine light but also to use it. By doing so, we are able to illuminate the light (光, *guang1*) through us. "Radiate her wisdom" is a translation of 复归其明 (*fu4gui1qi2ming2*).

It happens only when we can "keep to the Mother" and embrace Oneness. If we defy the teaching by allowing ourselves to overindulge and be distracted, we will not be able to "use her light" or "radiate her wisdom". When we can "keep to the Mother", not only do we "see small" with clarity, we are blessed by the divine light and are on our way to the "Fulfillment of Destiny".

There is no regret and misery

"Regret" paraphrases 遺身 (*yi2shen*1), which means a "dead body". If we perform evil, when our physical body passes, it is a body of "regret" that is full of bad karma. It brings "misery" (殃, *yang*1) to our real self. On the other hand if we radiate her wisdom, "there is no regret and misery".

This is inheriting the constancy

By "inheriting the constancy" (襲常, *xi*1*chang*2), we receive the wisdom and pass on the torch. I learned from my Master and pass on what I have learned to my disciples. Laozi passed on the philosophy of Tao to us. "Constant" is the eternal Tao. It is an inheritance, not an invention of anyone. Laozi didn't create Tao; he only gave it a name and explained what it is. He also "inherits the constancy". Wisdom of the major religions and scriptures like the *Yijing* are not an invention of anybody. They are "what is". They provide proper paths and success examples for us to follow. What we have to do is simply to follow in the footsteps and inherit the constancy.

Chapter 53
Easy Path of Tao 道夷

*Make Tao The Way.
I walk the great path,
And fear the winding trails.
Keeping to the great path is easy,
Yet people prefer to sidetrack.*

*Thus the court is corrupted,
The farms are neglected,
The granaries are emptying.*

*The leaders wear ornate clothes,
Carry flashy sword,
Overindulge in food and drink,
And amass excessive wealth.*

*This is blatant looting,
This is not Tao!*

Make Tao the Way

Here is the original text for this line: 使吾介然有知. The first character 使 (*shi*3) is made up of three elements: 亻, 一, and 史. 亻means "human", 一 means "one", and 史 means "history". It implies making Tao part of our daily life. 吾 (*wu*2) consists of two sub-characters. At the top is 五, which means "five", and below is 口, which means mouth. The number five symbolizes "the center" in the *Yijing*, and "mouth" refers to "speech". So, it implies "speech by a sage". 介然 means "honest and candid". 有 means "being" or Tao Use. So 有知 is to "see Tao from a practical perspective", implying that it should be made relevant to our lives. As a whole, we may also see the line as saying: "The Sage uses simple language to honestly and candidly explain the wisdom of Tao."

I walk the great path and fear the winding trails

"Great path" is a translation of 大道 (*da*4*dao*4), which implies Oneness. "Winding trails" paraphrases 迤 (*yi*3), which means a winding stream of water that deviates from the main waterway. Some editions use another pictogram: 邪 (*xie*2), which means "evil". Both mean a deviation. "Fear the winding trails" implies that we are fearful of wandering into an improper path.

Keeping to the great path is easy, yet people prefer to sidetrack

"Easy" paraphrases 夷 (*yi*2), which means "level". Although keeping to the great path is easy, people like to "sidetrack" (好径, *hao*4*jing*4). Laozi reminds us that there is no shortcut to the attainment of Tao. The only path is the great path. "Great pieces of art take time to complete," says the Sage.

Thus the court is corrupted, the farms are neglected, the granaries are emptying. The leaders wear ornate clothes, carry flashy swords, overindulge in food and drink, and amass excessive wealth

When a nation's leaders follow a different path, they no longer care for the people. Instead, they indulge themselves in earthly pleasures despite the widespread sufferings among their people.

"The court" is a translation of 朝 (*chao*2), which means the governing body of an organization. It implies the leadership of a country, a community, or an association. "Corrupted" is a translation of 除 (*chu*2).

"The farms" is a translation of 田 (*tian*2), and "neglected" 芜 (*wu*2). In an agricultural society, crops are the primary source of family income. When "the farms are neglected", there is no harvest, and naturally, "the granaries (仓, *cang*1) are emptying (虚, *xu*1)". People don't have enough to eat and are impoverished.

The irony is that, despite the suffering of the people, the leaders "wear ornate clothes". "Wear" is a translation of 服 (*fu*2), and "ornate" 文采 (*wen*2*cai*3). They dress up elegantly in expensive clothes. What a stark contrast to the people who are destitute! They "carry flashy swords" and look domineering. "Carry" is a translation of 带 (*dai*4), and "flashy swords" 利剑 (*li*4*jian*4). They use the sword to intimidate the people. With the misdeeds they have conducted, they are afraid of the people taking revenge. The sword, therefore, also serves to self-defend. Carrying a flashy sword, however, is combative. Tao loathes killing, and the displaying of weapons is against Tao.

"Overindulge" paraphrases 厌 (*yan*4), which means "feeling disgusted having done too much of something". "Food and drink" is a translation of 饮食 (*yin*3*shi*2). When the leaders are disgusted with food and drink, it implies overeating, over nourishment, and waste of food. It is such an irony when their people don't even have enough to eat. "Wealth" is a translation of 财货 (*cai2huo4*) which means "money and possessions"; and "excessive" 有余 (*you3yu2*), which means "having enough to spare". The wealth, however, is not the leaders' own creation. To have more than they need, they exploit the people who are already suffering.

This is blatant looting

These leaders are as vicious as robbers. "Blatant looting" paraphrases 盗夸 (*dao4kua1*). Most robbers would be shamed enough to conceal their acts, and these leaders don't even care to hide their misdeeds. It is as if they are saying, "I am a thief, so what?"

This is not Tao!

In this chapter, Laozi highlights the problems of being excessive. We have to know "when to stop" so as to "suffer no peril", as mentioned in Chapter 44. When there is "excess", there is chaos. While it is all right for the leaders to eat and dress well, they must not neglect their people. They must close the income gap between the rich and the poor, and create a balance. If the leader can, like what Laozi says, "Have less selfishness and desires", they are back to the great path and bring their country to a society of equality and Oneness.

Chapter 54

Firmly Rooted and Embraced 善建善抱

What a good builder plants,
Cannot be uprooted;
What a good embracer hugs,
Cannot slip away.
They are honored continuously
From generation to generation.

Cultivate it in self;
Te is genuine.
Cultivate it in the family;
Te abounds.
Cultivate it the village;
Te grows;
Cultivate it in the country;
Te thrives.
Cultivate it in the world;
Te is universal.

Therefore, let a self learn from another self,
A family learn from another family,
A village learn from another village,
A country learn from another country,
And a world learn from another world.

How do I know the ways the world behaves?
By doing these!

What a good builder plants, cannot be uprooted

The description "good" is a translation of 善 (*shan*4), which is the highest Te, as explained in Chapter 27. Tao is formless, Te is its use, and 善 is the highest Te. 善, therefore, is almost Tao. The "good builder" (善建者, *shan*4*jian*4*zhe*3) strongly believes in Tao, and consistent in their self-cultivation. The conviction is so firm it "cannot be uprooted" (不拔, *bu*4*ba*2).

What a good embracer hugs, cannot slip away

It is similar for people who embrace (抱, *bao*4) Tao. Tao is formless, so it doesn't "slip away" (脱, *tuo*1). By the same token, when a good embracer embraces Tao tightly, Tao will not leave them, neither will the embracer allow it to slip away.

They are honored continuously from generation to generation

Good builder and good embracer are staunch followers of Tao. They enjoy enduring respect from their descendants. Rituals of respect continue after their death.

The descendants here are more likely to be descendants of qi or a Tao lineage, rather than blood relations. Blood relations are primarily genetic. If the offsprings don't practice Tao, the relations fade away upon the death of either party. If parents practice qi together with their children, it converts the blood relations into a qi lineage, and the relations are enduring. Qi can be traced back to the primordial *taihe* qi energy, which is Tao. Qi lineage is thus inheriting the practices of Tao. "Honored" paraphrases 祭祀 (*ji*4*si*4), which means "ritual"; and "continuously" is a translation of 不辍 (*bu*4*chuo*4).

Cultivate it in self; Te is genuine

Te is "genuine" (真, *zhen*1) when we internalize the wisdom and put it into practice in the daily context. In other words, when we cultivate it in "self" (身, *shen*1), the Te is genuine, refined, and constructive. We conform to Tao and practice non-doing. Without doing so, what we attain is, at best, a blessing of fortune. The Te is not as refined, and it brings us good fortune but does little to the attainment of Tao.

Cultivate it in the family; Te abounds

"Family" is a translation of 家 (*jia*1). If we cultivate the highest Te together with our family, we bring the virtue to the members, including our spouses and children. If we bring in other relatives, we multiply the Te. Our Te "abounds". "Abound" paraphrases 余 (*yu*2), which means "having enough and to spare". Now, not only is our Te rich enough to help ourselves with our redemption, but it can be relied on for helping others.

Cultivate it in the village; Te grows

"Village" is a translation of 乡 (*xiang*1), which implies a community that consists of a number of families. "Cultivate it in the village" means a family of Tao inspires other families to practice Te. Now that the practice is expanded beyond an individual to include families and villages, it benefits even more people; Te grows (长, *zhang*3).

Cultivate it in the country; Te thrives

"Country" is a translation of 国 (*guo*2). Sizes of countries were small in ancient times. They can be just a number of villages in rural areas. When we "cultivate it in the country", the entire population practice the genuine Te. Not only does Te grow, but it also "thrives" (丰,

*feng*1). By the sheer increase in the number of people who observe it, Te is ever more impactful.

Cultivate it in the world; Te is universal

Of course, it is even better if all people in "the world" (天下, *tian-1xia*4) cultivate the highest Te. If our selves, our family, our village, our country, and the world are all cultivating it, then Te is "universal" (普, *pu*3).

Therefore, let a self learn from another self, a family learn from another family, a village learn from another village, a country learn from another country, and a world learn from another world

"Learn from" is a translation of 观 (*guan*1), which means to "view". It is reminiscent of the twentieth hexagram of the *Yijing* — Viewing — which is made up of the trigrams for Wind on top and Earth below. The "wind" (trend) of cultivating the highest Te blows around Earth (world). Firm "planters" and "embracers" are now everywhere, no longer few and far between.

There is a great number of spiritual paths for the cultivation of Te. While the approaches differ, the ultimate goals are the same. Taiji doesn't look like Tantra, for example, but they share common underlying principles. People from the paths must, therefore, respect and learn from each other. A self (身, *shen*1) can learn from another self. By the same token, a family can learn from another family, and a village from another village.

A country and a world are large communities. Taiji community can learn from, say, Tantra, Buddhism, or Christianity. As a community, the world is even bigger. The East, for example, can learn from the West, and vice versa. If we can do what the hexagram "Viewing" teaches, the wind of the genuine Te will blow over the entire Earth, and we shall build a world of harmony where people can live happily together.

How do I know the ways the world behaves? By doing these!

How does the Sage "know the ways the world behave"(天下然, *tian-1xia4ran2*)? "By doing these" (以此, *yi3ci3*). There is a simple underlying logic. Many of the world's problems today can be solved if we do what Laozi says: Cultivate Te among selves, families, villages, countries, and different worlds. We don't learn from others by just looking. We begin the process by viewing ourselves from within, and then enhance our practice by learning from others. If people can learn from one another and practice the genuine Te, honest communication can lead to world peace.

Chapter 55
Steeped in Te 含德之厚

A person steeped in Te
Is like a newborn
Whom deadly insects do not sting,
Wild beasts do not pounce on,
And raptors do not attack.

Despite their weak bones and soft sinew,
An infant's clench of fists is firm.

Their penis is erect,
despite not knowing sex,
Their vitality is intense.

They can scream all-day
And not grow hoarse.
Their body is in perfect harmony.

To understand harmony is to know the constancy.
Knowing the constancy is discerning.
Nourishing life is benign.
Exerting life energy is forceful,
A thing that is forceful begins its decline
And departs from Tao.
A thing departing from Tao perishes early.

A person steeped in Te

A person "steeped" (厚, *hou*4) in Te carries forward a richness of Te from their previous lives. To them, every rebirth is a "Fulfillment of Destiny", as explained in Chapter 16, which plays a part in the accumulation. Since the richness of Te is compounding, we must not let up in our cultivation so as to retain it.

Is like a newborn

"Newborn" is a translation of 赤子 (*chi*4*zi*3). Although not as formless as Tao, they are untainted, and their innocence keeps them close to Tao. If a person of Tao is steeped in the Te they inherited as a newborn, they are able to perform miracles like those explained in the following paragraphs:

Whom deadly insects do not sting

"Deadly insects" is a translation of 毒虫 (*du*2*chong*2); and "sting", a translation of 螫 (*zhe*1), which is the tail where venom is found. The deadly insects are not inclined to sting the person steeped in Te for the aura they exude.

Wild beasts do not pounce on

Neither would "wild beasts" (猛兽, *meng*3*shou*4) "pounce on" (据, *ju*4) them. As mentioned in Chapter 50, one-tenth of the population, "who knows truly how to live", don't fall prey to wild beasts. They include those who are steeped in Te.

Venerable Guangqin was among them. The legendary monk is said to rely on meditation alone for repose and did not have to sleep for years. Being steeped in Te enabled him to survive many an ordeal. One day, when he was meditating in stillness, a tiger approached him. Instead of fleeing, Guangqin calmly spoke to the tiger, "If I owe you anything, eat me up so that I can repay my debt. If I owe you nothing, then be my gatekeeper to keep me away from danger." The tiger obliged, and the two of them sat together in silence for ten days. The story is so fascinating; it has brought Guangqin the reputation of being "the Master who prevailed over the tiger".

And raptors do not attack

"Raptors" is a translation of 攫鸟 (*jue2niao3*), which means "a bird of prey". "Attack" is a translation of 搏 (*bo2*), which means "beating". Similarly, a raptor such as a vulture will not attack a person who is steeped in Te.

Despite their weak bones and soft sinews, an infant's clench of fists is firm

Bones and ligaments of an infant are soft and weak, never hard. "Weak bone" is a translation of 骨弱 (*gu3ruo4*) and "soft sinews" 筋柔 (*jin1rou2*). They grip their fists tightly. Some Taoists believe it is the richness of Te from a previous life that they hold in their clutches. The grip is especially firm for a sage reborn. Having attained enlightenment in their previous life, their *taihe* qi energy and divine light remain in the infant's body. Therefore, "deadly insects do not sting, wild beasts do not pounce on, and raptors do not attack" them. They are here in the current world to seek mentors for transcendence to a "Large Fulfillment of Destiny".

Their penis is erect, despite not knowing sex. Their vitality is intense

A man's genitals is erect when thinking of sex. But it happens to a baby boy as well who knows nothing about sex. Why is this so? "Sex" is a translation of 牝牡 (*pin4mu4*), which means "male and female"; and "erect" 朘作 (*juan1zuo4*) refers to the arousal of a male's genital. A baby's penis being erect is an indication of the vitality of Te. Be it boys or girls; we are gifted with the innate essence that generates the vitality of life, which is strong enough for the erection. The essence stays with us for the rest of our lives. We must not squander it if we want to stay healthy and robust. This explains why Laozi suggests in Chapter 52 that we must "shut the doors, guard the senses", and "exert only sparingly". With awareness, we will not deplete our vitality unwittingly.

They can scream all-day and not grow hoarse

An infant who is steeped in Te can "scream all day" 终日号 (zhong1ri4hao4) and "not grow hoarse" 不嗄 (bu4sha4). This is because not only are they rich in essence, but they are also filled with lavish qi and spirit. With strong *taihe* qi, their throat is strong, and their energy not easily exhausted.

Their body is in perfect harmony

"Harmony" is a translation of 和 (he2). "Perfect" paraphrases 之至 (zhi1zhi4), meaning "to the extreme". Intense qi energy enriches our spirit. Together with the well-conserved essence, our internal organs and meridians are optimized, enabling our body to be in "perfect harmony".

Decoding Notes: Tirelessly promoting the teachings of Tao blends us well with "Nature of Tao". This is another way that allows us to be in "perfect harmony".

To understand harmony is to know the constancy. Knowing the constancy is discerning

If we can "understand harmony" (知和, zhi1he2), we know "the constancy" (常, chang2) of Tao. While we are yet to attain Tao fully, we are on our way there. The awareness deepens our appreciation of

Tao and its profundity. "Discerning" paraphrases 明 (*ming*2), which means "clarity". It helps us to witness our "true self" (明心, *ming2xin*1) and subsequently, "realize our true nature" (见性, *jian4xing4*) if we can continue to work on the cultivation.

Nourishing life is benign

The first part of this chapter talks about the people of Tao. In the remaining portion of the chapter, Laozi writes about ordinary folk. "Nourishing life" (益生, *yi4sheng*1) refers to taking good care of our temporal body. This is what we must do in order to live well, and it is thus "benign" (祥, *xiang*2). We must not, however, forget the bigger purpose. The ultimate aim of a healthy body is to refine our perpetual self.

Exerting life energy is forceful

"Exerting Life energy" paraphrases 心使气 (*xin1shi3qi4*), which literally means "using our heart to force the qi energy". "Forceful" is a translation of 强 (*qiang*2). When we force our qi, we strain our bodies. Think about the moment when we lose our temper. It disrupts our mind and breath and very often doesn't help the situation, and it hurts.

Decoding Notes: During Taiji sparring, we maneuver our qi to repel the opponent. It uses force and can be stressful. While it is necessary during self-defense, Laozi reminds us to do it only sparingly. Similarly, we may have to use force occasionally in the course of problem-solving. Although it is called for, we must not overdo it.

A thing that is forceful begins its decline and departs from Tao

"A thing that is forceful" paraphrases 物壮 (*wu4zhuang4*), which means "thing that is boosted". "Decline" is a translation of 老

(*lao3*), which means "getting old". When something reaches its extreme, it reverses its course. If it turns for the worse, it can "depart from Tao" (不道, *bu4dao4*) and become harmful.

A thing departing from Tao perishes early

Things that don't conform to Tao perish early (早已, *zao3yi3*). This explains why we must stay humble, modest, and remain unfilled in life.

Chapter 56
Mysterious Union 玄同

Those who know do not talk.
Those who talk do not know.

Guard the desires,
Shut the doors,
Blunt the sharpness,
Untie the knots,
Blend in with the light,
Merge with the dust.

This is the Mysterious Union.

By doing so, we are not perturbed
By affinity or alienation;
Benefit or harm;
Honor or lowliness.

It is therefore
Treasured by the world.

Those who know do not talk. Those who talk do not know

"Those who know" are the 知者 (*zhi*1*zhe*3) who have realized their true nature. They do not "talk" (言, *yan*2). Tao is formless and cannot be adequately described by words. If anyone tells us they know it all, chances are they don't. It doesn't mean that we must not talk about Tao. It is just that there is a limitation we face when doing so.

To help us appreciate the profundity of the unspoken Tao, Laozi reiterates the six tenets outlined below. They are not new. We discuss them earlier in Chapters 4 and 52. But they are worth revisiting.

Guard the desires, shut the doors

We discuss "guard the desires" in Chapter 52. By keeping lust and meaningless babbles in check, we minimize a wasteful outflow of energy, keeping our essence, qi, and spirit intact. At the same time, by shutting the "doors" (senses), we prevent the external temptations from disrupting our inner peace. One is about outflow, the other inflow. It helps us to enter into a state of stillness, where we can appreciate the depth of Tao and realize our true nature.

The following four tenets are reiterations of material we introduced in Chapter 4.

Blunt the sharpness

Sharp corners cut. By blunting them, in words and deeds, we prevent injuries. If we can stay tactful, modest, and soft, we reduce the chances of hurting others, and this creates harmony.

Untie the knots

The knots to be untied include the inner knots such as worries; and outer knots, such as contention. When there are divides, there is greed, and we become calculative. This is a source of endless worries and disturbances. If we can, instead, turn our attention to the primary goal of refining our perpetual self, we naturally "untie the knots". Every form is transient; there is indeed nothing with which we need to contend.

Blend in with the light

"The light" here refers to the divine light of the sages, often portrayed by the halo circling their heads. It is the radiance of Tao that fuses the *taihe* qi and *Yuanyang*. The more accomplished the sages, the brighter their halo. When we "blend in with the light", we learn their virtues. If we can be as selfless as them, we live their virtue and enjoy their blessings. If our virtue is rich enough, we, too, can emit the halo and become a sage as well.

Merge with the dust

Not only do we learn the virtue of the sages, we merge with "the dust", which refers to the people in low positions who are trampled like dust. We don't just show our sympathy, we empathize with them and do whatever we can to help them.

This is the Mysterious Union

"Mysterious" is a translation of 玄 (*xuan*2). "Non-being, the beginning of heaven and earth. Being, Mother of all things," says Laozi in Chapter 1. "These two, share a common origin, yet come forth with a different name. Both are called a mystery." The mystery, another name of Tao, is the formlessness of Tao manifested in the forms of things. "Union" is a translation of 同 (*tong*2), which means "the same". "The Mysterious Union" is a union of being and non-being. It is, therefore, Tao.

Observation of the preceding six practices brings out the "Mysterious Union" manifested in the unspoken Tao.

By doing so, we are not perturbed by affinity or alienation; benefit or harm; honor or lowliness

"Affinity" is a translation of 亲 (*qin*1), and "alienation" 疏 (*shu*1). "Benefit" is a translation of 利 (*li*4), and "harm" 害 (*hai*4). "Honor" is a translation of 贵 (*gui*4), and "lowliness" 贱 (*jian*4). Be it affinity or alienation, benefit or harm, honor or lowliness; they are products of divides. When we understand the "Mysterious Union" of Tao, we see no differences among them and are not perturbed by any of them.

It is therefore treasured by the world

"Treasured" is a translation of 贵 (*gui*4). The pictogram consists of three components: 中, 一, and 贝; meaning "middle", "one", and "treasure", respectively. It implies that as long as we can keep to the center, we are able to enjoy the treasure of the "Mysterious Union".

Chapter 57
Govern a Country 治国

Govern a country with honesty,
Deploy an army with deceit,
Win the world by not imposing the will.

How do I know the ways things are?
By these:

The more the oppression,
The poorer the people.
The more weapons people possess,
The bigger the confusion in the land.
The more cleverness exists,
The more bad deeds are done.
The more the rules and orders,
The more the criminals.

Thus the Sage says:
"I practice non-doing,
and people naturally transform themselves.
I enjoy peace,
and people are naturally honest.
I do by not doing,
and people are naturally rich.
I am devoid of desires,
and people are simple and pure."

Govern a country with honesty

"Honesty" is a translation of 正 (*zheng*4). The pictogram consists of two sub-characters: 一, which means "one", on top, and 止, which means "to stop" below. We may thus interpret the word as "not to go beyond Tao One". The rulers have the interests of the country and its people close to their hearts. When they "govern a country" (治国, *zhi*4*guo*2), whatever they do is meant for the good of the country. They think little of themselves.

Deploy an army with deceit

"Deploy an army" is a translation of 用兵 (*yong*4*bing*1), and "deceit" 奇 (*qi*2), which means "surprising moves". It doesn't sound like the conformance to Tao. This is, however, what we must do in order to defend ourselves and uphold justice when we are attacked. Whether it is on a battlefield or in a meeting room, when we are forced into a position of divides, we must defend ourselves against the departure from Tao. Although we don't like it, we are left with no choice. If our tactics work, we catch the enemy by surprise and improve our positions. To do that, the "subtle insight" that leverages on the law of reversal, as mentioned in Chapter 36, comes in useful. Taoist military stratagems such as "Invisibility Warfare" (奇门遁甲) and "Mystifying Deployment" (摆阵), found in other ancient Taoist books, are derived from it. We "govern a country with honesty" when Tao prevails, not when Tao is pushed to the sidelines. We must be flexible.

This is what we do in Taiji sparring. When we want the opponent to go backward, we first get them to come forward. If we are going to hit their right side, we exert the force on their left. The deceit tilts the opponents off-balance and provides us with space to uproot them from their heels before we send them away.

Win the world by not imposing the will

"Not imposing the will" paraphrases 无心 (*wu*2*xin*1), which literally means "without the heart". It is another way of describing non-doing. We do things by tapping into the nothingness of Tao, not by allowing selfish desires to manipulate us. Good leaders serve without expecting anything in return. By doing so, they enjoy the support of their people. "Win the world" is a translation of 取天下 (*qu3tian1xia4*). In order to maintain harmony, the rulers must deploy the army with deceit when the occasion calls for. It creates lasting peace.

How do I know the ways things are? By these:

"The ways", here, is a translation of 然 (*ran2*). How does the Sage know that these are the ways? Because he knows what those ways are not.

The more the oppression, the poorer the people

"Oppression" is a translation of 忌讳 (*ji4hui4*). The first pictogram is 忌, which consists of 己 and 心, meaning "self" and "heart", respectively, and implying selfishness. 讳 means "misgivings", or "unwilling to tell the truth". Selfish rulers care only about what they want and think little of what the people need. They impose strict control and have no qualms with collecting high taxes to fleece the people of their hard-earned money. "Poorer" is a translation of 弥贫 (*mi2pin2*). Although the people are poor, they prefer to keep silent to avoid getting into trouble. Wealth is concentrated in the hands of a few, making people poorer.

The more weapons people possess, the bigger the confusion in the land

"Weapons" is a translation of 利器 (*li4qi4*), which means "sharp objects". They are tools of destruction. When weapons are freely available, the unscrupulous can use them to impose their will on others, bringing chaos to the community. "Confusion" is a translation of 滋昏 (*zi*1*hun*1). The "weapons" can be the psychological ones as well, such as betrayal and intrigue. If people are free to use whatever means to serve their selfish interests, trust among people is lost. If they don't seek harmony, more interpersonal strife will arise. How can a country not be in confusion in such a situation?

The more cleverness exists, the more bad deeds are done

"Cleverness" is a translation of 技巧 (*ji*4*qiao*3). 技 means "technical skills" and 巧 "craftiness". "Bad deeds" is a translation of 邪事 (*xie*2*shi*4), which means "wayward events". Technical skills are a double-edged sword. They can be used to improve productivity and bring about a better quality of life. Without the advance of technology, we wouldn't have been able to enjoy the many conveniences today, from flying and telecommunication to medicine. Unfortunately, when cleverness is used by crafty people, they can be harmful. High-tech scam and Internet hacking are some of the examples. The extent of damage and suffering they cause is beyond imagination. To prevent rampant evil, it is critical that the leaders "rule their country with honesty".

The more the rules and orders, the more the criminals

"Rules and orders" is a translation of 法令 (*fa*3*ling*4), which means "acts and law". And, "criminals" 盗贼 (*dao*4*zei*2), which means "robbers and thieves". While rules and orders are enacted to prevent crimes, introducing too many of them inspires more crimes to be committed. When a society is uncomplicated, simple rules and orders are sufficient to govern. With more crimes taking place, more of them have to be enacted. But the criminals will not simply swallow them, so more have to be enacted. The irony is, the more the rules and orders, the larger the number of outlaws. It doesn't seem to be the right solution. Laozi deplores the creating of more and more rules and orders. If only more people can turn their attention to self-cultivation, the number of outlaws will naturally shrink.

Decoding Note: Rules and orders are set by those in power. If the rulers are self-centered and driven by greed, more rules and orders are enacted not for the good of the people, but to protect the rulers' interests. In this way, the rulers are themselves criminals. In an average bank heist, robbers may take away thousands. But when the rulers plunder a country, what they take away is astronomical.

Thus the Sage says:

Laozi sums up the problems and offers solutions.

I practice non-doing, and people naturally transform themselves

When we practice non-doing, we work with the nothingness of Tao. "Transform themselves" is a translation of 自化 (*zi4hua4*). If the leaders govern a country by non-doing, the problems mentioned earlier would be naturally solved.

To walk the path of the formless Tao, one must know the implication of karma. If everybody knows that they are going to reap what they sow sooner or later, they become more cautious in the things they do. No one would do anything that brings them negative karma if they knew that they would have to pay for it, be it this life or future ones. As a result, people in leadership positions won't embezzle or abuse their power. Ordinary citizens dare not do anything unethical. An alignment between the leading and the led naturally emerges. When leaders don't have to worry about crime among the citizens, "people naturally transform themselves".

I enjoy peace, and people are naturally honest

"Enjoy peace" paraphrases 好静 (*hao4jing4*), which means "enjoy the quietness". 好 consists of two sub-characters, 女, and 子, which means "female" and "child", implying being modest and soft. 静 implies a focus of mind. When the leaders enjoy inner peace, they succumb to fewer desires, allowing them to be focused and disciplined. They are modest, humble, and conscientious. The people are inspired and willingly follow their lead to walk the path of Tao. They do what the *Tao Te Ching* teaches: To self-transform before transforming others.

Good leaders lead by setting good examples. If they are in a mess, the followers are in a mess as well. If they enjoy peace, so do their followers. With self-transformation, the leaders transform others. When the leaders of a country are conscientious, upright, and uncorrupted, so are their people.

I do by not doing, and people are naturally rich

"Do by not doing" paraphrases 无事 (*wu2shi4*), which literally means "nothing". Non-doing is a general guideline, and "do by not doing" is more specific. There is a subtle difference between them. "Naturally rich" is the translation of 自富 (*zi4fu4*). It refers to contentment, as mentioned in Chapter 33, rather than just wealth in the worldly sense. When the sages "do by not doing", they do what is good for the people and care little about their own interests. People are being inspired and "feel naturally rich", be it success or failure.

I am devoid of desires, and people are simple and pure

"Devoid of desires" is a translation of 无欲 (*wu2yu4*), and "simple and pure" is a translation of 自朴 (*zi4pu3*). The sages have no desire and are never greedy. They are happy with just basic subsistence and focus on their self-cultivation. By emulating what the sages do, the people are "simple and pure".

Chapter 58
Happiness and Misery 禍福

If rulers are plain,
Their people are simple and pure.
If rulers are fastidious,
People feel restless and insecure.

Happiness crouches in misery,
And misery lurks in happiness.
Is there an absolute?
No one can say for sure.
The honest can turn wayward,
And the decent can turn devious.
It has long been confounding.

Thus the sages are
Fair, but not cutting,
Virtuous, but not piercing,
Righteous, but not coarse,
Radiant, but not dazzling.

If rulers are plain, their people are simple and pure

"Plain" paraphrases 闷闷 (*men1men1*). The pictogram is made up of two sub-characters: 门 and 心, meaning "door" and "heart", respectively. It means to "keep the heart indoors". When the rulers allow their people to live their true nature by following the virtue of Tao, their people will not be easily distracted. The country may end up appearing "plain" since there is no fun and excitement found, yet the people are "simple and pure" (醇醇, *chun2chun2*). As a matter of fact, the people are not deprived of a good life. Spiritually, they are rich.

If rulers are fastidious, people feel restless and insecure

"Fastidious" paraphrases 察察 (*cha2cha2*); and "feel restless and insecure" 缺缺 (*que1que1*). When the leaders are fastidious, they tend to interfere with everything people do, and cannot wait to erect new laws to regulate more control. They like to find fault, making their people feel uneasy. Too much meddling is vexing. If people are penalized for even a small blunder, they grow "restless and insecure", and feel miserable.

Happiness crouches in misery, and misery lurks in happiness

"Happiness" is a translation of 福 (*fu2*), and "misery" 祸 (*huo4*). The passage aptly summarizes the first two stanzas. Being "plain" sounds like a misery, but crouched in it is a blessing that allows people to live a life that is happy and peaceful. Being fastidious sounds like a good thing. Lurking in it, however, is the misery where people are "restless and insecure".

Is there an absolute? No one can say for sure

"An absolute" paraphrases 其极 (*qi2ji2*), which means "the extreme". "Say for sure" paraphrases 定 (*ding4*), which means "certainty". Is there an absolute correlation between happiness or misery? "No one can say for sure" (其无定耶, *qi2wu2ding4ye1*), not even the exceptionally wise.

The honest can turn wayward, and the decent can turn devious

"Honest" is a translation of 正 (*zheng4*), and "wayward" 奇 (*qi2*). Sometimes, things that appear proper can become a mess. A birthday party that is supposed to be a happy occasion can end up a tragedy if someone loses their temper and pick a fight. "Decent" is a translation of 善 (*shan4*), and "devious" 妖 (*yao1*). By the same token, a decent person can become devious as a result of bad influence.

It has long been confounding

"It has long been" is a translation of 其日固久 (*qi2ri4gu4jiu3*). People have been "confounded" (迷, *mi2*) for a long time. They don't understand why the good can turn bad and vice versa. It is a difficult question, but observation of the four practices Laozi suggests in the next section could be part of the solutions.

Setting the blessing and the curse apart is not always easy. We must be able to see things beyond the surface. Sense the undercurrent, and many problems can be prevented. In the birthday party example, a little more vigilance could have helped avoid the tragedy from happening.

Thus the sages are fair, but not cutting

"Fair" paraphrases 方 (*fang*1), which means "square" and implies impartiality. "Cutting" is a translation of 割 (*ge*1), which means "hurting like a cutting knife". While the sages are honest and fair, hurting others, through words or deeds, is not warranted. Some parents love their children dearly and assume that the children must always react positively to their love. However, if the inspiration of a child is to be a playwright, the insistence of their parents to make them a lawyer can hurt, no matter how good the intention is. The parents are "fair", but it cuts. If the parents can round the edges and give the child the respect and empathy they deserve, they will be able to find a solution that doesn't cut.

Virtuous, but not piercing

"Virtuous" is a translation of 廉 (*lian*2), which carries the connotation of incorruptibility. "Piercing" is a translation of 刿 (*gui*4), which means "to cut". The pictogram is made up of the sub-character 岁, which means "age", and radical 刂, which means a "knife".

One can be virtuous and flexible. While it is respectable to be incorruptible, it can be unpleasant when it is done crudely. For example, when family and friends present a government official with gifts and receive a scolding, the official is "virtuous" but also "piercing". If he can accept the gifts or reject with grace, the family and friends would not have suffered from his piercing words.

Righteous, but not coarse

Being righteous (直, *zhi*2) is good, but it doesn't warrant us being "coarse" (肆, *si*4). When someone makes a mistake, we can candidly point it out. It, however, doesn't mean that we can be rude. We should give them due respect and be "righteous but not coarse".

Radiant, but not dazzling

When we are successful, be it in life or the attainment of Tao, we must dim the "radiance" (光, *guang*1) to avoid being "dazzling" (耀, *yao*4). We must stay humble, modest, and soft. Laozi mentions this in a variety of ways, such as "enlightenment looks insipid" in Chapter 41, and "although the Sage is draped in rough clothes, hidden within them are precious gems" in Chapter 70. When a person of Tao radiates the virtue of Te, they are gentle and warm; never dazzling.

Decoding Note: If we can observe these four practices suggested by Laozi and live the spirit of non-doing, we invite blessings rather than a curse. As a result, the confusion that bothers others hardly worries us.

Chapter 59
Longevity and Continuity
长生（啬）

Cultivating people and
Serving Heaven,
Nothing matters more than
Returning to the root.

Returning to the root brings early devotion,
Early devotion accumulates the virtue of Te,
With the accumulation of Te
There is nothing we cannot conquer,
When there is nothing we cannot conquer,
We are unfathomable.
When we are unfathomable, a country can be built.
With Mother of Tao guarding the country,
There is endurance.

It is having a deep and strong stem,
It is Tao of longevity and continuity.

Cultivating people and serving Heaven, nothing matters more than returning to the root

As human beings, we are gifted with intelligence for the attainment of Tao. It is a privilege, and we must make the best of it to refine our perpetual self. This is "cultivating people" (治人, zhi4ren2). We have to improve ourselves even if we are already steeped in Te. Every life is an opportunity for further refinement. It can be, say, to change some bad habits that hamper our progress. Since reading the *Tao Te Ching* helps us with the refinement, it is also an activity of "cultivating people".

"Serving Heaven" (事天, shi4tian1) is about emulating what Heaven does with Tao. Heaven was derived directly from Tao One. Upon its emergence, Earth was born. Only subsequently that the myriads of things, including the human being, came into existence. "Humanity follows Earth, Earth follows Heaven, Heaven follows Tao," says Laozi in Chapter 25. Heaven is, therefore, in the closest proximity of Tao. There is so much that we can learn from Heaven. For example, since Heaven benefits everything yet seeks no reward, then when we emulate what it does, we are compassionate and benevolent.

"Cultivating people and serving Heaven" is, therefore, the primary purpose of life. Through the observation of the Tao of Heaven, we refine our soul and, at the same time, motivate others to do so. To help us go about doing it, Laozi outlines the path below.

First, "returning to the root". This is summed up in the pictogram 嗇 (se4). Although this pictogram is crucial to the understanding of the *Tao Te Ching*, it is widely misinterpreted. It can be dissected into three sub-characters: 人, 土, and 回. They mean, respectively, "people", "Earth", and "return". At the upper half of the pictogram are two people (人). Sitting on the earth (土), they symbolize the sentient being. The lower half is the sub-character 回, which means "return". So, as a whole, we may interpret it as saying: All sentient beings will eventually return to the source.

Many people interpret 嗇 as "frugality". They probably derive the definition from dictionaries. The pictogram is often used together with 啬 to form the word "吝啬", which means "thrift". Although technically not wrong, the interpretation is insufficient to explain the Tao of longevity and continuity, which is the theme of this chapter.

Returning to the root takes time and is done by stages. It involves a process of "changing raft", as explained in the Buddhist scripture, the *Diamond Sutra*. Upon crossing a river, we discard the old raft and take a new one to cross yet another river. This is because each raft serves a specific purpose, and we have to discard the old one so that the new one can take its place to serve us on a new segment of the journey. The technique of Taijigong that I teach my disciples is a raft; it helps them to cross a river. Once they are on the other side, they pick up something more demanding and proceed further.

Every crossing of a river is a return and takes us closer to the root. Along the way, we must be ready for a new raft to begin a new crossing. Where do we find the new raft? No one can tell us for sure, but if we are devoted to the pursuit, the new raft will be delivered to us somehow. It is like how the Chinese saying puts it: "When the water arrives, a channel is formed." The answer will dawn upon us when the time comes. Someone may utter it to us, or an epiphany may strike us when we walk in a park. When we have "crossed a river", we will stumble into another "river" and find the need for another "raft". Metaphorically, it means we have to discard what we learned yesterday for the new things that appear today. It is a continuous renewal.

Regardless of our form of cultivation or level of attainment, we "return to the root". It takes us back to the source and helps us in the Fulfillment of Destiny. The completion of a stage takes us closer to the root.

Returning to the root brings early devotion. Early devotion accumulates the virtue of Te

"Early devotion" is a translation of 早服 (*zao3fu2*). It means "to begin the practice early". If our inclination is Tao, follow Tao. If our inclination is Buddhism, follow the Buddha. If our inclination is Christianity, follow God. Starting the practice early allows us more time and space to "accumulate the virtue of Te" (重积德, *chong2ji1de2*).

There are two types of Te that we accumulate. They, respectively, bring us happiness and wisdom. The first is Te of Fortune and the second Te of Wisdom. Through giving and caring, we help ourselves by helping others. When we take part in disaster relief, we feel good as the energy of Te rewards us with bliss and happiness. This is Te of Fortune. As for Te of Wisdom, it enriches our life through the assimilation of wisdom. For example, reading of the *Tao Te Ching* or other spiritual scriptures sheds light on the meaning of life, which helps us to derive more from our self-cultivation while refining our soul. This is Te of Wisdom. We need both.

With the accumulation of Te, there is nothing we cannot conquer

With the accumulation of both the Te of Fortune and the Te of Wisdom, we make headway in the journey of Tao, and there is "nothing we cannot conquer" (无不克, *wu2bu4ke4*). We can always find ways to overcome all sorts of challenges in life. Thanks to Te of Fortune that provides us with expanding energy; and Te of Wisdom that gives us the calmness, blunts the sharp edges that hurt and unties the knots that entangle. We accept what is and are adaptable. Even death bothers us little, and there is nothing that we cannot conquer.

When there is nothing we cannot conquer, we are unfathomable

When, to us, there is nothing that we cannot conquer, people cannot figure out our depth and potential. In fact, when we have tapped into the formless Tao, which is indefinitely big, there is no limit to what we can do. "We are unfathomable" (莫知其极, *mo4zhi1qi2ji2*).

When we are unfathomable, a country can be built

Although "country" (国, *guo*2) usually refers to a nation, here it also means organizations in general, be it spiritual, social, or business. Every spiritual path is unique, and may be seen as a "country". To build a "country", however, we will have to be "unfathomable", implying that the standard for spiritual attainment must be high. Any sage who is "unfathomable" can create a "country" they can call their own.

With Mother of Tao guarding the country, there is endurance

Mother of Tao is selfless and accommodating. Deserting the Mother (母, *mu*3) allows the country to be engulfed in divides and selfishness. When this is the case, the country will not last, no matter how big it is. Only when Mother of Tao prevails will the country thrive, and "there is endurance" 长久 (*chang*2*jiu*3).

It is having a deep root and strong stem. It is Tao of longevity and continuity

"Deep root" is a translation of 根深 (*gen*1*shen*1), and "strong stem" 固蒂 (*gu*4*di*4). When a country is built on Mother of Tao, it is as deep-rooted and enduring as a big tree. The deeper the root, the more robust is the tree, and the stronger is its stem. If the stem of an apple is weak, it is easily blown away, and the apple will not come into fruition. Without the fruit, there are no seeds and thus no renewal. When the root is deep, and the stem is strong, there is a continuation, and the "country" survives one generation after another.

"Longevity" (长生, *chang*2*sheng*1) is non-being, and it refers to the formless Tao. Tao is eternal. We don't know how old it is or how much older it will be. "Continuity" 久視 (*jiu3shi4*) is being. It is visible and refers to the use of Tao. Although Laozi died more than two thousand years ago, yet we still feel his presence. This is "longevity and continuity", which arise when we combine Tao Core with Tao Use. We pursue Tao by having it deeply rooted on solid ground.

Every country has to be built on faith, and the faith is the "Tao of longevity and continuity". It takes us back to Tao Core and Tao One. It is all about "Creating but possessing not. Doing but seeking no glory. Accomplishing but taking no credit". There are no divides, no selfishness. Laozi urges us at the beginning of the chapter that we must "return to the root". It is all about returning to the "Tao of longevity and continuity".

Chapter 60

Rule the World with Tao
道莅天下

*Governing a large country
Is like frying a small fish.*

*Govern the world with Tao,
The evil loses its power.
Not that the evil is powerless,
Its power is harmless to people.
Not only is its power harmless to people,
But even the Sage is harmless to people.*

*Alas! When both the evil and the Sage are harmless,
The Te is mingled and restored.*

Governing a large country is like frying a small fish

It is not easy to "fry a small fish" (烹小鲜, *peng1xiao3xian1*). If the fire is too strong, it burns the fish. If it is too weak, the fish is not properly cooked. For fear of burning, we flip the fish. But frequent flipping leaves the fish in tatters. "Governing a large country" (治大国, *zhi4da4guo2*) is equally delicate. The strength of the fire must neither be too strong nor be too weak; the frying cannot be forceful. Everything has to be just right. While the policies must be flexible and meticulous, we cannot change them at our whim. Otherwise, we create confusion and bring about a whole host of social problems.

Govern the world with Tao

If we can "govern the world" (莅天下, *li4tian1xia4*) with Tao, we can diminish problems associated with "frying a small fish". The "world" here refers not only to a country but also to any organization. When we rule the world with Tao, people are guided to follow the order of nature, rather than divides and selfishness. They see self-cultivation as their primary goal of life. When the leaders serve wholeheartedly, and the people are content, there is no need for micromanagement and the intricacy of "frying a small fish" is properly handled.

The evil loses its power

When everybody believes in Tao, they also believe in karma. It makes them conscientious about what they do, and avoid evil for fear of retribution. As a result, "the evil loses its power" (其鬼不神, *qi2gui3bu4shen2*).

Decoding Note: In a country ruled by Tao, everybody is focused on self-cultivation, while helping each other and the world. The good energy is so strong as if guardian angels are watching over them. It stops the evil from crossing over to disturb them.

Not that the evil is powerless, its power is harmless to people. Not only is its power harmless to people, but even the Sage is harmless to people

The word "power" paraphrases the character 神 (*shen*2), which means "spirit". With the good energy that prevails over the country, the evil cannot wreak havoc. As a result, its power is "harmless to people" (不伤人, *bu4shang1ren2*). It is like what Laozi says in Chapter 23, "Those who conform to Tao are one with Tao." "If we conform to Tao, Tao is with us." Since the people are blessed by Tao, both evil and the Sage are harmless to them.

Decoding Note: In a country ruled by Tao, people are devoted to self-cultivation, and the country is permeated with the abundance of happiness and qi. The country is in harmony, so blissful that evil prefers not to intrude. "Even the Sage is harmless to people." The deities and sages only punish the wicked who violate the order of Tao. They are delighted at what the people do and happy to help them transform. If we conform to Tao or Te, Tao or Te is with us.

Alas! When both the evil and the Sage are harmless, the Te is mingled and restored

Both the evil and the Sage are harmless when the good and bad people live alongside peacefully. It is possible in an environment where Tao prevails. Believing in karma, not only do the bad do no evil; they are transformed over time and turn over a new leaf. The good, on the other hand, are, by nature, harmless. They continue to improve and eventually become sages. So both the good and the bad are harmless. They stay where they are and do what they ought to. They learn from one another and work hard on their self-cultivation. "The Te is mingled and restored" (德交归焉, *de2jiao1gui1yan1*).

Chapter 61
Positioning Low 为下

*A large country stays
At the bottom of the flow.*

*It is where the world converges,
And where the feminine power
Rules the world.*

*The feminine overpowers
The masculine with calmness.
It positions low with calmness.*

*Thus when a large country lowers itself
Before a small country,
It wins over its heart.
When a small country lowers itself
Before a big country,
It wins over its trust.
One wins by positioning low;
One wins by remaining low.*

*The large country wants to unite and lead,
The small country wants to associate and serve.
Both get what they want;
The big should always lie low.*

A large country stays at the bottom of the flow

Water flows downward. The more receptive the concavity, the more water it gathers. This is how a large country can build up its leadership capacity. The more humble and modest a large country is, the more small countries it can attract to be its affiliates. "The bottom of the flow" is a translation of 下流 (*xia4liu2*).

It is where the world converges

It's where countries large and small meet and interact with one another. "Converges" is a translation of 交 (*jiao1*).

And where the feminine power rules the world

"Feminine" is a translation of 牝 (*pin4*), which means female and, in this context, implies motherliness. A large country must remain humble and modest and, at the same time, soft and affable. It must not be haughty and oppressive because of its privileged position. The bigger the country, the more this must be the case. It showers the small countries with empathy and support and cuddles them as a mother does a child.

The feminine overpowers the masculine with calmness

Soft and calm, the feminine is able to overcome the masculine (牡, *mu3*), which is hard and vigorous, and, at times, impatient. Let's use husband and wife as an example; the wife is able to overcome the harshness of her husband by being soft and counter his agitation with calmness (静, *jing4*). She wins the husband's devotion by being feminine. If, on the other hand, the wife is as hard as the husband, the couple will experience much conflict.

It positions low with calmness

By being calm and wise, the feminine prevails over the masculine who is unsettled. This is an excellent example of overcoming the agitated with calmness; and the harshness with softness.

Thus when a large country lowers itself before a small country, it wins over its heart

A large country, therefore, must lower (下, *xia*4) itself and treat a small country with humility and respect. By doing so, it wins over (取, *qu*3) its trust and affiliation.

China positions itself low when it deals with African countries, even though it is a more powerful country. It provides assistance to many developing countries to construct railways and bridges, develop hydroelectric power and mining, and promote education and healthcare. Even then, it remains humble and cordial. In return, it enjoys gratitude and support from these countries. Many African countries are appreciative and are now bosom friends of China.

When a small country lowers itself before a big country, it wins over its trust

Similarly, a small country should relate to a large country with modesty, humility, and respect, in return for its trust and protection. It must not become big-headed and take for granted the humility and respect extended to it by a large country. By remaining modest, the large country becomes a willing partner to take advantage of development opportunities that benefit both parties.

One wins by positioning low; one wins by remaining low

The large country wins affinity with the small country by "positioning low" (以取, *yi*3*qu*3). The small country wins the protection of the large country by "remaining low" (而取, *er2qu3*). One positions low to win affinity, the other remains low to win protection. Both get what they want.

The large country wants to unite and lead

The humility of the large country brings everyone together. When countries can identify common ground and ready for give-and-take, win-win opportunities that enrich every country can be found. It "unite and lead" (兼畜, *jian1xu4*) the small countries to generate abundance for everybody to share, leading to better lives for the people in each of the countries.

The small country wants to associate and serve

The small country wants to be of help and service to the large country. It wants to "associate and serve" (入事, *ru4shi4*). It stays modest so that it can win the trust and enjoy the audience of the large country.

Both get what they want

The large country enjoys the support and love of many small countries with whom they affiliate. The small countries, on the other hand, are able to serve. "Both get what they want" despite the difference.

The big should always lie low

Therefore, the larger the country, the more important that it always positions itself low.

Chapter 62

The Mysterious Secret of Tao 道奥

Tao is qi.
The mysterious secret of all things,
it is the treasure for a good person,
and refuge for the not so good.

Good words command respect,
Good deeds strengthen one's character.

If people are not so good,
Why do we abandon them?
So Son of Heaven is ordained,
And his three ministers installed.
Instead of offering them fine jade escorted by
A four-horse chariot,
Why not sit firmly in the arms of Tao?

Why did the ancients value Tao?
Not only does it respond to our request,
But it also spares us the punishment of guilt.
All things in the universe thus return to Tao.

Tao is qi

The version of the *Tao Te Ching* edited by Taoist Master Tao Hongjing begins this chapter with the statement "Tao is qi (炁)". Although omitted in most versions, it is highly relevant. I, therefore, include it here. Why is this statement omitted in most editions of the *Tao Te Ching*? A reason could be that the editors were scholars who did not practice qi. Even if they do, few were accomplished. People tend to associate qi with breathing and blood circulation, but the qi that we talk about here is a lot more profound. It's not just the oxygen (气) we breathe. Qigong (炁功) is not "air" gong (气功).

Taiji can trace its origin to the *Yijing*. "In the System of Change there is Taiji (易有太极)," says the *Yijing*. The System of Change is Tao Core, and Taiji is its use. The *Tao Te Ching* was written in the vein of the *Yijing*. There is a gap of more than two thousand years between the two works, similar to the time gap between Laozi and ours. Although Laozi is supposedly very remote from us, we can connect to him by qi, even as a novice of Taijiquan. Indeed, Tao is qi, and Tao is Taiji.

"Something nebulous was born before the emergence of the universe," says Laozi. Although we cannot be certain what exactly the "something nebulous" was, we know it consists of the *taihe* qi energy, which has been around since the dawn of time. We will have to rely on the "small *taihe* qi" in our body to make the connection when we return to Tao Core. Only when we have integrated with Tao Core can we tell with certainty what the "something nebulous" is. "The Tao that can be described is not the eternal Tao," says Laozi.

The mysterious secret of all things

"One mystery after another, the gate to all wonders," says Laozi in Chapter 1. It is the "mysterious secret" (奥, *ao*4) that lies beneath birth and death and departure and return. There is a law governed by Tao, which acts like a door. All things go through it to arrive in this world and go through it to return to their origin. It is a process that we describe as "returning to the root" in Chapter 59.

It is the treasure of a good person, and refuge for the not so good

A "good person" (善人, *shan4ren2*) is a person of Tao who sees Tao attainment as their ultimate goal in life and thus regard Tao as the treasure (宝, *bao3*).

Those who are "not so good" (不善人, *bu4shan4ren2*) don't regard Tao as a treasure. They don't believe in karma, and so can be unscrupulous. Even then, as long as they are ready to repent and change for the better, they can "find refuge" (保, *bao3*) in Tao. As the saying goes, "Lay down the butcher knife, and you are a buddha".

Good words command respect

The "good words" (善言, *shan4yan2*) are words of a person of Tao that are kind, virtuous, and magnanimous. They are well-received and "command respect" (市尊, *shi4zun1*) from people all over.

Good deeds strengthen one's character

"Good words" have to be put into practice to be useful. A person of Tao walks the talk and continuously improves. This is how they attain Tao. Through every good deed they perform, they "strengthen their character" (加人, *jia1ren2*), and make progress in their cultivation.

If people are not so good, why do we abandon them?

Since Tao is their "refuge", there is no reason for us to abandon "the not so good". They are "the average" and "the ignorant" as described in Chapter 41, who are yet to understand the implications of the "good words". When they have realized what they have missed and willing to accept the teachings, they too can benefit from the wisdom. There is no reason for us to "abandon them" (弃之, *qi4zhi1*).

So Son of Heaven is ordained, and his three ministers installed

Heaven was derived from Tao One. "Son of Heaven" is thus a "Son of Tao". It is a translation of 天子 (*tian1zi3*), which is used as a title for emperors in China. Tao is formless, and "Son of Heaven" is ordained to promote the teachings of Tao. The "three ministers" (三公, *san1gong1*) are *taishi* (太师), *taifu* (太傅) and *taibao* (太保) — the officials appointed to assist the "Son of Heaven" in promoting the "good words" and "good deeds". They help people to "blunt the sharpness and untie the knots" and to live a peaceful life. Spiritually, they guide them to transform themselves and refine their perpetual selves.

Instead of offering them fine jade escorted by a four-horse chariot, why not sit firmly in the arms of Tao?

Since "Son of Heaven" is ordained to promote Tao, if we want to pay respect to them, elegant tributes, such as a large piece of superior jade carried in a four-horse chariot, are inappropriate. Instead of expensive gifts, a far more pertinent tribute is to "sit firmly in the arms of Tao" (坐进此道, *zuo4jin4ci3dao4*). As the saying goes, "Mountain of wisdom is right in your heart." Don't seek externally for enlightenment. Go into the depth of the "absolute stillness" and dialogue with our inner self. Do what the sages do. Meditate in solitude, or simply as Mencius said, "I reflect internally three times a day." This is how the sages become enlightened.

Why did the ancients value Tao?

What is the reason for people to value (贵, *gui4*) Tao in this manner since ancient times?

Not only does it respond to our request, but it also spares us the punishment of guilt

Tao is with us when we conform to it. It is responsive and always comes to our aid when we need its help. "Not only" (不曰, *bu4yue1*) that, if we have drifted away from it, so long as we repent and mend our ways, Tao is ready to "spare us the punishment of guilt" (有罪以免, *you3zui4yi3mian3*). This explains why Tao is valued so much!

Decoding Note: We, however, must not take Tao's responsiveness for granted. Although Tao is responsive, we must do our share to internalize the teachings, so that Tao can "respond to our request" (求以得, *qiu2yi3de2*).

All things in the universe thus return to Tao

All sentient beings, good or bad, will eventually fulfill their destiny and return to Tao Core. Only then can we "return to the root" and permanently be spared the sufferings of reincarnations. It is, thus, Tao that "all things in the world must return to" (天下归, *tian1xia4gui1*).

Chapter 63
Nothing is Difficult 无难

Do by not doing,
Act by not acting;
Taste by not tasting.
Be it big, small,
More or less;
Greet hatred with Te.

See simplicity in the complicated;
Achieve greatness in small details.
Deal with the difficult
By working on the easy,
Deal with the big
By working on the small.
The Sage thinks not of
Doing anything great,
So they achieve greatness.

Alas! Casual promises
Are rarely fulfilled,
Things that appear easy
Have difficulties lurking within.
The Sage expects great difficulty,
So they do not experience difficulty.

Do by not doing

In this chapter, Laozi talks about applying the principles of Tao in things we do. "Do by not doing" (为无为, *wei2wu2wei2*) is to emulate Tao by practicing non-doing: "Create but possess not. Do but seek no glory. Grow but seek not to dominate. Accomplish but claim no credit." It provides a general direction.

Act by not acting

"Act by not acting" (事无事, *shi4wu2shi4*) is about the specific. In the handling of daily matters, we do as mentioned in Chapters 4 and 56: "Blunt the sharpness, untie the knot, blend in with the light and merge with the dust".

Tao is infinitely big; it is bigger than the entire universe. It is also infinitely small, so small that it is in the details of the things we do. Be it big or small; we can always benefit from the wonder of "act by not acting". Taste is a case in point.

Taste by not tasting

Taste (味, *wei4*) is small. It is in the flavors that tantalize our taste buds, or the little pleasures that impact the quality of our life. It is, nevertheless, also big. A person of Tao is not fussy about the taste of food, but find delight in self-cultivation, which is a big thing in life. They taste by "not tasting" (无味, *wu2wei4*). The "not" is a noun, which implies the taste of nothingness, i.e., Tao.

We sometimes laugh at people who have "no taste", teasing their out-of-fashion attire or ugly glasses. Does it mean that we have better taste? Taste is subjective. How it is perceived is subject to manipulation. An item that costs ten dollars to make can sell for thousands of dollars if it is worn by superstars we worship. Isn't it ridiculous? A person of Tao is down-to-earth. To them, clothes, food, shelter, and means of transport are meant for subsistence. There is no need to keep asking for more, not to mention keeping up with the Joneses or following the trends. They enjoy the taste of "not tasting".

"Do by not doing, act by not acting, taste by not tasting." With these tenets in mind, Laozi guides us on the ways to handle things big, small, more, and less, as well as hatred and virtue.

Be it big, small, more or less; greet hatred with Te

Big and small, more and less, hatred and virtue: They are products of divides. To the formless Tao, the world is One. There are no good and evil, not to mention "hatred" (怨, *yuan*4) and Te. Of course, we live in the mundane world of divides, and cannot hold on to Oneness all the time. Even then, our spiritual goal must be big, as big as that of the sages whose hearts go out to the people. Our worldly goal, on the other hand, must be small, so small that we are happy and content when basic subsistence is met. This is what the Buddha does. Although he is revered by the world, he has no qualms with begging for alms door-to-door. In contrast, people in the world want more, be it wealth, fame, or desires. A person of Tao, however, wants less: less ego and fewer desires. How one views the big (大, *da*4), small (小, *xiao*3) and more (多, *duo*1) and less (少, *shao*3) sets a sage apart from ordinary folk.

As for hatred and Te, it has to do with karma. Hatred may be recently incurred or brought over from a previous life. If someone hates us for what we owed him in a previous life, greeting their hatred with Te allows us to pay off the debt with interest and alleviate the bad karma we bear. It, at the same time, strengthens our cultivation. Is that not a good deal?

Besides, it is natural for a person of Tao to "greet hatred with virtue" because what they have for others is only Te. They harbor no grievances. This echoes what Laozi says in Chapter 49, "Those who are good, they are good to them. Those who are not good, they are also good to them."

See simplicity in the complicated

In the face of something difficult, begin by working on the easy parts. The first step to improving our health, for example, can be as simple as taking a walk. Similarly, for the spiritual pursuits, it is unrealistic to expect overnight attainment, so we may simply begin by doing what Laozi suggests: Bring down the ego and have fewer desires. It is hard for most people to have no ego and desire, although it sounds noble. We can, however, reduce them little by little. By the same token, in everything we do, identify "simplicity" (易, *yi*4) in the complicated (难, *nan*2). Once we have started, we will see progress along the way.

Achieve greatness in small details

If we want to "achieve greatness" (为大, *wei*2*da*4), we begin with the "little details" (细, *xi*4). If we cannot even get the small details right, how are we going to achieve something great? When interviewing candidates of senior positions, it is a common practice for companies to look not only at the big things candidates have done but also their intimacy with little details that make the big things viable. Small and big, easy and difficult are not absolute. They complement each other.

Tao is big, so attaining Tao is aiming big. To do that, however, we must be ready to do the small. Distractions are small, but we cannot achieve the big vision without weeding them out. The Buddha was wary of the little things he did. When he walked, he took pains not to step on any little living being. No good deed is too small to perform, neither a bad deed too small to avoid. Be it good or bad, the small details add up.

Deal with the difficult by working on the easy. Deal with the big by working on the small

Expanding on the previous two sentences, Laozi reiterates the importance of seeking simplicity. If we want to learn a new language, begin with simple daily phrases, and take every opportunity to practice them. Similarly, before a dispute develops into a conflict, contain it with conciliation. Don't expect overnight miracles. "Great piece of art takes time to complete", as Laozi says in Chapter 41.

The Sage thinks not of doing anything great, so they achieve greatness

Although the Sage has mastered non-doing and "achieved greatness" (成其大, *cheng2qi2da4*), they don't think that they are "doing anything great" (不为大, *bu4wei2da4*). It is reminiscent of what Laozi says in Chapter 15, "Since they are never filled, they can wear out and renew." This is the only way to achieve the complete attainment of Tao. A person of Tao remains humble and modest because they never assume they are great. Paradoxically, this is what allows them to be really big in whatever they do.

Alas! Casual promises are rarely fulfilled

Alas! Don't make casual promises (轻诺, *qing1nuo4*)! It doesn't mean that we don't make any commitment. But if we don't take the promises seriously, they are "rarely fulfilled" (寡信, *gua3xin4*). As far as cultivation is concerned, it is all the more important that we don't take our commitments lightly.

Things that appear easy have difficulties lurking within

When we take things lightly, we tend to underestimate the challenge they pose. As a result, something easy becomes difficult. Many good swimmers drowned because of their excellence in swimming. It makes them overlook the danger lurking in the quiet water. Complacency can be costly.

The Sage expects great difficulty, so they do not experience difficulty

The Sage always expects things to be difficult, so they don't take things lightly. In the end, nothing is difficult for them. A student who is thorough in his study doesn't assume anything is easy, so he covers every key aspect of his subjects of study, making his success in examinations a lot more assured. The same principle applies to Tao cultivation as well. The sages are able to fully attain Tao because they never think that Tao attainment is easy.

Chapter 64
Force Not 不敢为

What is at rest is easy to hold,
What is yet to happen is easy to plan.
What is brittle is easily shattered,
What is tiny is easily scattered.

Work on a problem before it arises,
Set things in order before they get out of control.

A giant tree grows from a tiny sprout;
A tower nine-story high rises from a pile of earth,
A journey of a thousand miles
Begins with a single step.

Those who force it, ruin it.
Those who grip it, lose it.
The Sage forces not,
So they never fail,
They grip none,
So they lose none.

People often fail
When they are about to succeed.
Give as much care to the end
As to the beginning;
Then there is no failure.

The Sage desires not to desire,
Values no precious goods.
They learn by not learning,
And reflect on the mistakes people are repeating.
They help all things to find their own nature
And do not impose their will.

What is at rest is easy to hold

A cup "at rest" (安, *an*1) is "easy to hold" (易持, *yi4chi2*). A country in peace and contentment is easy to govern. This explains why, in all forms of cultivation, peace of mind is first and foremost. It allows us to go deep. A mind unsettled can hardly focus. To calm our minds, we must do what Chapter 16 says, "Toward absolute nothingness."

If we can see the fleeting nature of things, we enjoy the benefits of calmness. Whatever we own today, be it fame or wealth or our body, is not going to be with us a hundred years from now. So, what is there for us to be bigoted about? With the understanding, we will not be perturbed by matters that divert our attention away from our primary goal of self-cultivation. We are not obstinate. We see everything as if an image in a mirror. When the object is in front of the mirror, it is there. When it is taken away, it vanishes. There is no baggage to bog us down. We are calm and easy and in peace. We hold fast to tranquility and enjoy the absolute stillness.

Another way to maintain peace of mind is to keep fear at bay. For that, it helps if we understand the impact of karma, and have faith in the good energy of the universe that blesses us for being kind. As the Chinese saying goes, "If our conscience is clear, we fear not of the knocks on our door deep in the night." When there is no fear, there is peace, and we find it easy to hold ourselves.

What is yet to happen is easy to plan

Everything in the universe moves in cycles. When summer settles into autumn, winter is around the corner. By knowing the cycles, we can plan. We sow in spring and worry not about harvest until autumn. We save for the rainy days because we know prevention is better than cure. "What is yet to happen" (未兆, *wei4zhao4*) is easy to "plan" (谋, *mou2*).

In Taiji sparring, we always plan before things happen. We scan the opponent for any potential movements. When the opponent starts moving, we either pre-empt them, or go with the move, but await opportunities to deflect the force back. The planning takes a split second, but it makes a world of difference. Similarly, during meditation, knowing that distractions can arise at any moment, we dive into stillness before any distraction can divert our attention. It makes the exercise a lot more effective.

What is brittle is easily shattered. What is tiny is easily scattered

We plan before things happen. But what if they have already happened? For example, we know that distraction drains our energy, but what if it has already intruded into our minds? Then we must deal with it when it is still small. "What is brittle (脆, *cui*4) is easily shattered" (破, *po*4)". When a tree is still a seedling, we can pluck it off with two fingers, but not when it has grown into a tree. In the social context, a criminal gang yet to gain big money and support is easily crippled. Once established, it becomes a lot harder to have them crushed.

"What is tiny (微, *wei*1) is easily scattered (散, *san*4)". When molding clay into a pot, we make adjustments before the earth is settled. Blow the powdery earth, and it scatters into the atmosphere. Similarly, for distraction, we must dispel it the moment it arises when it is still tiny and weak. This makes achieving a deep stillness a lot easier.

Work on a problem before it arises, set things in order before they get out of control

The best solution to a problem is prevention. Be it a personal, social, or political issue, we must, as far as possible, "work on a problem" (为之, *wei*2*zhi*1) "before it arises" (未有, *wei*4*you*3). If possible, nip off its source before the problem occurs. "An ounce of prevention is worth a pound of cure," so goes the saying.

In knowledge management, the practice implies securing a first-mover advantage. If we can invent something before someone else, we are leading the way. From the perspective of Tao, this is profound. "Before it arises" (未有, *wei4you3*) means there is yet to be anything. So, we work on a problem when it is still a non-being, and solve a problem before it is yet to be a problem. This is an important aspect of non-doing.

Also, we "set things in order" (治之, *zhi4zhi1*) "before it gets out of hand" (于未乱, *yu2wei4luan4*). In dealing with any situation, the best time for its management is before disorder sets in. Find out the source of disorder makes coping with it easier. To do that, see things in Oneness. Whenever possible, find common ground for a win-win solution. We must avoid countering evil with evil. Not only is it against Tao, but it is also the beginning of chaos and brings on a whole host of other problems. If everyone can walk the path of Tao One and Tao Core and practice non-doing, chaos can be avoided.

A giant tree grows from a tiny sprout

"A giant tree" (合抱之木, *he2bao4zhi1mu4*) is huge. Its beginning, however, is nothing but a "tiny sprout" (毫末, *hao2mo4*). The big begins small. It echoes Chapter 63, "Deal with the big by working on the small." Laozi reiterates it here to remind us of its importance. Like what is said in Chapter 63, "Achieve greatness in small details". Take one step at a time; more haste, less speed.

A tower nine-story high rises from a pile of earth

We don't build "a tower nine-story high" (九层之台, *jiu3ceng2zhi1tai2*) from the ninth story. Instead, we begin building it "with a pile of earth" (累土, *lei3tu3*) on the ground. We lay a solid foundation and build the tower one level after another. We allow the big to stay at the bottom, and the small to lie above. To do the reverse is against the law of nature, and the building is at the risk of collapse at any moment. It implies that the bigger we are, the more humble we must be to keep what we have built stable.

A journey of a thousand miles begins with a single step

Tao attainment is a long process. It is "a journey of a thousand miles" (千里之行, *qian*1*li*3*zhi*1*xing*2). However long the journey, we can never complete it if we don't take the first "single step" (足下, *zu*2*xia*4). If we don't even read, there is no point in talking about going to university. If we are serious about self-cultivation, take action now; don't just talk about it.

Those who force it, ruin it. Those who grip it, lose it

Those who "force it" (为者, *wei*2*zhe*3) are driven by divides to fulfill their personal agenda, a far cry from those who practice non-doing and seek no credit for the good deeds they perform. Those who force it "ruin" (败之, *bai*4*zhi*1) their attainment in Tao. There are also those who try to grab everything they want. They "grip it" (执者, *zhi*2*zhe*3) tight and refuse to let go, but "lose it" (失之, *shi*1*zhi*1) eventually because nothing is permanent in this world. No matter how tight the grip is, they can bring nothing with them when they die. In fact, what they lose are not only things they grip. An even bigger loss is an excellent opportunity for cultivation that refines their souls.

The Sage forces not, so they never fail. They grip none, so they lose none

The Sage practices non-doing by observing the law of nature. It allows them to do nothing and leave nothing undone, and so they "never fail" (无败, *wu*2*bai*4). In addition, the Sage lets go of everything. They grip nothing and worry about nothing, "so they lose none" (无失, *wu*2*shi*1).

People often fail when they are about to succeed. Give as much care to the end as to the beginning; then there is no failure

Whether it is spiritual or worldly pursuits, people often fail when they are "about to succeed" (几成, *ji4cheng2*). They do not give as much care to "the end" (终, *zhong1*) as to the "beginning" (始, *shi3*). Many entrepreneurs begin humbly. It wins them the support of their employees and customers. When they are successful, they forget what has brought them there and become big-headed. Soon, the pillars of their success erode, and their business goes into decline. Similarly, there are Tao cultivators who are conceited upon initial success and become inconsistent in their practice. In the end, they lose the attainment that they took pains to accumulate.

Here, Laozi uses the character 慎 (*shen4*), which means "cautious". The pictogram consists of radical 忄, which means "heart", and the sub-character 真, which means "true". So 慎 may be interpreted as the "true heart" or deep devotion to Tao. Whether we are at the beginning or already enjoying success, we must consistently adhere to Tao and embrace it with the "true heart". It takes us to full attainment, and "there is no failure" (无败事, *wu2bai4shi4*).

The Sage desires not to desire

We may, therefore, say that the "desire" (欲, *yu4*) of the Sage is "not to desire" (不欲, *bu4yu4*). If they don't desire, then there are neither forms, divides, nor self-interests to worry about. There is simply no desire.

Values no precious goods

For the Sage, whatever that goes beyond subsistence to keep going is "precious goods" (难得之货, *nan2de2zhi1huo4*). They see them as dispensable and don't "value" (贵, *gui4*) them.

They learn by not learning and reflect on the mistakes people are repeating

The Sage "learns by not learning" (学不学, *xue2bu4xue2*). They learn not worldly knowledge, but the eternal wisdom ignored by most people. They reflect on "the mistakes" (之所过, *zhi1suo3guo4*) that trap people in the cycles of suffering. They make progress in Tao attainment by not "repeating" (复, *fu4*) what they do.

They help all things to find their own nature and do not impose their will

The Sage teaches people the law of nature and the rights and wrongs of things. No one can go against the will of Heaven. What the Sage can do is "to help", rather than to alter the ways the law of nature works. They, therefore, "don't impose their will" (不敢为, *bu4gan3wei2*) on anybody. Instead, they help (辅, *fu3*) them to find their own "nature" (自然, *zi4ran2*).

Chapter 65
The Great Path of Flow
大顺

*The ancients who knew Tao
Did not teach people to be clever,
Only helped them to remain simple.*

*People are difficult to govern
When they are clever.
Thus, rulers of cleverness
Are their country's curse.
Rulers of no cleverness
Are their country's blessing.*

*By comparing the two,
We see a pattern.
Seeing the pattern,
We know the Mystery of Te.*

*The Mystery of Te is profound and far-reaching,
It is a reversal of all things!
It takes us to the great path of flow.*

The ancients who knew Tao did not teach people to be clever, only helped them to remain simple

The "ancients" refers to people who lived before the times of Laozi, a time when the world was in the proximity of Tao Core. The ancients "who knew Tao" (善为道者, shan4wei2dao4zhe3) were leaders of true wisdom. They, however, did not "teach people to be clever" (明民, ming2min2). "Clever" here refers to shrewdness in earthly matters, rather than the attainment of Tao. Being "clever", people are savvy and obsessed with the pursuit of glory and wealth. They fail to see the fleeting nature of things and neglect the refinement of their souls. Knowing this, enlightened leaders prefer to help their people to "remain simple" (愚之, yu2zhi1). 愚 is often associated with stupidity, but Laozi uses it here to describe those who look stupid yet are truly wise. "Simple", but not simplistic, they break the worldly confine and are constrained by neither forms nor divides. With few desires and self-interests, they think little of glory and wealth. In the eyes of ordinary folk, they look stupid. To the enlightened leaders, however, this is what their people should be.

People are difficult to govern when they are clever

When people are "clever" (智, zhi4), they are driven by divides and selfishness. To satisfy their thirst for glory and wealth, they may resort to dishonesty. As a result, it is hard to tell whether they are genuine in what they say or just trying to pull a fast one. Furthermore, being savvy, they are elusive, and it is hard to track them down. They are indeed "difficult to govern" (难治, nan2zhi4).

Thus, rulers of cleverness are their country's curse. Rulers of no cleverness are their country's blessing

It is worse if a country is ruled by leaders who are "clever". They care primarily about their own interests and will do anything to fulfill their personal agenda. The country and people suffer as a result. They are, therefore, "the country's curse". "Curse" paraphrases 贼 (*zei*2), which means "thief". Since they are in the position of power and influence, the size of wealth they plunder can be unusually huge. It is not easy for a bank robber to lug away a million dollars from a bank, but a corrupt leader can easily rack up hundreds of millions through their influence. Indeed, bank robbery appears to be a petty crime in comparison to such leaders. Describing them as a curse is, therefore, not an exaggeration.

This explains why "rulers of no cleverness" are their country's "blessing" (福, *fu*2). They genuinely care for the country's, rather than their own, interests. Moving toward Tao One and Tao Zero, they "create but possess not, do but seek no glory, grow but dominate not, accomplish but claim no credit". They are magnanimous and always have the best interests of the people close to their hearts. They bring good fortune to the country.

By comparing the two, we see a pattern

There are leaders who are a curse and those who are blessings of their country. What is the difference between them? "By comparing the two" (知此两者, *zhi*1*ci*3*liang*3*zhe*3), we can see an underlying "pattern" (楷式, *kai*3*shi*4). Seeing the pattern is to see the ways nature works.

Seeing the pattern, we know the Mystery of Te

The underlying pattern is the "Mystery of Te" (玄德, *xuan*2*de*2). Laozi talks about the mystery in Chapter 1, "One mystery after another, the gate to all wonders." It is another name of Tao. Why doesn't Laozi use the word "Tao" directly? Because Tao is formless, while both the "mystery" and Te itself are Tao Use, which can be perceived, allowing us to see and reflect on it. The power of simplicity and evil of cleverness, as explained earlier in this chapter, are examples of the "Mystery of Te".

The Mystery of Te is profound and far-reaching

"The Mystery of Te is profound (深矣, *shen1yi3*) and far-reaching (远矣, *yuan3yi3*)". It's beyond the comprehension of most people. Only the enlightened who know it are not hesitant to walk the path as it takes them to the attainment of the eternal Tao!

If we govern a country based on the Mystery of Te, we build a nation that lasts. With the Oneness of Te, there are no divides, we are not overly-materialistic, and we don't turn a blind eye to vices that deviate from Tao. Walking the path of Tao, we don't go against our conscience to make a quick buck by doing things that we are going to regret for the rest of our lives. While we provide for the people, we make sure that they are content and happy. A person's desires are endless. Only when we help them stop wanting more when they have enough will they be happy and calm.

It is a reversal of all things! It takes us to the great path of flow

"Returning is the way Tao works," says Laozi in Chapter 40. A person of Tao sees things in a reverse way. When most people want it big and to have more, they want it small and to have less. "It is a reversal of all things" (与物反矣, *yu3wu4fan3yi3*). It takes us to the "great" (大, *da4*) path of "flow" (顺, *shun4*). "Great" refers to the formless Tao. "Flow" means smoothness and refers to the movement of Tao. "We let go and let go till we do nothing" (Chapter 48) is a way of walking the "great path of flow".

Chapter 66
Staying Low 善下

*Why are seas and rivers
Rulers of the streams of hundreds of valleys?
It is because of their low positions.*

*Thus, if the Sage wishes to
Command from above,
They speak from a position below.
If they wish to lead at the front,
They follow the people from behind.*

*So the people feel no burden
When the Sage commands from above,
Feel no threat of harm
When the Sage leads them at the front.*

*Praises for the Sage are unflagging.
Since the Sage competes with no one,
No one can compete with them.*

Why are seas and rivers rulers of the streams of hundreds of valleys? It is because of their low positions

The seas and rivers (江海, *jiang1hai3*) lie low, allowing streams from hundreds of valleys to converge in them, resulting in them becoming their natural "rulers" (王, *wang2*). What if they position themselves high up instead? They cannot be the rulers. By the same token, if we want to be a respected leader, we must lie low; stay humble and modest like the seas and rivers. The lower we are, the more streams from hundreds of valleys can flow to us, and the more support we garner from the people.

Thus, if the Sage wishes to command from above, they speak from a position below

When the Sage has to "command from above" (上民, *shang4min2*), they must humbly "speak from a position below" (言下之, *yan2xia4zhi1*), and bear the best interests of the people close to their heart. Similarly, if we are a business leader and want to earn loyalty from the employees, we must not order the people around us. The more modest we are, the more respect we receive. We earn respect not from the salaries we pay, but humility in words we use and deeds we perform.

If they wish to lead at the front, they follow the people from behind

If the Sage wants to "lead the people at the front" (先民, *xian1min2*), they listen to the people, address their concerns, and let the people enjoy the benefits first. They "follow the people from behind" (以身后之, *yi3shen1hou4zhi1*).

So the people feel no burden when the Sage commands from above, feel no threat of harm when the Sage leads them at the front. Praises for the Sage are unflagging. Since the Sage competes with no one, no one can compete with them

When the Sage leads from above, because they are modest, humble, accommodating, non-divisive, and selfless, the people feel "no burden" (不重, *bu4zhong4*). They don't feel any pressure and willingly follow the Sage's command.

Since the people's concerns are addressed first, the people feel "no threat of harm" (不害, *bu4hai4*) when the Sage leads them at the front. Spiritually, with the Sage guiding the way, they keep to the center and will not go astray while pursuing the attainment of Tao. The people will enjoy only benefits and no harm. "Praises" (乐推, *le4tui1*) for the Sage are "unflagging" (不厌, *bu4yan4*). The people are happy to have such a leader forever. Furthermore, the Sage "competes with no one" (不争, *bu4zheng1*). Having been enlightened, they have no divides and treat everybody as equal, so who do they have to compete with? Since the Sage competes with no one, no one can "compete with them" (与之争, *yu3zhi1zheng1*).

Chapter 67
Three Treasures 三宝

People in the world are saying,
"My Tao is so big as if having no form."
Indeed Tao is indefinitely big,
And it has no form.
If it has form,
It would have long been small.

I have three treasures
That I hold dear to my heart:
The first is compassion,
The second is thrift,
The third is not to be ahead of
The world under Heaven.

From compassion comes courage,
From thrift comes magnanimity,
From not being ahead of the world of Heaven
Comes leadership.

Now discard compassion for foolhardiness,
Discard thrift for extravagance,
And forsake humility to rush ahead.
This is certain death!

With compassion, we will win
When there is a battle,
And impregnable when in defense.
Heaven will come to our rescue
And protect us with compassion.

People in the world are saying, "My Tao is so big as if having no form."

This chapter is written in a tone as if the Sage is talking to us directly. The word "big" is a translation of 大 (*da*4). It refers to Tao Core, which is indefinitely big and as if "having no form" (不有, *bu4you3*).

Indeed Tao is indefinitely big, and it has no form. If it has form, it would have long been small

When something has a form, it is something that can be measured and compared with. We can find out whether it is bigger or smaller than something else and make all sorts of comparisons that we can think of. What if it has no form? Then we have no way to make a comparison. Tao is formless. Nothing physical can be bigger than it. So enormous it covers the entire universe and beyond, and everything we can think of is small in comparison. This explains why if Tao had form, "it would have long been small" (其小久矣, *qi2xiao-3jiu3yi3*).

Decoding Notes: If our spiritual practice is based on form, what we can accomplish is at best a "small feat", never attainment of the formless Tao Core. Laozi thus emphasizes that the only path to complete enlightenment is non-doing.

I have three treasures that I hold dear to my heart:

Here, Laozi introduces the "three treasures" (三宝, *san1bao3*) that serves as a code of conduct while he seeks complete enlightenment.

The first is compassion

"Compassion" is a translation of 慈 (*ci2*), which is a genuine concern for others. It is derived from empathy, love, and care. Full of

Yang energy, it is life-giving. Sages are known for their compassion, which propels them to do their utmost to help relieve the sentient beings of their sufferings.

The second is thrift

"Thrift" is a translation of 俭 (*jian*3). We lower our ego and desires and keep life simple. In terms of self-cultivation, it also means the conservation of energy, in the sense of essence, qi, and spirit, notably the *taihe* qi. External disruptions drain our energy, so we have to keep them to the minimum. "Let go and let go, till we do nothing," as Laozi says in Chapter 48. When our essence, qi, and spirit are strong, and the *taihe* qi in our body is rich, it makes integration with the *taihe* qi energy in the big environment easy, thus allowing us to bask in the radiance of Tao. "Thrift" also means dimming our "sparkle", so that we can do what Laozi says in Chapter 58, "Radiant yet not dazzling." We don't trumpet our Te. Even if the radiance of Tao illuminates through us, we remain modest.

The third is not to be ahead of the world under Heaven

Many people find the sentence confusing. To understand what it means, we need to know what "the world under Heaven" 天下 (*tian*1*xia*4) is. "Heaven" was derived directly from Tao One. Its existence predates Earth and the myriads of things, and enjoy the closest proximity to Tao. A person who is entrusted with the "world under Heaven" is "Son of Heaven" (天子), a title accorded to emperors in China for centuries. How can the "Son of Heaven" ever be "ahead" (先, *xian*1) of the world under Heaven when they are under its auspices? The sentence speaks of respect for Tao. No matter how powerful we are, even if we were an emperor, we dare not be ahead of "the world under Heaven". Similarly, for the sages who have fully attained Tao. They don't dare to be ahead of

Tao, because they know they are yet to truly know. There are those, nevertheless, who claim themselves to be bigger than the world under Heaven. This is incompatible with a person of Tao, who is always humble, gracious, and respectful to Tao. They are devilish.

From compassion comes courage

Great compassion gives us courage (勇, *yong*3) to do what we can to help free the sentient beings from their suffering. The courage refers not to the foolhardiness of a thug who blindly picks a fight. It is the resolve exemplified by the sages who share and serve selflessly.

From thrift comes magnanimity

There are two aspects of "magnanimity" here. The word paraphrases 广 (*guang*3), which means "broad". First, by being thrift, we enrich our energy. We enhance the essence, qi, and spirit, as well as the *taihe* qi energy through the conservation. Second, with the enhanced energy, we can more effectively integrate with Tao to boost the capacity of our Te, allowing us to perform more tasks of magnanimity.

From not being ahead of the world of Heaven comes leadership

"Leadership" is a translation of 器长 (*qi4zhang3*). 器 literally means "apparatus", and 长 a "superior". We may interpret the word as "a leader of the material world". By "not being ahead of the world of Heaven", we respect Tao and do everything in the spirit of Tao. We are ever so humble because no matter how high the leadership position that we are holding, we are small before Tao. We bear the interest of the world close to our hearts, and never impose our ego on others. We are doing what Laozi says in Chapter 66: "So the people feel no burden when the Sage commands from above, feel no threat of harm when he leads them at the front."

Now discard compassion for foolhardiness

Unfortunately, people today tend to discard compassion for "foolhardiness" (勇, yong3). Do note that the very same pictogram 勇 found in the earlier clause "from compassion comes courage" reappears here. In there, the "courage" is selfless. Here, it refers to the foolhardiness many people display today. Instead of being compassionate, they are smug, aggressive, and egoistic.

Discard thrift for extravagance

"Thrift", as mentioned earlier, is the conservation of resources. On a personal level, it refers to personal energy. Many people unwittingly dissipate the energy they have taken pains to accumulate. Here, the pictogram 广 found in the earlier clause, "From thrift comes magnanimity", reappears. In there, the thrift brings forth "magnanimity". Here, the very same pictogram is translated as "extravagance". Instead of conserving energy in the pursuit of Tao, many people dissipate it in the pursuit of extravagance.

And forsake humility to rush ahead. This is certain death!

A Tao person is humble and dares not be ahead of the world of Heaven. They don't "forsake humility" (舍后, she3hou4) to "rush ahead" (且先, qie3xian1). Heaven derived directly from Tao One. Without it, there is neither Earth nor the myriads of things. Who can be ahead of it? Only the wicked will make such claims. However brazen they are, nevertheless, they are no match for Heaven. "This is certain death" (死矣, si3yi3).

With compassion, we will win when there is a battle

If we have compassion and are wholehearted in helping the sentient beings, we will win; no matter what type of battle that we are fighting. Tao and evil exist side-by-side, but Tao will not allow evil to go unchecked. If, having tried to educate them, the evil still refuses to change for the better, they have to be eliminated. A battle must be waged. If we are fighting for Tao and since Tao always prevails, "we will win when there is a battle" (以战则胜, *yi3zhan4ze2sheng*4).

And impregnable when in defense

A person of Tao conducts only self-defense. They don't invade. Because they conform to Tao, they are "impregnable" (固, *gu*4) in their "defense" (守, *shou*3).

Heaven will come to our rescue and protect us with compassion

When a person of Tao runs into trouble, Heaven will "come to their rescue" (救之, *jiu4zhi*1), and "protect" (卫, *wei*4) them with compassion. Compassion is not just empathy. It is an unwavering devotion typical of a sage who helps free the sentient beings from sufferings and guide them to walk the path of Tao. It is not unlike the spirit of a hidden guardian angel.

Chapter 68
Use the Strengths of People 用人之力

The best warrior avoids combat,
The best fighter is driven not by anger,
The best conquerer avoids conflicts,
The best leader serves.

This is Te of non-contending,
It is using the potential of people,
It is in unity with nature.
It is an ultimate since the dawn of time.

The best warrior avoids combat

"The best" (善, *shan*4) refers to the "highest Te", as explained in Chapter 27. So "the best (善为, *shan*4*wei*2) warrior" (士者, *shi*4*zhe*3) is a warrior of Tao. They are "the wise" as mentioned in Chapter 41, who are unwaveringly devoted to Tao. Most people are inclined to use force at the time of conflicts. "The best warrior", who conforms to Tao, however, is driven by Te. Their first approach is always to find a peaceful solution. They reason and don't give up reasoning easily. It is only when the other party is adamant and refuses to be reasonable that they counter it with the use of force. Even then, the force serves more as deterrence and self-defense than to start a war.

The best fighter is driven not by anger

The "fight" here is a metaphor and refers to more than a physical war or a scuffle. It can, say, also be a debate or negotiation. When a fight is to take place, "the best fighter" (善战者, *shan*4*zhan*4*zhe*3), who is a person of Tao, is "driven not by anger" (不怒, *bu*4*nu*4). Why is it so? Fury is like a fire that devastates and wipes out whatever that we have built. When we lose our head in anger, we lose our calm and drives away the divine energy that is supposed to protect us, exposing ourselves directly to dangers. Like "the best fighter", we must stay calm under all circumstances.

Taiji sparring is an illustration of such a fight. To overcome the hard with softness, Taiji practitioners avoid losing their cool. Without the calmness, it is hard to keep to the center and counter the attacking forces with softness. To keep the calmness, we regulate our breath before engaging in any contact. Once contact is made, we "wrap" the opponent up with our qi, and deflect the force of the opponent to uproot them effortlessly. The same approach can be used in all kinds of situations in life to bring us tremendous advantages, be it a meeting or a negotiation. "The restless lose their master," says Laozi in Chapter 26.

When there is a fight, there are likely to be casualties. Heaven is life-giving and loathes killing. Combative behavior is, therefore, against Tao. If we can talk calmly to find a peaceful solution, fight, more often than not, can be avoided. As the saying goes, "Those who conform to Tao prosper. Those who go against it perish." We must learn to avoid anger and, whenever possible, fight.

The best conquerer avoids conflicts

"Avoid conflicts" paraphrases 不与 (*bu4yu3*), which means "not to meddle with something". "The best conquerer" paraphrases 善胜者 (*shan4sheng4zhe3*), which means "a person who is good at winning". A person of Tao wins by wisdom and virtue when handling disputes. Whenever possible, instead of contention, they initiate collaborations and build win-win relationships. When applying the principle to geopolitical disputes, they, as far as possible, find common ground that benefits all parties and identify solutions. Fighting a war is to nobody's advantage.

The best leader serves

"The best leader" paraphrases 善用人者 (*shan4yong4ren2zhe3*), which means "a person who is good at deploying people". As a leader, we must know that people don't like to be forced into doing anything. If we are humble and ready to listen, we win them over by persuasion. When the boss in a high-up position is humble and affable, they can be firm and yet are respected by their employees, who are also more ready to work hard.

This is Te of non-contending

There is no fight, no anger, nor pettiness. Instead, we must stay humble, modest, and tolerant. These are Te of "non-contending" (不争, *bu4zheng1*).

It is using the potential of people. It is in unity with nature. It is an ultimate since the dawn of time

"People" is written as 人 (*ren*2). The pictogram, which consists of two strokes, is easy to write but extremely profound. The two strokes lean against each other, symbolizing mutual support. If we take the upper stroke off, the lower stroke cannot stand on its own. If we take the lower stroke away, the upper stroke falls because of the withdrawal of support. They are mutually reliant. This underlines the importance of having no fight, no anger, and staying humble.

No person is an island. When we deal with others, we must always find common ground despite differences. By supporting and helping each other, we live and prosper together. "Using the potential of people" is a translation of 用人之力 (*yong*4*ren*2*zhi*1*li*4). It is the basis that makes us the "intelligence of the universe". Heaven loathes killing and prefers to give life. To coexist and avoid suppression and killing is in line with the behavior of Heaven. It is "in unity with nature" (配天, *pei*4*tian*1). We enjoy benefits from unity and sharing. It is an "ultimate" (极, *ji*2) since "the dawn of time" (古, *gu*3).

Chapter 69
The Military Maxim
用兵有言

Says the military maxim:
"I dare not be an invader,
And rather be a guest.
I dare not advance an inch
And prefer to retreat a foot."

This is to move the invisible move;
Raise the invisible arms;
Fling the invisible enemy;
Deploy the invisible army.

There is no greater disaster
Than to make light of the enemy.
Making light of the enemy
Almost deprives me of my three treasures.

So when two armies engage in conflict,
Victory goes to the one who grieves.

Although we must avoid war, it happens. This chapter illustrates how we may apply being and non-being in such situations. In the second stanza, the word "invisible" is used repeatedly. It refers to the invisible Tao, i.e., the non-being. In contrast, the army and people are visible, and being. Taiji sparring simulates a conflict situation, and the principles introduced here are very relevant. We are going to elaborate more about it in the Chapter: Apply the Wisdom to Taijiquan. Specifically, its use in the advanced Taiji technique *lingkongjin* (凌空劲) is introduced. The technique enables a Taiji practitioner to lift their opponent up or even bounce them around without having to make any physical contact.

Says the military maxim

"Military" paraphrases 用兵 (*yong*4*bing*1), and "maxim" 有言 (*you*3*yan*2), which is advice for a person of Tao on self-defense. The application is the same, whether we are defending ourselves or a country.

I dare not be an invader, and rather be a guest

"Invader" paraphrases 主 (*zhu*3), which literally means "the host". "The guest" is a translation of 客 (*ke*4), which refers to the "victim of an invasion" or a "defender". As an army commander of Tao, instead of being an "invader", they prefer to be "the guest", i.e., the defender. During the Second World War, for example, Japan was the "host", in this context, and China a victim and thus the "guest".

I dare not advance an inch and prefer to retreat a foot

Having driven out an invader, what most commanders do is to pursue the enemy to their base. This is to "advance an inch" (进寸, *jin*4*cun*4). It is, however, not what a commander of Tao would do.

They adhere to the principle of non-aggression despite having the upper hand. Instead of pursuing the enemy, they "retreat a foot" (退尺, *tui4chi3*). They give up more so that their troops can return to their own land. This exemplifies the virtue of "greeting hatred with Te", as mentioned in Chapter 63.

When there is an armed conflict, both the victor and the loser suffer casualties. Tao is life-giving, so it is against wars. In Chapter 68, we use the pictogram 人 (human being) to illustrate the importance of mutual support. People rely on one another, the fall of one party in a conflict inflicts pains on the other. We must avoid war, and don't compromise our moral high ground by turning ourselves into an invader. This doesn't mean that we should not defend ourselves. A commander of Tao will not be hesitant to strike back with all their might should an invader strike.

There is another way to interpret "retreating a foot": To prevail over movement with stillness. "The calm lords over the restless," says Laozi in Chapter 26. The impulse to give chase is a restlessness that makes us lose our cool. Although we are winning, we are no longer in full control of the situation. This endangers our position and has the tendency to turn ourselves from a defender into an invader. "Retreating a foot" helps us to stay calm and keep to our center.

"Retreating a foot" is also the basis of Taijiquan, and it can take us to a very high level of practice. It makes advanced techniques, such as *lingkongjin* possible. As mentioned, this is explored in the Chapter: Apply the Wisdom to Taijiquan.

This is to move the invisible move; raise the invisible arms; fling the invisible enemy; deploy the invisible army

"Move the invisible move" paraphrases 行无行 (*xing2wu2xing2*). "Invisible" here refers to the invisible Tao. To move the invisible move is to move with the flow of Tao. Instead of being an invader, we defend by adhering to the principle of non-contention. We do not wage war, not to mention such cruelty as deploying chemical weapons of mass destruction. We only fight back if need be for self-defense. We maintain the moral high ground of Tao.

Raising arms is a metaphor for the call for justice. When we "raise the invisible arms" (攘无臂, *rang3wu2bi4*), we appeal to the like-minded to defend the principle of the invisible Tao. When an invasion happens, we garner support from other countries to defeat the invader. This is what happened during the Second World War. The Allies were formed to oppose the invasion of the Axis countries, including Germany, Japan, and Italy.

As for "fling the invisible enemy" (扔无敌, *reng1wu2di2*), it refers to tossing off an enemy of the invisible Tao. We isolate the invader by making it a common enemy of the people of Tao. This is, however, not in the sense of giving an eye for an eye. It doesn't mean that if they kill one of our people, we must kill ten of theirs. This will move us on to a vicious cycle that is against the teachings of Tao.

"Deploy the invisible army" (执无兵, *zhi2wu2bing1*) refers to the deployment of an army of the invisible Tao. With the blessings of Tao, we will prevail. Was this not the concerted efforts of the armies of Tao that defeated the invaders and ended the Second World War?

There is no greater disaster than to make light of the enemy. Making light of the enemy almost deprives me of my three treasures

The "military maxim" highlights a profound message: Never "make light of the enemy" (轻敌, *qing1di2*). It is "disastrous" (祸, *huo4*) if we do so, be it in the handling of personal matters or defending a country. Of all the enemies, the first and foremost is our ego. When it gets the better of us, it is equivalent to making light of Tao and ends up with us losing the blessings of Tao. It deprives us of our "three treasures" as mentioned in Chapter 67: Compassion, thrift, and not to be ahead of the world under Heaven.

We must not forget compassion when fighting a battle. We don't kill the innocent and, unless it is absolutely out of self-defense, we don't use weapons of destruction. Even when we have the upper hand, we don't kill the enemy if we can help it. Instead, we do whatever we can to educate and transform them.

We observe "thrift" and impose restraint. We do not indiscriminately attack. Upon victory, we adhere to the primary objective of self-defense and don't allow ourselves to become an invader by "advancing an inch".

Similarly, we don't stay "ahead of the world under Heaven". We know how insignificant we are before Tao. We are always humble and kind to all.

So when two armies engage in conflict, victory goes to the one who grieves

When two parties are in conflict, "the one who grieves" (哀者, *ai1zhe3*) is the one that remains soft and humble. They are most likely to be the victim of the conflict. If they bear in mind the three treasures, they will be able to prevail by being calm and soft and adhering to Tao.

Chapter 70

Find Gems in Rough Clothes 被褐怀玉

My words are easy to understand
and easy to put into practice.
Yet few under Heaven can follow
And put them into use.

A word has its ancestor,
And a matter has its ruler.
Alas! When we see the invisible law,
Then we will not be confused
By what we think we know.

Those who know me are rare,
Those who emulate me are invaluable.
Although the Sage is draped in rough clothes
Hidden within them are precious gems.

My words are easy to understand and easy to put into practice. Yet few under Heaven can follow and put them into use

Laozi laments that although his words "are easy to understand" (易知, *yi4zhi*1) and "easy to put into practice" (易行, *yi4xing*2), yet few under Heaven "are able to follow" (莫能知, *mo4neng2zhi*1), and "put them into practice" (莫能行, *mo4neng2xing*2). What Laozi teaches is simple: To return to the Oneness of Tao, and not to be obsessed with the divides or keep wanting more. A person of Tao does what most people don't. While most people want things bigger, they are happy with the small. When most people are fighting to have more, they are contented with less. Are the teachings difficult to understand? Why are people not following and practicing?

A word has its ancestor

A word's "ancestor" (宗, *zong*1) is Tao. It predates Heaven and Earth and is what Laozi's teachings are based on. When he says, "Create but possess not, do but seek no glory, grow but seek not to dominate, accomplish but claim no credit", he is talking about the magnanimity of Tao that we must emulate. When he teaches us to "blunt the sharpness, untie the knots", he teaches us to practice non-doing in things we do. Every "word" (言, *yan*2) can be traced back to the "ancestor".

And a matter has its ruler

A "matter" (事, *shi*4) here refers to anything we do, be it negotiating a deal or mopping the floor. Within every matter, there is a "ruler" (君, *jun*1), which is like the king of a country, or the boss of an organization. If we know the "ruler", we can identify the "officials". While each "official" has a role to play, they impact one another and contribute to the overall picture. This is what a medical doctor does when treating a patient. If the patient is suffering from a headache, they find out the "ruler", i.e., the source of the problem. Then, they examine the various factors or the "officials" that contribute to the problem. By knowing the "ruler" and roles each of the "officials" plays, they are able to assess the situation and prescribe a cure.

When we analyze a matter by consulting the *Yijing*, we identify the ruler and its officials by observing the line of a hexagram. In a company, the boss is the ruler, and they take up the fifth line; the general manager takes up the fourth line, and other employees the second. Each of the lines carries its own implications. If we are unfamiliar with the *Yijing*, we should view the organization in Oneness and how each role contributes to the whole, so as to identify answers to many of the questions that we face.

When we have identified the "ruler" of a matter, we must also link it back to the "ancestor". Things change all the time but not the "ancestor". It remains unchanged. It is the immutable principles. Although matters vary and come in all shapes and sizes, they always follow the "ancestor", which we may also see as the law of the universe. Within the law, there are sub-laws. The law of reversal that we mentioned earlier is one of them. Knowing the law, we understand how changes revolve around a cycle. We know, for example, when things reach their peak, they go into decline. As a result, we are cautious when enjoying success. We know that if we are not humble and don't continue to seek renewal, we will soon lose relevance and go into decline. This is why in the first hexagram of the *Yijing*, the phase after "flying dragon in Heaven" is an "arrogant dragon who has cause to repent". By following the ruler, we adhere to the immutable principle and can be in better control of things we do.

We can apply the "ancestor" to everything, be it governing a country or cooking a meal. This is what TCM (Traditional Chinese Medicine) doctors do. Based on the universal law of Yin Yang, they can figure out a remedy for a headache that deprives their patients of a good night's sleep.

Alas! When we see the invisible law, then we will not be confused by what we think we know

It is easy to "think we know" (我知, *wo3zhi1*) based on what we see. Unfortunately, what we see may not be real. Is our body real? It is, but only during our lifetime. It is temporal, and it will vanish from this world one day. If we can see the "invisible law of Tao" (无知, *wu2zhi1*), then we will not be confused by the things we see.

The word "only" is a translation of 惟 (*wei2*). The pictogram consists of the radical "heart" (忄). It implies that we have to listen attentively with all our hearts. It helps us to discover our invisible real self. With that, we are unlikely to be confused or blindly follow the crowds.

Those who know me are rare. Those who emulate me are invaluable

"Those who know me" (知我者, *zhi1wo3zhe3*) are people who can see the value of their perpetual self. They are "rare" (希, *xi1*). Similarly, those who can "emulate me" (则吾者, *ze2wu2zhe3*) to cultivate the perpetual selves are "invaluable" (贵, *gui4*).

From the spiritual perspective, the "ancestor" mentioned earlier in this chapter may also be interpreted as the perpetual body. By the same token, the "ruler" is the temporal body. However complex the world is, as long as we get our temporal body to serve the perpetual body, we free ourselves of divides and selfishness, and we are safely on the course to the attainment of Tao.

Although the Sage is draped in rough clothes, hidden within them are precious gems

Although the Sage is "draped in rough clothes" (被褐, *bei4he4*) and look plain and dull to the eye of ordinary folks, underneath their simple appearance are precious gems of Tao. Self-cultivation, which is about the inner strength, goes deep below the surface. The Sage has successfully refined their perpetual self. They don't need a flashy appearance to impress.

Decoding Note: When Laozi says that "a word has its ancestor", he suggests how a word in the *Tao Te Ching* can be decoded. Chinese words are pictograms, the images they project help us to trace them to their "ancestor". By dissecting the pictograms, we see the nuances. A wealth of hidden messages can be found in the radicals and sub-characters of the pictograms to help us decipher the text and go deeper. This is something we cannot achieve by checking the dictionaries alone.

Chapter 71
Sick the Sickness 不病

Knowing we do not know,
Supreme!
Not knowing yet think we know,
Sick!
If we are sick of sickness,
We do not fall sick.
The Sage is not sick,
Because they are sick of sickness,
And thus, they do not fall sick.

Knowing we do not know, supreme!

A person of Tao sees the invisible, so they "know" (知, *zhi*1) that they "do not know" (不知, *bu4zhi*1). Tao is formless. This explains why many people cannot perceive it. Even if we want to, as Laozi says in Chapter 1, "The Tao that can be mentioned is not the eternal Tao", what we can know is very limited. In addition, learning is one thing; talking about it is another. Even if we know it, it is very difficult for us to utter the experience in words.

This is why the pursuit of Tao is a journey of "one mystery after another". What is our destiny, and how do we fulfill it? What does our true self look like, and how do we refine it? What is Tao attainment like, and how does it lead to complete enlightenment? Most of the mysteries remain mysteries. We cannot learn it by just thinking or talking about it. We must know that we do not know and slowly learn by experiencing it. We thus emulate the "Supreme" Laozi mentioned in Chapter 17, and enjoy the quality of "the wise", as mentioned in Chapter 41.

Not knowing yet think we know, sick!

There are people who think they have already attained Tao and go around to brag about what they know. In fact, they have achieved nothing more than scratching the surface. This is "sick" (病, *bing*4). Since Tao cannot be thoroughly explained, there is always imperfection in what we know. Those who don't know yet claim that they know may well be devils who intentionally mislead. A true person of Tao recognizes the imperfection and, therefore, always stay humble and are ready to learn the wisdom with practice. They will not brag that they know when they don't know.

If we are sick of sickness, we do not fall sick

When we are "sick of sickness" (病病, *bing*4*bing*4), we will take precautions. Chances are, "we do not fall sick" (不病, *bu4bing*4). The "sickness" here refers to "not knowing yet think we know".

The Sage is not sick, because they are sick of sickness, and thus, they do not fall sick

The Sage is aware that this is a sickness, so they "sick the sickness". As a result, they never think they truly know, so they "do not fall sick" (不病, *bu4bing4*). As Laozi says in Chapter 34: "By not claiming to be great, the Sage achieves greatness." The Sage has attained Tao, yet never thinks that they have attained Tao. This is how they attain Tao and achieve greatness.

Decoding Note: Beware of those who claim full attainment of Tao to advance their evil intent. If we end up as their captive, it can be hard to break ourselves free. As the saying goes, "It is easy to host a ghost but difficult to send it away." Having given their victims some sweetener, they will stack up their demands, and the victims will be hapless. Stay away from them even when they are friendly and helpful. They are dangerous!

Chapter 72
Fear of Menace 畏威

When people fear no menace,
A serious menace is approaching.

Lament not our narrow dwelling,
Agonize not the misery of life.
Alas! Since we lament not,
There is no lament,

So the Sage knows their self,
And are not bigoted.
They value their self
And are not infatuated with it.
They let go of one
And choose the other.

When people fear no menace, a serious menace is approaching

The "menace" (威, *wei*1) here refers to the inevitability of karma. When people "fear no menace" (不畏威, *bu4wei4wei*1), they don't believe in karma and have no fear of retribution. When this is the case, "serious menace is approaching" (大威至, *da4wei1zhi*4). Retribution may target an individual. It can also target a group, and the scale can be enormous. Disasters like tsunamis, earthquakes, and hurricanes that destroy lives are some of the examples.

Lament not our narrow dwelling, agonize not the misery of life

Knowing the implications of karma and rebirth, we see beyond our current life. The "dwelling" (居, *ju*1) refers literally to a physical abode, but here it means the current life that we are living. This is a "narrow" (狹, *xia*2) dwelling, so we must see beyond it.

Things happen to us for a reason, which can be traced back to what we did earlier — in this life or an earlier one. They are the fruits of the seeds that we sowed earlier. While the effect is clear, the cause, unfortunately, is usually not known. If we don't like what has happened, the best thing to do is to ensure we don't plant a bad seed. While we have no control over our next life, we can impact it with the types of seeds we plant in this life.

"Agonize" is a translation of 厌 (*yan*4), and "life" 生 (*sheng*1). Many people lament their lack of luck and complain about life being unfair. They wail that others are not working as hard as them, but, unlike them, are able to have things their way. Everything happens for a reason. Drowning in despair is not a solution. If everything has a cause, then work on the cause, and bring on the good energy. Enriching our perpetual selves is a good option.

Alas! Since we lament not, there is no lament

Knowing the impact of karma, we don't blame others for the hardship that we endure. Instead, we take the opportunity to atone by planting good seeds for the future. Since we "lament not" (不厌, *bu4yan4*), our attention is on doing good. We conform to Tao, and Tao will not desert us. There is "no lament" (不厌, *bu4yan4*). The pictograms 不厌 appear twice in the sentence, but carry different connotations. One is "Not to complain", the other is "There is no reason to complain".

So the Sage knows their self, and are not bigoted

The Sage knows the impact of karma, the fleeting nature of life, and the importance of self-cultivation. They "know their self" (自知, *zi4zhi1*), so they are not "bigoted" (自见, *zi4jian4*). Bigotry arises from divides, selfishness, and an obsession with glory and wealth. When the Sage knows their selves, they steer themselves clear of the bigotry that sways them away from Tao.

They value their self and are not infatuated with it

With the self-awareness, the Sage "values their self" (自爱, *zi4ai4*). They take good care of their temporal body, so that they can rely on it for self-cultivation. They cherish their temporal body but are not "infatuated with it" (自贵, *zi4gui4*). The temporal body ages, not their real selves. They know where the real value is.

They let go of one and choose the other

We, therefore, let go of bigotry and self-infatuation and choose true wisdom and perpetual self.

Chapter 73
Net of Heaven 天网

Those who dare, die,
Those who dare not, survive.

Of these two,
One is good, and the other harmful.
There are things Heaven detests.
Who knows why?
Even the Sage has no answer.

Tao of Heaven:
Does not compete, yet wins;
Does not speak, yet responds;
Does not command, yet obeyed,
It accomplishes, without obvious design.

The net of Heaven is cast wide.
It is loose, but nothing slips through it.

Those who dare, dies

"Dare die" is a translation of 勇于敢 (yong3yu2gan3). A person who "dares, dies" is a daredevil who is easily provoked and enraged. Among them are young hooligans who misconstrue violence as bravery and do not hesitate to harm so as to earn glory. They are victims of their own devices. When they clash with others or the law, it can be fatal. With the loss of life, they miss the opportunities for refining their soul, and this is an even greater loss.

Those who dare not, survive

On the other hand, those who "dare not, (勇于不敢, yong3yu2bu-4gan3) survive". It sounds as if Laozi is applauding cowardice, but this line leaves more than meets the eyes. In the first place, why must we dare death? The path of Tao we walk is formless, and without divides, what is there for us to contend or to be angry with? Seeing the ephemeral nature of life, a person of Tao conforms to Tao and is modest, humble, and soft. When there is a dispute, they prefer to find common ground and seek solutions rather than to start a fight. They preserve their life not out of cowardice, but for a bigger purpose: To cultivate their perpetual self.

Of these two, one is good, and the other harmful

"Of these two" (此两者, ci3liang3zhe3) refers to the dare and dare not. Which of them is good and which is harmful? They are two types of bravery. "Those who dare not" are driven by true courage, while "those who dare" by sheer recklessness. The courage the sages display when saving the sentient beings is the true bravery. It is derived from compassion, as Laozi says in Chapter 67. Not the courage of "those who dare die", as it is driven by divides and selfishness. They allow their fury to run wild, even when it hurts the innocent. While there are people who regard their behaviors as bravery, this is not the type of bravery we want. Of these two, one of them is "good" (利, *li*4) and the other "harmful" (害, *hai*4). We must know the difference between them so that we will not be confused.

There are things Heaven detests. Who knows why?

Heaven is life-giving and loathes killing. "Those who dare" love to fight and kill. It is against Tao, and it is what the Heaven "detests" (恶, *wu*4). Without the blessings of Heaven, it is hard for them to survive. "Those who dare not" preserve life. They conform to Tao, and thus enjoy its blessings and survive. "Who knows why?" Instead of giving an assertion, Laozi makes us ponder. Indeed, there is something more in this than meets the eye.

Even the Sage has no answer

While the principle is easy to understand, what actually happens is not always clear. "Has no answer" paraphrases (犹难之, *you*2*nan*-2*zhi*1), which means "still find it difficult". It is a question that requires us to revisit, so we must not expect a straightforward answer.

It is puzzling. There are "those who dare not" who meet a sudden death as well. Why? It has to do with negative karma, and the "narrow dwelling" Laozi mentions in Chapter 72. They are reaping what they sowed. It could be a punishment for what they did wrong in a previous life, despite having turned over a new leaf in this life. The bad seeds are still growing, and the fruit is in the form of a tragedy. Should this happen, even the Sage cannot help much. They may help alleviate the pains, not to nullify the retribution.

Tao of Heaven

"Tao of Heaven" (天之道, *tian*1*zhi*1*dao*4) refers to the spirit of Tao. Changes are not always predictable and hard to explain, but they must be properly handled. To do that, Laozi introduces the four precepts below.

Does not compete, yet wins

Tao is constrained not by divides or ego. If we can learn from the Tao of Heaven and "do not compete" (不争, *bu4zheng*1), we go with the flow of nature and win, not by forcing our will. As Laozi mentions in Chapter 22, "As we contend not, the world cannot contend with them." We are blessed by Tao in our undertakings and are natural in winning. We don't have to compete, yet "win" (胜, *sheng*4) naturally.

Does not speak, yet responds

Tao of Heaven "does not speak" (不言, *bu4yan*2) and yet "responds" (应, *ying*4). So, we don't communicate with Tao by talking, but by feeling it deeply. Tao of Heaven is responsive. If we are sincere, we are heard. This is the way we interact with the sages as well. Tao is the energy of qi. If we want to interact with the sages, we connect to them through qi in all sincerity.

Does not command, yet obeyed

Be it a blessing or a curse, there is no need to "command" (召, *zhao*1), and it is "obeyed" (自来, *zi4lai*2). It comes without us making any effort to command. It is determined not by the individual but by karma. If what we do invites a curse, a curse happens. If what we do attracts blessing, a blessing emerges. A thought of robbing a bank triggers an evil deed, so it invites a curse that gets us into trouble sooner or later. By the same token, we can invite a blessing by doing good. Whether it is a blessing or a curse, it all depends on what we do.

It accomplishes, without obvious design

"Accomplish" paraphrases 繟然 (*chan1ran2*). 繟 means "continuous, consistent, never-ending". 然 means "in the manner of". The pictogram 繟 consists of the radical 纟 and the sub-character 单,

which means "silk" and "single", respectively. We may interpret it as referring to "individual cases". Everything in this world, big or small, carries with it its own karma and moves along with its own destiny. It is so as an individual or collectively as a group, such as a country. In other words, as much as we would like to plan, as part of a bigger whole, we are under the constraints of the Tao of Heaven by default. The best way to plan is to accept our karma and go with the flow of nature. If we do what is called for and do not see immediate results, it does not mean that we are doomed for failure. It could well be that the time is yet to arrive. When the time comes, which may not be in this life, it bears fruit. We accomplish, despite having no "obvious design" (谋, *mou*2).

The net of Heaven is cast wide. It is loose, but nothing slips through it

We are under the auspices of the net of Heaven (天网, *tian1wang3*) and reap what we sow. The net is so big that it has no boundary and no form. Although it is invisible, "loose" (疏, *shu*1), and apparently disordered, "nothing slips through it" (不漏, *bu4lou4*). It is completely just and fair.

Chapter 74

Mess with the Blades of a Master Carpenter
代大匠

If people are not afraid to die,
Why intimidate them with death?
If they are made afraid of dying,
And I can seize and kill the unruly,
Who dares?

There is always a lord of death.
Whoever takes their place to kill,
Is messing with the blades of a master carpenter.
Those who mess with the blades of a master carpenter
Rarely escape injuring their own fingers.

If people are not afraid to die, why intimidate them with death?

Most people are "afraid to die" (畏死, *wei4si3*). But there are those who don't. They include refugees who do not see life to be any better than death. When they flee their country in an overloaded boat, are they not aware of the risks? They know they can be gobbled up by the rough sea anytime, but still move ahead because the only way for them to survive is to risk death. There is not much one can do to "intimidate them" (惧之, *ju4zhi1*) with death.

Others are not afraid to die because of intense hatred. Just imagine! An entire family — grandparents, father and mother, and children — is having a blissful moment together. All of a sudden, a bomb plummets and kills everyone except the two grandchildren. Do you think the young men who survive the ordeal can brush the memory off and bury the hatchet? The acrimony makes them an easy target for terrorists on their recruitment drive. When hatred breeds hatred, there is no end to conflicts and wars.

There is also the third type of people who defy death. They are the bigots who are fixated on getting what they want, even at the expense of killing others.

If they are made afraid of dying, and I can seize and kill the unruly, who dares?

To maintain the harmony of the world, we must make the unruly "afraid of dying" (畏死, *wei4si3*). At the same time, if the Sage can "seize" (执, *zhi2*) and "kill" (杀, *sha1*) the unruly (为奇者, *wei2qi2zhe4*), it is enough to contain them.

Laozi uses the pronoun "I" here, indicating speech of the Sage. It implies that the punishment is not to be meted out by just anybody. They have to be a sage or a law enforcer endorsed by Tao, just to ensure that the enforcement is fair.

Under such circumstances, "who dares" (孰敢, *shu2gan3*) to commit evil?

There is always a lord of death

This line implies the constancy of Tao, which presides over life and death. "Lord of death" is a translation of 司杀者 (*si1sha1zhe3*). Those who commit evil will receive retribution from Heaven. They will either be punished by humankind's laws or the invisible arms of Heaven. Since everyone carries with them their own karma, the retribution may not be immediate. Even then, it will come when the time arrives.

Whoever takes their place to kill, is messing with the blades of a master carpenter

We must, therefore, be patient. If we are not in the position of enforcement and yet take the law into our own hands, we are metaphorically messing with blades of a "master carpenter" (大匠, *da4jiang4*).

Those who mess with the blades of a master carpenter, rarely escape injuring their own fingers

If someone who is not a master carpenter and yet performs the delicate task by using the master's tools, what will happen? They risk "injuring their own fingers" (伤手, *shang1shou3*), probably also hurting other people. Eradicating the criminals is the responsibility of the law enforcers, including Heaven. If we try to do it on their behalf, we are countering violence with violence. Since we do not know the karma involved, we may injure or kill a wrong person and invite negative karma upon ourselves. We injure our own fingers!

Chapter 75
Live Wisely 贤于贵生

People starve,
When the rulers eat up
too much of their income through taxes,
leading to starvation.

People are difficult to govern,
When the rulers
Force on them their will,
making people difficult to govern.

People think little of death
When they are eager to make a living,
So they think little of death.

Thus only those who can
See the true value of life,
Are able to wisely live an invaluable life.

People starve, when the rulers eat up too much of their income through taxes, leading to starvation

When "the rulers" (其上, *qi2shang4*) of a country are selfish and greedy, they "eat up too much of (the people's) income through taxes" (食税之多, *shi2shui4zhi1duo1*), even when their people have barely enough to eat. It leads to "starvation" (饥, *ji1*). Isn't it deplorable? If only the rulers walk the path of Tao, the miseries could have been avoided.

People are difficult to govern, when the rulers force on them their will, making people difficult to govern

People are "difficult to govern" (难治, *nan2zhi4*) when the rulers are selfish and greedy and "force on them their will" (有为, *you3wei2*). Instead of sitting in silent acceptance, however, the people often respond by being selfish and greedy as well. This makes them difficult to manage.

This would have been avoided if, instead of forcing on their will, the rulers can govern in the spirit of the non-being of Tao: "Create but possess not, do but seek no glory, grow but seek not to dominate". At the same time, "Blunt the sharpness, untie the knots". If they can go with the flow of Tao and serve the people wholeheartedly, people will respond with the same magnanimity, and will not be difficult to govern anymore.

People think little of death when they are eager to make a good living, so they think little of death

When people fail to see the impermanence of life and the importance of refining their perpetual self, they do not know how much they will have missed and "think little of death" (轻死, *qing1si3*). As a result, they spend their entire life amassing wealth and living a good life. "They are eager to make a good living" (求生之厚, *qiu2sheng1zhi-1hou4*), and end up dying with an empty soul.

Thus only those who can see the true value of life, are able to wisely live an invaluable life

Be it the ruler who makes light of the people's suffering or the people who belittle death, when a person does not know the ultimate purpose of self-cultivation, they don't know the "true value of life". "The true value" paraphrases 无 (*wu2*), which is the non-being of Tao. In other words, only when we can live *wu*, i.e., Tao and enrich our perpetual self, then we can "wisely" (贤于, *xian2yu2*) live an "invaluable life" (贵生, *gui4sheng1*).

Chapter 76
Father of Maxims 教父

A person is born soft and supple,
At their death, they are hard and stiff.
Green plants are born soft and tender,
At their death, they are brittle and dry.

Thus being rigid and stiff
Is courting death;
being soft and supple
Is living life.

An army that is rigid is easy to defeat,
A tree that refuses to yield is easy to break.
Although the teeth are stronger than the tongue
They are first to decay.

The big and powerful stays below,
The strong and supple reigns from above.

What I have learned from others, I teach.
The "strong beam" dies not a natural death
I see it as "Father of maxims".

A person is born soft and supple, at their death, they are hard and stiff

A person is "born" (生, *sheng*1) "soft and supple" (柔弱, *rou2ruo4*). The body turns "hard and stiff" (坚僵, *jian1jiang1*) at death (死, *si4*). It is used as a metaphor to highlight the importance of softness. During self-cultivation, for example, our essence, qi, and spirit are properly integrated, allowing our qi to travel smoothly and making our bodies soft. At death, the *taihe* qi that harmonizes a person's body is depleted, turning the body hard and stiff.

This explains why practices like Taijigong is good for health and longevity. We allow the *taihe* qi to move around, making our body softer than usual. Without *taihe* qi, our body is stiffened easily. Although in my 70s, I still adhere to the daily training to ensure proper movements of *taihe* qi in my body. It pays off. During my recent lecture series for my disciples on the *Tao Te Ching*, I spoke non-stop for more than ten hours every day for over a week, and yet there was no sign of fatigue. Thanks to the *taihe* qi energy that I have been nurturing.

Green plants are born soft and tender, at their death, they are brittle and dry

Similarly, a green plant is "soft and tender" (柔脆, *rou2cui4*) at birth, and "brittle and dry" (枯槁, *ku1gao3*) at death. The plant relies on qi for survival as well, which nourishes it with vitality. If it has no qi, it is dead. During the Taijigong training, we like to stay around ancient trees. If the qi in them can allow them to remain robust for millennia, just imagine the qi it emits. It must be enriching and able to boost the *taihe* qi energy in our body.

Thus being rigid and stiff is courting death; being soft and supple is living life

"Courting death" paraphrases 死之徒 (*si3zhi1tu2*). The pictogram 徒 is made up of radical 彳, which is often associated with "moving";

and the sub-character 走, which means "walk". As a whole, it refers to a path and implies the direction we take. So those who are "rigid and stiff" (坚强, *jian1qiang2*) are heading towards demise. It follows the cycle of nature. The heat of summer is stiff, and it leads to autumn, before winter, which is a metaphor for death, is around the corner.

Being soft and supple like a newborn baby, on the other hand, is "living life" (生之徒, *sheng1zhi1tu2*). It is like a lovely spring that breathes life. All life begins soft and hardens at death. Our body is in the highest state of softness during infancy. It gets harder and harder when we grow older and become totally stiff at death. It applies to every form of life, be it a human, animal, or a plant.

To stay soft and supple is fundamental to Taijigong. We are not just talking about the softness of the body, but that of the mind as well. It is because of the softness that my Master Wu Tunan was able to perform the "posing as a pheasant standing on one foot" (金鸡独立), a highly demanding single-foot stance, at the advanced age of 102 years old. The posture requires us to stand on one leg while having the other hanging halfway in the air. The stance is a challenge even for people one-third his age. Of course, no one can escape death, and a couple of years before his death, my Master's body was slowly stiffening as well. It was, however, still remarkable that he lived to the ripe old age of 105. In contrast, many kungfu fighters die at a young age because they train their bodies overly-hard.

An army that is rigid is easy to defeat

No matter how strong an "army" (兵, *bing1*) is, if it is "rigid", it accelerates its own decline. "Rigid" is a translation of 强 (*qiang2*), which usually means "strong", but is used here to imply being arrogant and belligerent. No matter how strong an army is, when it is conceited, it exposes its weaknesses, becoming "easy to defeat" (则折, *ze2zhe2*). It is also likely to make more enemies. If the enemies band together, they accelerate the army's demise.

A tree that refuses to yield is easy to break

The pictogram 强 is used again here, and translated as "refuses to yield". When a tree is unyielding, it is "easy to break" (折, *zhe*2). In addition, a tree can also become a target of builders when it is hard. The builders are hunting for durable wood to be the middle beams, and they may fell young trees simply for them being hard.

Although the teeth are stronger than the tongue yet they are first to decay

The teeth and the tongue are born at the same time. As people age, however, the teeth decay (敝, *bi*4), but the tongue remains. Even at death, the tongue is still intact. It shows that the hard deteriorate sooner than the soft. This is why Taijiquan improves its practitioners' endurance through softness. It is based on the teachings of Tao.

The big and powerful stays below, the strong and supple reign from above

"Returning is the way Tao works," says Laozi in Chapter 40. Tao of Heaven weakens the strong and strengthens the weak. It favors those who are modest, weak, and soft. When we build a house, the stones lie beneath to form a foundation. The sturdier the stone is, the more stable the house is. Thus, "the strong" (强大, *qiang*2*da*4) "stays below" (处下, *chu*3*xia*4), while the "soft and weak" (柔弱, *rou*2*ruo*4) "reigns from above" (处上, *chu*3*shang*4). It sounds paradoxical, but it reflects a law of nature.

When practicing Taijiquan, we prevail over the opponent by following the law. We make every contact with the opponent soft. With no stiff muscles, we are supple, flexible, and agile. As a Taiji adage puts it: "Those who exert force has no qi, those with qi exert no force." Without stiff muscles and brute force, we can "repel a thousand pounds of weight with four ounces of strength". Staying soft also allows us to have more space for listening. We can listen more accurately to the flow of the opponent's energy, and deflect it back. The principle can be applied to every aspect of life. Be it politics, business, or family. For example, being soft brings us friends, and by helping others, we help ourselves. It brings us success.

What I have learned from others, I teach

Having learned the law of nature from the enlightened, the Sage passes it on to others. It, of course, includes the principle that we have learned in this chapter.

The "strong beam" dies not a natural death

Laozi uses another word to describe the unyielding: "the strong beam", which is a translation of "强梁" (qiang2liang2). It refers to people who believe in using force and impose their will on others. They do not understand the power of softness and how it can prevail over the hard and strong. They are short-tempered, afraid to lose, and eager to pick a fight. The chances of them being killed by someone or dealt with by the law are high. They are against Tao of Heaven and are prone "not to die a natural death" (不得其死, bu4de2qi2si3).

I see it as "Father of maxims"

"Father of maxims" is a translation of 教父 (jiao4fu4). It refers to teachings of wisdom, like patriarchal advice that warns against danger. Implications of the "strong beam" is a case in point. If we can stay soft and weak and refrain from being forceful, it spares us the prospect of an unnatural death caused by recklessness.

Chapter 77
Tao of Heaven 天之道

Tao of Heaven
Is like bending a bow.
The high is pressed down,
And the low is raised up.
Take from the excess,
And give it to the lacking.

Tao of Heaven,
Takes from the excess
And gives it to the lacking.

Not the way most people do,
They take from the lacking,
And give it to the excess.

Who can take from their excess
And give it to the world?
Only a person of Tao!

Thus the Sage
Does but seeks no glory;
Accomplishes but claims no credit.
They do but do not
See themselves as eminent.

Tao of Heaven is like bending a bow. The high is pressed down, and the low is raised up. Take from the excess, and give it to the lacking

Heaven is in the closest proximity of Tao Core. By observing how Heaven behaves, we gain profound insight into Tao and the meaning of life. A simple illustration of "bending a bow" (张弓, *zhang1gong1*) is enough to offer us a series of life lessons.

Before releasing their arrow, archers aim at the bullseye and adjust the angles for a hit. What is the lesson of Tao of Heaven that we can learn from it?

The aim has to be precise. "The high" (高者, *gao1zhe3*) is "pressed down" (抑之, *yi4zhi1*), and "the low" (下者, *xia4zhe3*) is "raised up" (举之, *ju3zhi1*). At the same time, the exertion of force has to be just right. We "take from" (损, *sun3*) the "excess" (有余, *you3yu2*), and "give it to" (补, *bu3*) "the lacking" (不足, *bu4zu2*).

High or low? More or less? A good archer strikes a balance to achieve a precise shot. The lesson on Tao of Heaven it offers is: If we are just and fair, we will neither miss the target nor experience failure. This is what we do when practicing Taiji sparring. We always hold to the center and do neither too much nor too little. There is always a counterbalance.

Tao of Heaven, takes from the excess and gives it to the lacking

In a social context, we take from the rich who have more than enough to spare and give it to the poor who are struggling to make ends meet. This is what Tao of Heaven does. Hexagram 15 of the *Yijing* has a fascinating account of this. "The gentleman weighs things and makes them equal," it says. The image of the hexagram, known as "Modesty", consists of the trigram "Earth" on top and "Mountain" below. It suggests cutting down the mountain from the middle to level the land. It creates equality, and irons out social imbalances. In Taiji sparring, we listen to the opponents to identify the void in their body, then fill the void up with our qi to tilt their balance. It is like "flowing of water" — the name of an advanced technique.

Not the ways most people do. They take from the lacking and give it to the excess

What most people do, unfortunately, is often the other way round. Being divisive and selfish, they "take from the lacking", i.e., exploit the poor, and give it to the rich who already have more than enough. Tao does the reverse; it takes from the excess and gives it to the lacking. The "Great flow", as described in Chapter 65, is thus a reverse course.

Who can take from their excess, and give it to the world? Only a person of Tao!

Who can "devote" (奉, *feng*4) whatever the excess they have and give it to the world, keeping just enough for subsistence? Only "a person of Tao" (有道者, *you3dao4zhe3*)! They know the impermanence of life and see the cultivation of their souls as the primary focus. Just like what Laozi says in Chapter 48, "Let go and let go, till they do nothing. Do nothing, and nothing is left undone." When they have let go of everything, they become indifferent to the worldly possessions and naturally devote their excess to help the world.

Thus the Sage does but seeks no glory; accomplishes but claims no credit

The Sage gives away their excess to the world because they are selfless. They "do but seek no glory, accomplish but claim no credit". They are wholehearted in serving the world and see giving as a matter of course. Even when they have saved others, they never see themselves as saviors.

They do but do not see themselves as eminent

Despite having attained Tao, the Sage remains modest and humble. They are indifferent to praises, as they don't "see themselves as eminent" (见贤, *jian4xian2*). "The richness of Te looks inadequate," says Laozi in Chapter 41. Although they don't seem to be doing anything spectacular, their impact on the world is tremendous. Like what is mentioned in Chapter 34, "By not claiming to be great, it achieves greatness".

Here, Laozi introduces a three-step methodology in the attainment of Tao. First, we are "just and fair" as the ways we adjust the bow. Second, "we take from the excess and give it to the lacking". Finally, we emulate the sage who "takes from their excess and gives it to the world".

Chapter 78
Te of Water 水德

*Nothing in the world
Is as soft and yielding as water.
Yet nothing does better than it
In overcoming the hard and rigid.
It has no equal.*

*So the weak can defeat the strong,
And the soft can prevail over the hard.
Everyone knows it,
but few can put it into practice.*

*Therefore the Sage says:
"Those who can take the smear for the country
Are fit to lead the country.
Those who can brave the calamity for the country
Are fit to reign over the world."*

Words of Tao sound paradoxical.

Nothing in the world is as soft and yielding as water

"Soft and yielding" is a translation of 柔弱 (*rou2ruo4*). Water has no shape but can be in any shape. Few things, if any, are as soft, yielding, and modest. It adapts to changes in any situation with ease and grace.

Yet nothing does better than it in overcoming the hard and rigid. It has no equal

Although water is soft and yielding, it is able to "overcome" (攻, *gong1*) "the hard and rigid" (坚强者, *jian1qiang2zhe3*). A river dam is formidable, but water can infiltrate it with time. Hard rock is impenetrable, but water can drip through it with persistence. Aided by technology, water is so sharp it can slice through stone and steel.

Conversely, can an iron bar, which is apparently a lot harder, beat water? Not really. Water yields and splits. No matter how hard we hit it with an iron bar, the force exerts no impact on water. This is how Taijiquan enables the weak to counter the formidable. We move as soft and weak and flow like water to neutralize all forms of attack.

As far as overcoming the hard and rigid is concerned, nothing "does better" (胜, *sheng4*) than water. "No equal" is a translation of 无以易之 (*wu2yi3yi4zhi1*), which means irreplaceable.

So the weak can defeat the strong, and the soft can prevail over the hard. Everyone knows it, but few can put it into practice

The power of softness that can overcome the hard is not difficult to understand. "Everyone knows it" (莫不知, *mo4bu4zhi1*). However, "few put it into practice" (莫能行, *mo4neng2xing2*). Why is that so?

It has to do with the mindset. We tend to think that soft and weak make us a loser; or that we are on the losing end when we give. It is, therefore, difficult for us to stay modest or to swallow humiliation. Because it is difficult to do, few people are motivated enough to make it work.

Therefore the Sage says: "Those who can take the smear for the country are fit to lead the country

"Smear" is a translation of 垢 (*gou*4), which refers to dirt, such as the dirty deposit at the bottom of the water flow. Metaphorically, it implies insults. Despite being wronged and hurled a barrage of grave insults, "those who can take the smear" is able to accept it gracefully and softly for the country. They are as yielding as water. Only people of such endurance are fit to be the "ruler of a country" (社稷主, *she*4*ji*1*zhu*3).

If we want to be a responsible ruler of a country, the readiness to endure humiliation is more vital than the ability to manage. With endurance, we are naturally modest and humble. The process shapes our character, making us more accommodative. It helps the leader of a country to gain its most important strength: Trust of the people. There is no need for a leader to be good at everything. When people trust them, people will come forward to help them when it is called for.

This is how I lead my team. I am weak in many areas, be it technology or finance. I just make sure that I am a leader that my disciples respect and the support is forthcoming. They will help me with things that I am weak in. What I need to do is simply to delegate the tasks to the right people. What if I am a selfish leader and bulldoze to protect my personal interests? The support will trickle away. This is another good example of how being soft and weak is capable of overcoming the hard and rigid.

Those who can brave the calamity for the country are fit to reign over the world."

To take the smear is tough, but more often than not, we don't risk our lives to do it. To "brave" (受, *shou*4) the "calamity" (不祥, *bu4xiang2*) is different. We must face up to the calamities that wreck the country and be ready to sacrifice our lives. If we can survive the calamity, we are ready to "reign over the world" (天下王, *tian1xia4wang2*), and enjoy even greater support of the people. If we can survive the ordeal, sacrificing our temporal body to save the country brings our attainment of Tao to an all-new level. Although our physical body has perished, our perpetual selves become the "Kingly" capable of connecting to Heaven and Earth (see Chapter 25). We become a sage. If we have a chance to be reborn, we will perform even better. One life builds on another; we get closer and closer to complete enlightenment in this manner.

Words of Tao sound paradoxical

"Words of Tao" (正言, *zheng4yan2*) "sound like paradox" (若反, *ruo4fan3*). Most people are divisive and selfish. In contrast, a true person of Tao is selfless and ready to die for people. Most people want to be hard and strong, yet a person of Tao wants to be soft and weak. What a person of Tao does appears to be contrary to what most people do.

Chapter 79
Hold the Left Deed 执左契

*Patching up an animosity
Is sure to leave hatred behind.
How can we regard it as a good ending?*

*Therefore the Sage
Holds the "left deed"
Yet does not force payment.*

*A person of Te holds the deed,
A person of no Te exacts payments
Like a tax lord.*

*Tao of Heaven does not take sides.
It is always with those who do good.*

Patching up an animosity is sure to leave hatred behind. How can we regard it as a good ending?

"Animosity" is a translation of 大怨 (*da4yuan4*), which refers to an intense bitterness resulting from, say, injury or loss of life or family. After a war, victims are likely to carry with them deep animosity. It does not matter even if the invaders are repentant or have been punished by law. It is hard to have a total resolution and is insufficient to be "regarded as a good ending" (以为善, *yi3wei2shan4*).

Imagine a victim who has lost their loved ones or is deprived of their vision or limbs during a war. Do you think they can ever forget? The thought of it is enough to rekindle hatred. The culprits, on the other hand, cannot escape the torment of their conscience as well. There is retribution, and they can never be at peace. Even when there is a "patching up" (和, *he2*), things don't end well.

Therefore the Sage holds the "left deed" yet does not force payment

In ancient China, deed for debts was cut in halves. The lender kept both. Upon full settlement, the lender kept the "left deed" (左契, *zuo3qi4*) and gave the "right deed" to the debtor. When the Sage held only the "left deed", it implies that he did not keep the right deed and would have nothing to give to the debtor when the debt was paid in full. This is another way to say that the lender had no intention to press for repayment. If the debtor paid up, fine! If the debtor did not, the lender would not force it. "Force payment" paraphrases 责于人 (*ze2yu2ren2*), which means to "blame someone". In life, monetary disputes are major causes of grievances, which often lead to tussles in both business and personal life, from harassment for repayment and threat of physical harm to murder. Laozi reminds us that if someone genuinely needs help financially, we must help them if we can and hold the "left deed". We see the help and any ensuring debt as a donation to charity and accumulation of our good deeds.

A person of Te holds the deed

"A person of Te" (有德, *you3de2*) walks the path of Tao. Their priority is self-cultivation and, to them, every form is illusory. They clinch to nothing and thus care little about worldly possession. Genuinely giving, they hold the "left deed" and expect no repayment.

A person of no Te exacts payments like a tax lord

A person of no Te (无德, *wu2de2*) behave like tax lords (司彻, *si*1che4). Divisive and self-centered, they expect repayment of every single cent. They care little about self-cultivation and are obsessed with the pursuit of wealth, even to the extent of creating animosity or evil. Things will not end well for them.

Tao of Heaven does not take sides

"Heaven" is a direct derivative of Tao. It has no divides and does not "take sides" (无亲, *wu2qin*1). Since Tao is formless and thus "nothing" (无, *wu2*), we may interpret the sentence as: "Tao of Heaven is a family of nothingness or Tao".

It is always with those who do good

"If we conform to Tao, Tao is with us," says Laozi in Chapter 23. Tao of Heaven, which is in the proximity of the formless Tao, favors people "who do good" (善人, *shan4ren2*). At the same time, a person rich in Te does good and aims to be in the proximity of Tao. Although Tao of Heaven does not take sides, since "those who do good" have the inclination of Tao of Heaven, it is always with them.

Chapter 80

A Small Country with Few People 小国寡民

It is a small country with few people.
Give them ten or a hundred times more tools,
And they use them not.
Teach them to take death seriously
And they do not travel afar.
Despite the boats and wagons they own,
They journey not on them.
Despite the armors and weapons they have,
They do not put them on display.
Teach them the simplicity of life,
And to knotting cords, they return to record events.

They enjoy what they eat,
Put on elegant clothes,
Live peacefully at home,
Enjoy the culture.

Although neighbors are within sight,
Where cock crows and dog barks are in harmony,
They leave each other alone in peace,
Till their ripe old age and death.

In this second-to-last chapter, Laozi gives a summary of the book. At the same time, he elaborates further on the art of self-cultivation.

It is a small country with few people

The "country" (国, *guo2*) here refers to a small community, and the "people" (民, *min2*) are its members. "It is a small country with few people" is a utopia of Laozi, where people of Tao congregate. They are "the wise", as described in Chapter 41, who diligently put the teachings of Tao into practice. The size of the population, however, is tiny as compared to the general population, and thus described as small.

It is an apt description of the community of Taijigong. The community is very small because much of the teaching is conducted face-to-face, and it limits the class sizes to rarely more than twenty. The members, however, enjoy close attention from the teachers. The teachers "feed" the students with qi, guide them in-person techniques to generate qi movements, and teach them to integrate with the universe. The impact is hard to achieve when the classes are big or conducted via distance learning attended by hundreds or thousands of attendees.

Give them ten or a hundred times more tools, and they use them not

"Ten or a hundred times more tools" is a translation of 什伯之器 (*shi2bo2zhi1qi4*). 什 means "ten times", and 伯 "a hundred times". Both come with radical 亻, which means "people". The pictogram 器 means "tools" or "instruments". As a whole, we may interpret them as tools that people use. When there are too many tools, however, they confuse the mind.

In the modern context, an excellent example of such tools is the computer. Life used to be simple, but information technology has complicated it. With the massive inflow of all sorts of information, people today spend too much of their time on tools like computers and smartphones to watch movies, read the news, and follow gossip. These activities deprive them of precious time for spiritual cultivation. It does not mean that the tools are bad. But when they crowd the important things out, they are bad.

Different priorities dominate the various stages of our life, which may be divided into four phases, like the seasons. The priority of the spring and summer of our life is growth. We study hard and build our careers. At these stages of our life, more of the tools are needed. When we are in the autumn and winter of our life, the focus is on harvest and conservation. In these stages, fewer of the tools are used, so that we can allocate more of our time to spiritual cultivation.

In the "small country", spiritual cultivation takes center stage. The fewer tools its people have, the better. It allows them to be truly focused so that they are hardly distracted. They are in control of the situations, not the other way round. They control the tools, rather than allowing the tools to control them. The fleeting nature of life must not disrupt the cultivation of our real self.

Teach them to take death seriously, and they do not travel afar

People in the "small country" "take death seriously" (重死, zhong4si3). They prefer to have their mentor around to recite and fortify their mantras during their passing, so they do not "travel afar" (远徙, yuan3xi3). The sentence can also be interpreted metaphorically. It implies that at the moment of dying (rebirth), they must keep to their mantra and "never travel afar". In other words, when the consciousness of the physical body is about to vanish, the mind must be aligned to the awareness of the perpetual body. For a person of Tao, it is all the more important that their faith is unwavering at the moment of death so that they can find perfect harmony with their real selves. If they "travel afar" at this critical moment for whatever reason, it is going to affect the quality of their "Fulfillment of Destiny".

Despite the boats and wagons they own, they journey not on them

"Boats and wagons" (舟輿, *zhou1yu3*) are means of travel, one by sea and the other by land. Since people of the "small country" do not travel afar, they "journey" (乘之, *cheng2zhi1*) not on them. Traveling is easy today. We can fly thousands of miles and back on the same day. It was not like that in ancient times. It took years for Zhang Qian (164 BC–113 BC), the renowned imperial envoy of the Han Dynasty, to travel to the Western Regions of China. He went as far as Xinjiang, a journey that takes only a few hours by flight today. The statement, therefore, is especially relevant for ancient times. Still, travel is exhausting even today. Can we quietly cultivate on a hectic journey? Travelling can be disruptive. Whatever approach of cultivation we choose, we cannot do it well without stillness. By cutting down long-distance travel, there are fewer distractions, and we are more prone to stillness. Like what Laozi says in Chapter 37, "No desiring is tranquility, and the world is in peace."

Despite the armors and weapons they have, they do not put them on display

"Armors and weapons" (甲兵, *jia3bing1*) are fighting tools meant for defending a country. People of the "small country" are spiritual. They know that killing is against Tao, and they do not force their will on others. They are aware that "a country's weaponry should not be displayed to anyone", like what Laozi mentions in Chapter 36. Weaponry is meant for defense, not showing off. Besides, if everybody respects Tao and values Te, we learn from each other, and no one would think of invading others. There is no need for anyone to put the armors and weapons "on display" (陈之, *chen2zhi1*).

Teach them the simplicity of life, and to knotting cords, they return to record events

The primitives are illiterate, so they rely on "knotting cords" (结绳, *jie2sheng2*) to record events. It is used here as a metaphor, implying returning to the basics. It sounds anachronistic. It is like marking events on a wall calendar when everyone else uses a digital calendar to do so. It, nevertheless, reminds us of the simplicity of life. It saves us precious time that would have been squandered on the diversions. It puts us back to focus on the cultivation of *taihe* qi, harmonization with the universe, and refinement of our perpetual selves.

They enjoy what they eat, put on elegant clothes

If we can focus on self-cultivation, we will gradually feel its impact on our daily life.

People of the "small country" "enjoy what they eat" (甘其食, *gan1qi2shi2*). Since they have no divides, they find whatever they eat delicious. During the lecture series on the *Tao Te Ching* in the mountain, the participants were served only vegetarian meals. The foods were simple and coarse, but everyone found them appetizing. Cucumber and radish-omelets, alone, are good enough to cheer them up. When our heart is filled with the joy of Tao, everything is beautiful.

They put on "elegant clothes" (美其服, *mei3qi2fu2*). Similarly, when we are content, anything we wear is elegant. Clothes are meant to keep warm and present a decent appearance. People of the "small country" have no divides. They shine with their inner purity and look beautiful in whatever attire they choose.

Live peacefully at home, enjoy the culture

When our mind is peaceful, everything is cozy. A wooden bench is as comfortable as a bed. As the saying goes, "A clear conscience lets you sleep through thunder." People of the "small country" are calm and in harmony with qi. They "live peacefully at home" (安其居, *an1qi2ju1*).

"Culture" is a translation of 俗 (*su2*). The pictogram consists of radical 亻, which means "human", and the sub-character 谷, which means "valley". Valley is echoic and implies responsiveness. 俗, therefore, may be interpreted as "the faith", through which we interact with the divinity. It can be in the form of a religion or simply a belief. For people in the "small country", they are happy to follow a culture that teaches them to be kind and guide them on their return to the Source, be it their own or others'.

Although neighbors are within sight

The "country" referred to here is small, which can be a district or a community. Neighbors (邻国, *lin2guo2*) are "within sight" (相望, *xiang1wang4*), so near that they can learn from one another. There is no border between them. Since everyone lives in peace and there are no conflicts, why bother to set up a defense?

Where cock crows and dog barks are in harmony

As the Chinese saying goes, "When a person has attained Tao, even their chickens and dogs ascend to heaven". Chickens, dogs, and other domestic animals are close to people, so they are susceptible to our influence. Our commitment to Tao is sounded through the "cock crows and dog barks" (鸡狗之声, *ji1gou3zhi1sheng1*). They, too, are cordial when interacting with the neighbors and are in harmony. "Harmony" paraphrases 相闻 (*xiang1wen2*), which means "hearing one another".

They leave each other alone in peace, till their ripe old age and death

They don't get in other's way during self-cultivation until they die a natural death at the ripe old age. Of course, they do help and support each other in times of need, but that is about it. They behave like a recluse in a temple, whose focus is on cultivating the temporal body for the refinement of the perpetual self. They are indifferent to external intrusion, not to mention creating conflicts and inviting trouble.

Chapter 81

Do and Contend Not
为而不争

True words are not beautiful;
Beautiful words are not true.
The wise do not argue;
Those who argue are not wise.
The enlightened are not erudite;
The erudite are not enlightened.

The Sage does not hoard.
The more they do for others,
The richer they are.
The more they give others,
The greater is their abundance.

Tao of Heaven,
Benefits and brings no harm,
Tao of the Sage,
Does and contends not.

This final chapter of Tao Te Ching echoes the first. The first chapter begins with "The Tao that can be mentioned is not the eternal Tao", and ends with "The gate to all wonders." It teaches us that whatever we talk about Tao is just an interpretation, which is limited by what we know. They are not constant and eternal.

In this final chapter, descriptions like "true words", "the wise" and "the enlightened" refer to the "eternal Tao". Contrasting them are descriptions like "beautiful words", "argue" and "erudite". They are all related to the "wonders", as in the phrase "the gate to all wonders" of Chapter 1. As explained, "wonders" is a translation of 妙, which has a connotation of being soft, weak, tolerant, modest, and humble. Underlying it is the secret of Tao attainment.

True words are not beautiful

"True words" (信言, xin4yan2) are true but not always "beautiful" (美, mei3) to the ear. They can even sound jarring. Truthfulness, however, is the essence of Te, and critical to self-cultivation and the pursuit of Tao. We need it.

Tao is paradoxical. It tends to contradict the entrenched thoughts. It teaches us to desire less, always ready to give, and focus on self-cultivation. While most people think highly of themselves, and yet Tao wants us to be modest and humble. Its words are true but not always soothing to the ear. They, however, are critically important, and we must listen even when they are unpleasant.

Beautiful words are not true

The "beautiful words" (美言, mei3yan2) here refers to "flattery" and "sweet talks". Although not always true, they are music to the ear. They, however, are words of divides, selfishness, and short-sightedness. The speakers are obsessed with glory and wealth and like to contend. Even then, they are well received because they go along with most people. However pleasing they are, they are not true. They go against Tao, and if we follow them, it can compromise the quality of our perpetual selves. As the saying goes: "Good medicine is bitter, true words are jarring to the ear". The true words help us in our attempt to attain the constant Tao. A person of Tao must be discerning and know what to embrace.

The wise do not argue; those who argue are not wise

"Those who are wise" (善者, *shan*4*zhe*3) live the virtue of Te. They convince others by what they do, not what they say. They "do not argue" (不辩, *bu*4*bian*4). Rather than arguing with cleverness and knowledge, they inspire and guide. By the same token, "those who argue" (辩者, *bian*4*zhe*3) "are not wise" (不知, *bu*4*zhi*1). They are not and unlikely to be enlightened. In this final chapter, Laozi recaps the two important things that we learned earlier: "The Tao that can be mentioned is not the eternal Tao", as mention in Chapter 1; and "Know that we do not know, Supreme! Not knowing yet think we know, sick!" as mentioned in Chapter 71.

The enlightened are not erudite; the erudite are not enlightened

"The enlightened" (知者, *zhi*1*zhe*3) are those who truly know what Tao is. "Erudite" (博者, *bo*2*zhe*3) refers to people with a wealth of worldly knowledge, but not the true wisdom. Worldly knowledge is important. It helps us to earn a living. Every field of work has its experts, and knowledge is so vast no one can learn it all in a lifetime. The richness of knowledge, however, cannot replace wisdom and does not lead to the attainment of Tao. We must know the difference between them and not miss the forest for the trees, so to speak. The true wisdom is simple. It boils down to consistently walking the path of Tao attainment. To truly understand what this means is not easy. It is even harder to put it into practice. It is, however, far better than having only the worldly knowledge. Unless they are open-minded, the erudite will never truly know.

The Sage does not hoard

There are many paths to attain enlightenment. Whatever path we take, we must "discard the raft having crossed the river." Crossing a river is a "Small Fulfillment of Destiny". As previously discussed, we must discard the old raft so that we can continue the journey with another one. Before we can attain the "Big Fulfillment of Destiny", many rafts would have been discarded along the way.

The Sage does not "hoard" (积, *ji*1). Instead of hoarding, they give. Instead of keeping the old rafts, they give them to others, so that they can forge ahead to venture new territories. The more they share, the wiser they are.

The more they do for others, the richer they are. The more they give others, the greater is their abundance

The Sage doesn't hoard. They give wholeheartedly without reservation. "The more they do for others" (尽以为人, *jin4yi3wei2ren2*), the more that they are rewarded. They become "richer" (愈有, *yu4you3*) in both virtue and wisdom.

This is similar to the discarding rafts. "Raft" or 筏 (*fa2*) in Chinese sounds like 法 (*fa3*), which means an "approach" or a "method". Only when we cast away a "raft" (method) of a lower-level practice are we able to access a better one of a higher level. The more rafts we cast away, the higher is our attainment. Our wisdom grows by the day.

This is what I have learned as well. When I share new insight with my students, I gain new insight into the process. Therefore, I do whatever I can to teach and enjoy self-enrichment in the process. So do the sages. The more they "give others" (予人, *yu3ren2*), the more resources they acquire, and "the greater is their abundance" (愈多, *yu4duo1*).

Tao of Heaven, benefits and brings no harm

As we have discussed before, "Heaven" is derived directly from One Source, i.e., the formless Tao. It is life-giving and loathes killings, and thus it "benefits" (利, *li*4) all and "brings no harm" (不害, *bu*4*hai*4). If everything conforms to the Tao of Heaven, then the world is in peace. Unfortunately, the human race does not follow Tao all the time, resulting in the collective karma that cannot help brings on calamities. When the calamities strike, even Heaven.

Tao of the Sage, does and contends not

People are contentious because they are divisive, and can't see the Oneness among all individuals. Not the Sage, though. Having attained Tao, they understand the formlessness of Tao, and see no reason to contend with anyone. Instead of contending, they make the best of non-being, which is the nature of Tao Core. They "create but seek no possession, do but seek no glory, grow but seek not to dominate, accomplish but claim no credit." They "blunt the sharpness, untie the knots, blend in with the light and merge with the dust." In a nutshell, the Sage "does" (为, *wei*2) and "contends not" (不争, *bu*4*zheng*1).

Decoding Note: Why does Tao Te Ching consist of 81 Chapters and more than 5,000 characters? We can find the secret in the *Yijing*, which uses numbers as a means for encoding. Heaven is great Yang, which is 9. The Sage is a crusader of Heaven and is also 9. 9 multiplied by 9 is 81. "Return is how Tao works," says Laozi. 9 plus 9 is 18. Reversing 18, we get 81 as well. Furthermore, 8 plus 1 is also 9.

Multiplication and addition are growth, and so they are Yang, which is life-giving. This echoes what Laozi says in Chapter 48: "Acquire knowledge, we add on something every day." Division and subtraction are reductions and are thus Yin. 9 divided by 9 is 1. 1 is One of Tao. It is the use of Tao. 9 minus 9 is 0, and 0 is the formlessness of Tao. They are Yin and so about letting go. This is again echoed in Chapter 48: "Listening to Tao, we let go of something every day." "Let go and let go, till we do nothing." The first "let go" is 1, and the second "let go" is 0. If we can "do nothing and nothing is left undone", we reach the ultimate and unleash our potent power. We have connected ourselves to both 0 and 1 Tao, and we switch between the Tao Core and Tao One.

Furthermore, the *Tao Te Ching* consists of just over 5,000 Chinese characters, beginning with the digit 5. In the *Yijing*, 5 is the center and implies conforming to the center and Tao. Laozi uses the numbers as a hint to us that the *Tao Te Ching* is a book of cultivation and renewal. We find in it the Tao of Heaven, the wisdom of the sages, and ways to keep to the center. It takes us to the Tao of 0 and 1 ... a treasure trove for self-discovery!

My Wish: Whether you are a practitioner of Taijigong or otherwise, I hope you have found *Decoding the Tao Te Ching* useful. I hereby wish you abundant blessings of Tao.

Apply the Wisdom to Taijiquan

The Translator's Notes

Taijiquan is not only an exercise for health and self-defense but also an inspiration for wisdom. Embodied in the practice are teachings of the *Tao Te Ching*. It enables us to draw on the enormous power of the universe for self-discovery, which is essential to the unleashing of our latent potential. It makes us both physically and spiritually stronger.

"The Tao that can be mentioned is not the eternal Tao," says Laozi. Tao is invisible and cannot be precisely explained. Through Taijiquan, however, it can be felt. Not only does it make the potency of silence, softness, and humility palpable, it also enables us to use it to good advantage. By harnessing to the power of softness, a demure lady can defeat an opponent bigger and stronger than her. The practice, however, involves apprehending the dynamics of Yin and Yang, which requires devotion and years of rigorous training to achieve. It is a process of building competence in Taijiquan, training of the mind, and refinement of character.

This explains why the book of wisdom *Tao Te Ching*, together with its ancestor the *Yijing*, plays such a central role in the Taiji lineage that the author inherits and now leads. In his attempts to decode the scripture, he repeatedly refers to Taijiquan and uses it as a source of countless examples to illustrate the wonders of the teachings.

When I was entrusted with the task of translating the book, my first attempt was to keep the commentaries on Taijiquan intact. It, nevertheless, led to some unexpected problems. Because the author goes deep in his elaborations, readers with no martial arts background may find them bewildering. In fact, the references often disrupt the flow of their perusal. As a compromise, I decided to take the passages out to form a separate chapter, and here you have it. I hope the arrangement is helpful to both the general readers and Taijiquan enthusiasts.

The Taijiquan the author teaches is known as Taijigong (太极功). It is from a lineage that goes back centuries. He inherited it from Grand Master Wu Tunan, a highly acclaimed Taiji doyen.

Taijiquan used to be taught on a one-on-one basis. The highly individualized approach is good, but it also limits the number of people who can benefit from it. In order to make Taijiquan accessible to more people, Grand Master Wu saw it as his mission to systemize the training. The system faithfully follows the teachings of Tao and incorporates centuries-old wisdom of the ancestral masters, including the legendary Taiji Master Zhang Sanfeng of the 13th century and Song Yuanqiao, his senior disciple. The author continues the tradition. The school he established since 1964 is now in more than 20 countries. Known as "Nam Wah" (南华), it is named after the book of Chuang Tzu, a Taoist sage who complements Laozi very well.

Below are some of the passages on Taijiquan found in the Chinese version of the book.

Tao is qi

"Tao is qi", says Laozi in Chapter 62. Many people are aware that qi is the life energy that keeps us alive. In the *Tao Te Ching* and Taijigong, however, its significance goes beyond that. We see qi also as the *taihe* qi that predates Heaven and Earth. As mentioned in several chapters of the book, especially Chapter 1 and 25, the *taihe* qi is in the Tao Core. It is omnipresent, underlies every existence, and keeps the entire universe in order. Connecting to it not only helps strengthen our health but also nourishes our minds.

It is important to have a clear understanding of what qi is. Many people see qi as the air we breathe. This is a misunderstanding. While oxygen is indispensable to our survival, it does little to the realization of our true nature and is limited in its role in the mastery of Taijiquan. Oxygen is for the present or being. *Taihe* qi is for the non-being and is Nothingness. We need both.

The author explains in Chapter 10 of the Chinese text the non-being aspect of qi; specifically, *Yingqi* (营气) and *Weiqi* (卫气) and how they can be blended into the *taihe* qi.

Yingqi (营气) is the qi energy found in our internal organs. The first step of Taijigong training is to relax the internal organs to enrich the qi energy in them. In our beginner exercise for health, known as Yangshenggong (养生功), this is done through the mind focus, body movements, and hand massages. We massage the organs, vibrate the body, and rock the internal organs against one another. The ultimate aim is to loosen up the *yingqi*. Subsequently, we relax the fifteen primary joints, from wrists and elbows to shoulder joints and more. It allows the qi to move freely along the meridian lines, circulate amidst the internal organs, and travel to the most remote parts of our body, such as the fingertips and toe tips and the skin. This warms up our entire body and brings along sensations such as tingleness and body expansion. The healthy circulation of energy enriches the *yingqi*, nourishes our internal organs, and helps us achieve an inner balance that is essential to health.

Weiqi (卫气) is innate qi energy. It keeps our body warm, regulates our sweat glands, smoothens our breath, and firms up the pores of our skin. It protects our body like a guard watching over a house. Although it works hard day and night, we hardly realize its existence. Under normal circumstances, the *weiqi* in our body is good enough for health. But if we want to use it for self-defense through Taijiquan, it is insufficient. A series of exercises have been designed to strengthen it, leading to attainment of *linpijin* (临皮劲), which literally means "qi energy that floats on skin". It is a fine layer of cloud-like qi energy that wraps our skin, indicating that our *weiqi* is now integrated with the *yingqi* as one.

A prerequisite for *linpijin* is the fullness of qi in our body. A way to achieve this is to open the "three gates". We begin with opening the "Earth gate", i.e., the *yongquan* acupuncture points on our feet, and allow the qi energy to surge from the earth to feed our body. When we open the "human gate" subsequently, the qi energy multiplies. It is followed by the opening of the "Heaven gate". It integrates the qi in our body with the *taihe* qi of the universe. The sequence fills our body with qi like a ball and brings our Spirit and Qi together in Oneness, a reminder of what Laozi says in Chapter 10, "Embrace our vigor and soul as one".

Linpijin is very useful in Taijiquan practice. It is crucial to the use of qi during Taiji sparring for the flexibility it offers. The presence of *linpijin* is an indication of the fullness and refinement of the qi energy, which can be one moment as smooth as the surface of a piece of paper and twisted like strips the next, or in the shapes of little cubes or dots. By altering the shape of our qi, we have better flexibility in meeting the challenges of different situations. It is reminiscent of water, which is in the shape of a cup when it is in a cup, but not when it is in a bottle. With *linpijin*, any point of contact with external forces becomes a springboard that intuitively wards off the attack with the richness of qi in our body.

The soft can prevail over the hard

As Laozi says in Chapter 78: "Nothing in the world is as soft and yielding as water. Yet nothing does better than it in overcoming the hard and rigid. It has no equal." Taijiquan follows the principle through, and this explains why by practicing it, an old Taiji Master is able to fight an opponent half his age and double his size. It is also the reason why our Grand Master Wu Tunan was able to perform "Posing as a pheasant standing on one foot" (金鸡独立), a demanding single-foot stance, at the advanced age of 102 years old.

When we are faced with an opponent, no matter how tough they are, we make every contact with the opponent as yielding as water so that we can instantaneously deflect the energy and nullify the attack. By being yielding, we open up a space, however tiny, for maneuver and return the force back to the opponent. Since we are re-using the opponent's force, the harder the attack, the stronger is the rebound. This is known as "Beating a thousand pounds by quietly rallying four ounces of strength" (牵动四两拨千斤) in Taijiquan.

Being soft and yielding is known as *song* (松) is Taiji. The word has no equivalent in English, as it encompasses qualities of softness, expansiveness, spaciousness and malleability. It is unfettered. An interesting aspect of being *song* is that it allows us to "dismantle" our body into parts so as to confine the impact of attack locally. If the opponent grabs our hand, for example, we disengage the hand to keep the remaining parts of the body steady. Concurrently, we quietly reposition the body from within to effect a counter-attack. It catches the opponent unprepared and disrupts their balance.

In Taijigong, there is a series of training to attain the state of *song*. Yangshenggong is one of them. It relaxes our internal organs, one at a time, before loosening up the primary joints. We stay calm and free of emotional baggage, allowing Nothingness to prevail and softness to arise. We scan for points of tension and release them one at a time. Softness is easier to maintain when we are static, but harder to keep when we are moving about, especially during sparring. Our body is built to ward off danger, so it tenses up when sensing attack. It implies that to remain soft, we have to subdue the reflexes. It is not easy. This explains why, although Taijiquan is easy to get started on, it is not easy to master.

Do not confuse softness with mushiness. Softness of Taijigong has to be buttressed by firmness, or it is dangerous. One of the basic techniques that we learn to keep softness firm is "buoyancy" (浮定劲), which enables our body to be as resilient as water. It allows us to float the opponent in a way similar to water floating a boat. In this case, our body is as if a buoy. When the attack is slight, it yields slightly. We yield more when the attack is strong. The speed of response improves with mastery. On average, it takes less than three seconds but can be as fast as a split second when we are accomplished. Although the technique takes a long time to hone, it is so vital to the success in Taijigong that it is an aspiration of every Taijigong student.

To maintain the buoyancy, it is imperative that we keep to the center at all times. Keeping to the center is in the heart of Taijigong training. It is amplified in an exercise known as "Nine Square of the Eight Trigrams" (九宮八卦), as shown in the diagram below. It is taken from the *Yijing*, and explained in Chapter 20 of the Chinese text. During the training, we walk from one square to another. Because the number 5 is in the center, we cannot help but keep coming back to it. It is central to the walk; every return accentuates the role it plays. Within the circle are nine small boxes with their respective numbers. Each number has its significance that is beyond the scope of this book. Add them in whatever order — horizontally, vertically or diagonally — the total is always 15. The number 5 is the center and in the Nothingness. The remaining numbers are the present. When we are in the present, it is important to come back to the Nothingness now and then. Applying the principle to Taiji moves, no matter what we do, we are always back to the center of 5.

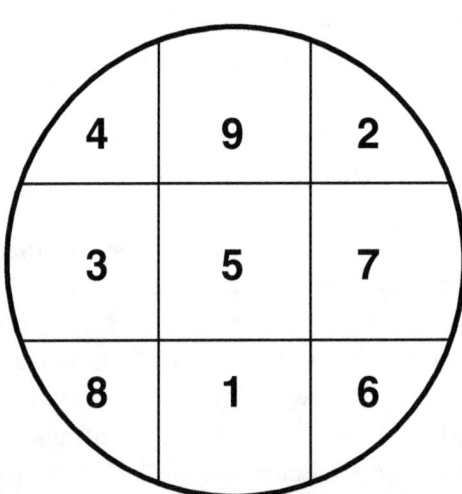

To shrink it, allow it to expand

In addition to softness, Taijiquan is known for its application of the law of reversal. "To shrink it, allow it to expand. To weaken it, allow it to go strong. To eliminate it, allow it to flourish. To take, we give," as Laozi elaborates in Chapter 36 of the *Tao Te Ching*.

According to the law of reversal, things take the reverse course upon reaching the extreme. We squat low to jump high. This is a law that we observe all the time in Taijiquan. If we want the opponent to go right, we go to the left, and ditto front and back. Otherwise, the Taijiquan is ineffective no matter how elegant it looks.

The techniques of *zhan* and *ti* (沾提) are good examples. *Zhan* means "to stick". It is a technique unique to Taiji. We are as if glued to the opponent and follow the opponent wherever they go. If they go forward, we follow. If they move to the left, so do we. In the process, we listen to their weak links and wait for the right moment to *ti*, i.e., lift them up before sending them away.

Interestingly, although we stick to the opponent all the times, the actual intention is to lift them up. To be effective with *ti*, we have to precede it with *zhan*. *Ti* requires the palms to be soft and contracted, while *zhan* firm and expanded. So, in the process of expansion and contraction we lift the opponent up. It allows us to suck up their qi energy from beneath their feet to lift their body up and tilt their balance, before throwing them off the ring. It is known as "Uproot and throw" in Taiji sparring.

If we apply the law and the opponent doesn't, we can destabilize them with ease. If we enhance it with the use of qi, we are in total control. Ancestral Master Xu Xuanping once said, "Add reverberation of qi to expansion and contraction; we are in full control." It allows a demure lady to beat a brawny rascal gracefully.

Application of the law of reversal is so quick and subtle most bystanders don't notice it. Laozi thus says in Chapter 36: "Seeing small is clarity, staying soft is a strength." Taijigong teaches us to perceive subtlety in the energy field to make the mystical energy or the so-called "black objects" discernible. It helps us to see the presence of Tao and Yin Yang to attain clarity.

Hold fast to tranquility

Although the soft can prevail over the hard, it is not a matter of course. We have to be soft and firm and keep to the center, like a tumbler doll that never falls. Otherwise, we are easily crushed.

To keep to the center in Taijiquan, it is important that we don't lose our serenity, so that we can prevail over movements. We smoothen our breath before engaging any contact and "wrap" the opponent up with our qi, looking for leverage and uprooting them effortlessly.

We must, like what Laozi mentions in Chapter 16, "Hold fast to tranquility". We are as still as a mountain. We don't move if the opponent doesn't. If they move, we pre-empt them if need be. With tranquility, we are like the languid winter in all readiness to rise for the arrival of spring. Sometimes, we have no choice but to instigate the opponent to act. Even then, we let the opponent's movement peak and hit back only when it begins its decline. "When a thing is strained with force, it will soon decay," says Laozi in Chapter 30. When the opponent's movement wanes, we marshal our latent energy to turn the lethargy of winter into the vibrancy of spring. We soar when the opponent is on the decline, enabling us to turn the tables with ease.

Tranquility is often viewed as a weakness because people fail to see its potent power. Laozi talks about its importance time and again in the *Tao Te Ching*, such as Chapters 16 and 26. Thanks to tranquility, we are able to connect to Tao and see the "subtle insight", as mentioned in Chapter 36.

"Great dexterity looks awkward," says Laozi in Chapter 45. "Awkward" is a translation of 拙 (*zhuo*2). It is reminiscent of what ancestral Taiji Master Xu Xuanping said: "With the honesty of the heart and calmness of the mind, we're always agile and nimble in our moves." In the *Tao Te Ching*, "Great" refers to Tao, so "Great dexterity" is the use of Tao. 拙 is made up of radical 扌 and the sub-character 出, which consists of two 山, one on top of the other. 山 means "mountain". In the *Yijing*, the hexagram of Mountain (艮卦) implies "stillness" and "quietude". We may see the "mountain" on top as Nothingness or our real self, and the one below as calmness or the present. Radical 扌 means "hand", which implies dexterity of Taiji. In Taiji sparring, tranquility brings us an advantage, because we are in both Nothingness and the present. We sense the undercurrent of movements and hear the inaudible. Although we are "agile and nimble", we "look clumsy" because of the stillness. The "Great dexterity" is not an overt display of outer movements, but a mastery of the inner nimbleness. The choice of the pictogram 拙 is indeed subtle.

"See how the old man in his seventies fights back a young and strong man. So deft and swift! Only when we dance to the flow of our heart are we practicing the art," according to a well-known saying of Taijiquan. What it says is precisely "Great dexterity looks clumsy". A master who has accomplished the "Great dexterity" of Taiji works on the inner discipline, not the outward movements.

Conservation of energy

In Taijigong training, we end our exercise routines with a sequence that conserves energy. When we are totally relaxed, we draw in energy from the surroundings and conserve it in the *dantian* — the reservoir of qi energy located in the lower abdomen. The energy warms up our body. The calmer and more relaxed we are, the warmer it is. This is an example of how "stillness generates heat" as mentioned in Chapter 45.

Laozi reminds us that we must be prudent with the energy we conserve. Use it only sparingly and preserve it for primary purposes like health, self-defense, and longevity. In addition to the sequence mentioned in the last paragraph, there are several other exercises that help us with the conservation. Among them is "Cultivating the Elixir" (养丹), which gets us to "embrace the innate qi and keep to the center" (抱元守中). We "stay calm and serene", as mentioned in Chapter 45 of the *Tao Te Ching*. When there are no distractions, we are totally focused, and our world is "in peace".

To assess how good we are with the conservation, we may perform an exercise known as "Jumping on Dan". To do that, we lie back on the floor and get a partner to jump from a height of 1 to 1.5 meters, landing vertically on our Dan, where our *dantian* is. If we can sustain the impact, it shows that our qi energy is rich enough. Obviously, this is not for the faint-hearted, and we must not do it without proper guidance.

Flow like water

"The highest good is like water," says Laozi in Chapter 8 of the *Tao Te Ching*. In Taijigong, we aspire to be as fluid as the flow of water and simulate its virtues. Here are about two of the seven virtues that Laozi enumerates in the chapter.

First, "Working with competence". This may be illustrated by the advanced technique of Taijigong known as "Flowing like water" (水性流法). At the points of contact, we dribble our qi energy like water into the opponent's bones, allowing it to flow and wriggle through curvatures in their body to destabilize them. When the time is right, we "suck", i.e., lift the opponent up with qi and throw them off the ring. With the technique, a demure lady or a frail old man can manipulate their opponents with the use of their fingers alone. They can even move the opponent remotely without touching their body if they are accomplished.

Second, "Watch timing for actions". An example is "Flowing of qi like tiny balls rolling through a tortuous tunnel" (行炁如九曲珠). The image suggests flowing through and overcoming a series of obstacles. Our qi flows like gushing water into the opponent's body. It is unstoppable no matter how tortuous the flow is, or how nimble the opponent is in evading the influx. The qi energy dashes right to the opponent's heels and upsets their balance. In the nick of time, we *zhan* (stick to) the opponent and *ti* (lift) them up before sending them away effortlessly. This is what "Watch timing for actions" means. What if the opponent does the same thing to us? Instead of resisting, we simply relax and let the qi flow through unimpeded, like allowing water to flush down a pipe. When there are no obstructions like disconnection or jerkiness, the opponent doesn't have any opportunity to hold us down. Not only do we evade their *zhan*, but we can also effortlessly *zhan* them back and tilt them off balance.

Flinging the opponent in the air

It sounds miraculous, but a Taiji Master can remotely control his opponents and toss them like a ball in the air. It is enabled by the highly advanced technique of Taijigong known as *lingkongjin*, which literally means "flinging the opponent in the air". The author uses the principles introduced in Chapter 69 of the *Tao Te Ching* to explain how this is done.

> *Says the military maxim:*
> *"I dare not be an invader,*
> *And rather be a guest.*
> *I dare not advance an inch*
> *And prefer to retreat a foot."*
>
> *This is to move the invisible move;*
> *Raise the invisible arms;*
> *Fling the invisible enemy;*
> *Deploy the invisible army.*

The military maxim says: "I dare not be an invader, and rather be a guest." Instead of an aggressor, we prefer to be a guest, i.e., a defender. Someone asked a Taiji Master, "You put me in an impasse. I can neither press on nor withdraw. How do I fight?" The Master replied, "Then don't fight!" When practicing Taijiquan, we don't initiate an attack. Rather, we prevail over movements with stillness. We listen attentively to the opponent, predict the direction of their moves, and flow with their qi to uproot them. In Taijigong, this involves the use of techniques such as *zhan*, *nian*, *lian* and *sui* (沾、粘、连、随). They work together to deflect the force back to the opponent.

When an opponent is eager to win and exert brute force, they put themselves in a detrimental position. We can easily *zhan* (stick to) and follow them around. If they take flight, we drive them out with their fleeing force. For those who stay put, we lock them in an impasse, giving them no room to move. While we refrain from initiating an attack, we make the best out of the opponent's attack. Although we don't take the lead, we follow through. We deflect the force falling on us and turn it into a blow on the opponent.

The maxim also says, "I dare not advance an inch and prefer to retreat a foot." It brings to life the technique 离空劲炁 (*li2kong1jin4qi4*), which may be loosely translated as "Retreat for space". First, we move backward to wrap the opponent up in a mass of qi. In appearance, we don't "advance an inch". Rather, we "retreat a foot". What actually happens, however, is the other way around. The retreat is not actual. What is retreating is our physical body, not the qi, which still adheres to the opponent. Thinking that we are moving away, the opponent dashes forward. Since our qi is still adhered to their body, we take the opportunity to stretch and expand the qi downward and backward, and quietly return it to the opponent. The mass of returning qi collides with the opponent's onward movement and bounce the opponent off. To be precise, we "retreat a foot" to release countless of arrows to the opponent. Only with the retreat do we have space to draw the arrows. If we, say, grab the opponent's body and refuse to retreat, there is no room for the maneuver. See how vividly the line depicts the process!

In the stanza that follows, Laozi uses the word "invisible" repeatedly. As explained earlier in several chapters, he uses "invisible" to describe Tao. Since Tao is qi, as mentioned in Chapter 62, the word also refers to qi.

The meaning of "Move the invisible move" is clear. Qi drives every movement in Taijiquan. Thus, when we are moving our body with the invisible qi (以炁运身), we are making an invisible move.

The "Invisible arms" of the next line refers to arms permeated with qi. We are wielding the arms full of qi, rather than using the muscles. Although only arms are mentioned, it can mean any part of our body. We can, for example, subdue an opponent with the ten fingers, or spring an opponent off with the tummy or a shoulder.

"Fling the invisible enemy" is to fling the enemy of Tao. Be cautious that we can be our own enemy if the opponent is adept in the use of qi. They can plunge our force of attack into a pocket of emptiness (引进落空) and nullify our attack, which makes room for their counteraction. The bigger the force we exert, the stronger is the rebound. In this way, we make ourselves our own enemy! We are using the visible to attack the invisible. This is dangerous!

Brute force of muscle impedes the movements of qi, and prevents the release of our potent power. Legendary Taiji Master Zhang Sanfeng said this when teaching the 13 Forms: "Those with qi use no force, those with force use no qi. By not using force, we enjoy the pure strength of Yang." The force that he referred to is the brute force.

The final line of the stanza is "Deploy the invisible army". It refers to our qi energy for combat. Imagine the scenario: An opponent charges at us with a weapon, what shall we do? A way to react is to get hold of any object at hand to block the weapon, then move close to the opponent and stick our empty hands to their body with qi. Concurrently, we "wrap" their body up with a mass of qi and lock them down in an impasse, so that they can neither press forward nor move away. When the moment is right, we throw them off the ring. A Taiji master doesn't rely on physical "army", i.e., weapons, for self-defense. They deploy the "invisible army" of qi.

With the mastery of the techniques mentioned in this section, a Taiji master is able to deploy *lingkongjin* to toss an opponent remotely. Do bear in mind, nevertheless, that the technique works only with the opponent who is rich in qi or inner strength. Otherwise, our qi energy can have no effect on them. In this case, instead of *lingkongjin*, we must resort to other sparring techniques to handle the opponent.

Integration with Heaven

Laozi gives an interesting portrayal of Tao in Chapter 14 of the *Tao Te Ching*: "Look at it, yet it cannot be seen, we name it *"ji"*. Listen to it, yet it cannot be heard, we name it *"xi"*. Grab it, yet it cannot be grasped, we name it *"wei"*. These three are indefinable, so we see them as One."

Although "The Tao that can be mentioned is not the eternal Tao", we can feel it. In Taijigong training, we engage with Tao Core through qi. With the connection, not only are *ji*, *xi*, or *wei* palpable, we can also use them to good advantage. The feel of qi gets stronger with training, which becomes evident when we are thoroughly relaxed.

Grand Master Wu Tunan used to say, "Oh, *wei*, *ji*, *xi*! They're full of wonders!" In Taijigong, we don't just fill our body with qi, but also listen attentively to what it does in the opponent. It makes *lingkongjin* a reality. From *wei* to *yi* to *xi*, it is indeed a journey of wonders.

In addition to feeling the qi energy in the immediate environment, we also perform regular integration with Heaven. It connects us to the *taihe* qi energy of the universe and we bask in the radiance of Tao, allowing our Essence, Qi, and Spirit to work as one. We "embrace our vigor and soul as one, with no gap between them", as Laozi says in Chapter 10. When we dialogue with Heaven, messages trickle down to us, inspiring answers to difficult questions on our minds. It enables self-discovery and actualization.

In Taijigong, we resort to a sequence "By being feminine" for the connection to Heaven. In the process, we expand and contract our cells to assimilate the energy, in a manner reminiscent of what Laozi says in Chapter 10: "Can we interact with the universe, with (without) femininity?"

"By being feminine" is important for the integration, because we need a huge amount of Yang energy to keep our body warm and active. For that, we must "supplement our qi energy" (补炁). We must "know the masculine (Yang), but keep to the feminine (Yin)", as mentioned in Chapter 28. To attract the Yang energy, we must be in Yin or "being feminine" by relaxing our body. The more relaxed we are, the more Yin we are, and the more Yang energy we assimilate to warm our body. We don't obtain Yang through Yang; we obtain it through Yin. With the abundance of Yang, we are able to amalgamate the *taihe* qi in us with that of the big universe and, subsequently, *Yuanyang* the Primordial Yang. This is what "Interact with the universe", or "Open and close the gate of Heaven" in

Chapter 10 mean. "Being feminine", therefore, is of vital importance. It paves the way to a state where we are "without femininity" — a culmination of Taijigong. By then, we are completely integrated with the pure Yang. Legend has it that the early ancestor of Taiji, Xuanwu was one of the very few who attained the level. Since his body was totally integrated with Heaven, it dissolved into thin air, leaving not a trace, when he died. Those who can attain this level of attainment are few and far between. Most of us stay at the level "being feminine" for many, many years (probably billions of years), or forever.

One step at a time

Although the mastery of Taijiquan is arduous, it is not beyond reach. "A journey of a thousand miles begins with a single step," as Laozi says in Chapter 64. We need to start somewhere.

The training of Taijigong is divided into four stages: *Shi*, *Jin*, *Qi*, *Hua* (势、劲、炁、化). *Shi* (势) means "posture". At this level, we make sure that our forms, such as postures and basic movements, are right. *Jin* (劲) means "inner energy". The level involves a series of exercises that loosen up our body to make it soft and supple. The focus is on the nurturing of inner strength. It is followed by the level of Qi (炁), where we begin the pursuit of Nothingness (虚). The final stage is *Hua* (化), also known as "transcendence". It is the apex of Taijigong training that takes us to the "absolute Nothingness". By then, we "hold fast to tranquility", and are free of any disruption to our serenity. It softens our body further to access the state of Nothingness.

In Chapter 50, Laozi mentions that only ten percent of the people "know truly how to live". They are able to do so because they constantly cultivate their Essence, Qi, and Spirit (精、炁、神), and have themselves integrated with Heaven. In Taijigong, we also make the cultivation a step-by-step training.

We begin with "Refinement of the Essence for Qi" (炼精化炁), then "Refinement of the Qi for the Spirit" (炼炁化神), and "Refining the Spirit for Nothingness" (炼神还虚), before we finally arrive at

"Embracing Tao in Nothingness" (炼虚合道) that takes us to Tao Core. For convenience, let's simplify the names of the four stages as Essence, Qi, Spirit, and Nothingness. The progression corresponds with the questions Laozi asks in Chapter 10.

The stage of Essence is related to "Holding our vigor and spirit as one". The stage of Qi corresponds to "Focus our life energy and become supple, like a newborn baby". For an average student, training for the first two stages take several years. In these stages, in addition to Yangshenggong that we mentioned earlier, we also take up a series of exercises for cultivating inner energy and qi. The primary focus here is "Blending the Yin and Yang", as mentioned in Chapter 4, which helps us maintain the vigor of life.

The stage of Spirit is related to the question, "Feeling throbbing of a baby when we reverberate the life energy to attain Nothingness?" The question is not found in most editions of the *Tao Te Ching*. It is, however, highly relevant to *Taijigong,* so the author includes it in the book. What puzzles many people is the phrase "Reverberating the life energy to attain Nothingness" (搏炁致虚). What it says is we pit the yin and yang energy in our body against each other. It is an unusual way to nurture qi in our body, but when properly done, we feel a sensation as if a baby is kicking in their mother's womb. This is an indication that the qi in our body, especially in the *dantian* (丹田), is so robust it is throbbing. It is an indication that we are on the way to the stage of Nothingness. Unlike the first two stages, in addition to loosening up, we also void our body. It is a critical step that leads us to the formless Tao Core.

Initially, the throbbing sensation is felt only in the *dantian*. When the qi circulation is more robust, we can feel it at any part of our body. Any external force that lands on our body is "kicked back" by the qi energy. The "baby" is more like a "divine infant" derived from Tao One, rather than an ordinary baby created by Yin and Yang. It is not just the oxygen we breathe, but an amalgamation of the pristine qi of *taihe* and *Yuanyang*. It is so rich it brings about the sensation of "throbbing of a baby".

With the foundation, we may advance to the stage of Nothingness. It is similar to the level of Transcendence (化) that we mentioned earlier. Now, we "embrace Tao in Nothingness", and are in one with Tao. We answer the questions, "Can we interact with the universe without femininity?" and "Can we stay not-knowing when acquiring true wisdom?"

We may see the stage of Nothingness as a process of "Blending into Nothingness" (冲虚) that takes us back to Tao Core.

"Tao generates One, One generates Two, Two generates Three, and Three generate the myriads of things," says Laozi in Chapter 42 of the *Tao Te Ching*. The training of Taijigong takes a reverse order: from Three to Two to One and then Zero. Three is the "Essence" (精), Two is "Qi" (炁), "One" is Spirit (神), and Zero" is Nothingness (虚). The ultimate goal of the training is to take us back to The Original (本体), i.e., One Source (一本) or "Zero".

Chongxu Jing (冲虚经) or "The Scripture on Blending the Nothingness", was written by Taoist Master Liezi. Heavily influenced by Laozi, the book is a good reference for cultivation during the stage of Nothingness. We open the "three gates" and assimilate energy from around us to accentuate the qi energy in us. The qi flows around the twelve meridians and eight extraordinary channels to "blend the Yin and Yang". The Yang energy rises, and the Yin descends. A Yin-Yang harmony is created in our internal organs. It provides conditions for the attainment of "Realigning the Five Organs" (五炁朝元), a precursor of "Three Flowers Gather on the Crown" (三花聚顶), one of the most advanced techniques taught in Taijigong. When this happens, our three fundamentals — the Essence, Qi, and Spirit — converge on the crown, and are at one with Heaven. We are in the proximity of *taihe* qi. Everything is in Oneness and without divides. We are back to *Yuanyang* and integrated with Heaven.

Tao follows what is naturally so

Chapter 25 of the *Tao Te Ching* says: "Humanity follows Earth; Earth follows Heaven; Heaven follows Tao; Tao follows what is naturally so." The passage describes the ways the universe works. We may also use it to illustrate the progress of training in Taijigong.

"Humanity follows Earth" may be seen as the cultivation of the "inner energy", when our energy is firm yet soft (刚柔). During the training, we open the "earth gate", i.e., the *yongquan*, for connection to Earth. The gush of qi fills our internal organs and permeates the twelve meridians. Our body is as if made up of thousands and thousands of dots, which are either joined together or detached from others. The body is empty yet agile.

"Earth follows Heaven" may be seen as the cultivation of qi when our qi hovers between the "Nothingness" and "substance" (虚实). We draw the qi energy not only through the "earth gates", but also the "human" and "heaven" gates. When we open the three gates all at the same time, we elevate the Earth energy to the qi of Heaven and enter into a state of Nothingness. The Nothingness allows the qi to move freely and penetrate every part of our body, from the internal organs, bones, sinews to all. It fills our entire body with qi and turns it into a refined Small Taiji. Now, we arrive at the Qi level of Taijigong.

"Heaven follows Tao" may be seen as a state of transcendence (化功), or the stage of Spirit, where we "cultivate the Spirit for the Nothingness" (炼神还虚) and progress toward Oneness with the universe. We have realized the nature of existence and, as mentioned in Chapter 16, "Toward absolute Nothingness", we "hold fast to tranquility".

Finally, "Tao follows what is naturally so". At this level, we are highly accomplished in the attainment of Tao, in which we "cultivate the Nothingness to conform to Tao" (炼虚合道). The *taihe* qi energy in our body is now integrated with Tao Core. We are in the state of "ultimate silence and emptiness", as mentioned in Chapter 25.

Turning of river and flipping of sea

Every technique that we use in Taijigong is traceable to the teachings of Tao. Taijiquan is, therefore, not just an exercise for health and self-defense, but also one for wisdom. This, however, doesn't mean that by taking up the practice, we are naturally enlightened. Ancestral masters reminded us that practice of the law of reversal is only a set of *moji* (末技) — "trivial skills"— associated with the "subtle insight", as mentioned in Chapter 36. It is at best the feat of a "small achiever". To attain the ultimate Tao, we have to be at the level of transcendence.

In his secret Taiji manual, Master Song Yuanqiao — the most senior disciple of Master Zhang Sanfeng — explains the concept of "Turning the river and flipping the sea" (翻江播海), which illustrates the time we take to achieve the complete attainment.

"Turning river" is a forerunner of "flipping the sea". Look at the stone forest in the Yunnan province of China. It is on the land, but some 270 million years ago, it was lying on the seabed. Can you visualize its actual look underwater? We can if we have the power of seeing things that happened hundreds of millions of years ago. This is the power of "turning the river". With it, seeing what Taipei was like when it was a lake more than 300 years ago is easy. With training, we can acquire the faculty, and see in stillness incidents of thousands of years ago. This is what my Master Wu Tunan did when he saw himself living as an "old leopard of thousands of years in Heaven."

What about "flipping the sea"? If the South China Sea and the Pacific Ocean were flipped over, what would it be like? It sounds like the end of the world, doesn't it? "Flipping the sea", nevertheless, does happen. It is said that it takes at least 1 "Kalpa" (about 4,320 million human years) for it to happen. Only sages like the Buddha can see it! "Flipping the sea" is "a great realization of true nature" (大见性), an accomplishment beyond those who can "turn over the river". We have to experience many rounds of "turning the river" before seeing "flipping the sea". It is not something that happens immediately. It will take many returns of cycles, as we describe in Taijigong, "one cycle builds on another" (往复须有折叠). Let's assume it takes a thousand points to achieve "flipping the sea", and one point to achieve "turning the river". It means after we have attained the level of "turning the river" the first round, there are at least another 999 points to score before we can arrive at the level of "flipping the sea". We have to experience many "small enlightenments" before achieving the "big enlightenment".

While the ultimate goal of Taijiquan practice is unlikely to be attained in our lifetime, just a tiny part of it is enough to make our life rich and fulfilling beyond imagination.

About the Author

Master Sim Pooh Ho has been practicing martial arts since the age of six. In 1964, while still a teenager, he founded Nam Wah Martial Arts Federation of Singapore, and grew it into a chain of more than ten branches in less than a decade, with disciples clinching top prizes in local and international competitions. As a recognition of his achievement in the martial arts, he was invited to appear in Tokyo TV's The World of Wonders in 1972.

From 1978 to 1988, Master Sim was President of Singapore Martial Arts Instructor Association (SMAIA) for five consecutive terms. He was behind several major events, including International Martial Arts Meet in Singapore in 1986. In recognition of his contributions, he was awarded PBM Public Service Medal by the President of Singapore in 1986.

Master Sim became An "inner-chamber" disciple of Grand Master Wu Tunan in 1978. The doyen of Taiji of China, Grand Master Wu subsequently adopted him as a son. He inherited from the Grand Master the lineage of Taijigong, which can be traced back centuries. In addition to the teachings of Taiji ancestors, such as Xu Xuanping, Li Daozi, Zhang Sanfeng and Song Yuanqiao, he imbibed the teachings of scriptures such as the *Tao Te Ching*, *Yijing*,

Diamond Sutra and *Nanhua Jing*. This explains why his approach to training goes beyond the honing of physical skills to embrace the cultivation of one's self and attain harmony with Heaven.

Master Sim's disciples and students come from a variety of backgrounds and can be found in no less than 20 countries, from Asia, North and South America to Europe. In addition to excellent martial artists, they include high achievers in a variety of fields, from academics, politics to the businesses.

He is regarded highly by his disciples not only for the skills he teaches but also for the wisdom he imparts. He guides them to recognize the subtlety of Yin-Yang and the Five Elements that are essential to the mastery of Taijiquan, and directs them to the observation of the law of nature and the transcendence of self.

In 2016, upon requests of his disciples, Master Sim conducted a series of lectures on *Decoding the Tao Te Ching*, which culminated in the publication of the Chinese version of this book. During the lectures, he shared the epiphanies he had experienced and the ways to verify the teachings of the *Tao Te Ching* through the progressive training of Taijigong.

About the Editor/Translator

Tekson Teo combines his quest for Tao with investigation of management excellence, while verifying what he has learned through the practice of Taiji and Qigong and observation of organizational behaviors. The fusion results in his unique approach to leadership and personal development. It instills calmness and quiet confidence as antidotes to meeting the demands of a highly competitive and frenzied world.

An avid reader of Taoist literature, Tekson is familiar with classics such as the *Yijing*, the *Tao Te Ching*, and *The Art of War*. Spellbound by the rare insights they offer, he observes with immense curiosity how the laws of the universe embedded in these works manifest in the modern world. Decades of practice as a management consultant across countries in the Asia-Pacific region allow him ample opportunities for the observation. So does the rigorous training of the ancient lineage he follows. He examines the subtleties in the people he observes, and the energy flows that he experiences in the practice of Taiji and Qigong.

Tekson became Master Sim's disciple in 1999. He was awarded BSc (Econ) Hon by the University of London, and MBA and DIC by Imperial College London.

The Tao Te Ching in Chinese

第一章

道，可道，非常道。名，可名，非常名。无，名天地之始。有，名万物之母。故常无，欲以观其妙。常有，欲以观其徼。此两者同，出而异名，同谓之玄。玄之又玄，众妙之门。

第二章

天下皆知美之为美，斯恶已。皆知善之为善，斯不善已。故有无相生，难易相成，长短相形，高下相倾，音声相和，前后相随。是以圣人处无为之事，行不言之教。万物作焉而不辞，生而不有，为而不恃，功成而弗居。夫惟弗居，是以弗去。

第三章

不尚贤，使民不争，不贵难得之货，使民不为盗。不见可欲，使心不乱，是以圣人之治，虚其心，实其腹，弱其志，强其骨。常使民无知无欲，使夫智者不敢为也，为无为，则无不治。

第四章

道盅（冲），而用之或不盈（久弗盈）。渊兮，似万物之宗。挫其锐，解其纷，和其光，同其尘。湛兮，似或存。吾不知谁之子。象帝之先。

第五章
天地不仁，以万物为刍狗。圣人不仁，以百姓为刍狗。天地之间，其犹橐籥乎。虚而不屈，动而愈出。多言数穷，不如守中。

第六章
谷神不死，是谓玄牝。玄牝之门，是谓天地根。绵绵若存。用之不勤（觐）。

第七章
天长地久。天地所以长且久者，以其不自生，故能长生。是以圣人后其身而身先，外其身而身存。以其无私，故能成其私。

第八章
上善若水。水善利万物而不争。处众人之所恶，故几于道矣。居善地，心善渊，与善仁，言善信，政（正）善治，事善能，动善时。夫惟不争，故无尤。

第九章
持而盈之，不如其已。揣而锐之，不可长保。金玉满堂，莫之能守。富贵而骄，自遗其咎。功成名遂身退，天之道。

第十章
载营魄抱一，能无离乎？专气致柔，能如婴儿乎？搏炁致虚，能有婴乎？涤除玄览（目览），能无疵乎？爱国治民，能无为乎？天门开阖，能无雌（为雌）乎？明白四达，能无知乎？生之、畜之、生而不有、为而不恃、长而不宰，是谓玄德

第十一章
三十辐共一毂，当其无，有车之用。 埏埴以为器，当其无，有器之用。 凿户牖以为室，当其无，有室之用。故有之以为利，无之以为用。

第十二章
五色令人目盲，五音令人耳聋，五味令人口爽。驰骋田猎，令人心发狂。难得之货，令人行妨。是以圣人为腹不为目。故去彼取此。

第十三章
宠辱若惊。 贵身若大患。何谓宠辱若惊？宠为上，辱为下，得之若惊，失之若惊，是谓宠辱若惊。 何谓贵身若大患？吾所以有大患

者，为吾有身。及吾无身，吾有何患？故贵以身为天下，则可寄于天下，爱以身为天下，乃可托于天下。

第十四章

视之不见，名曰夷（几）。听之不闻，名曰希。搏之不得，名曰微。此三者，不可致诘，故混而为一。其上不皦，其下不昧。绳绳兮，不可名，复归于无物。是谓为无状之状，无象之象，是谓惚恍。迎之不见其首，随之不见其后。执古之道，以御今之有。能知古始，是谓道纪。

第十五章

古之善为道者，微妙玄通，深不可识。夫惟不可识，故强为之容：豫兮若冬涉川，犹兮若畏四邻，俨兮其若客，涣兮若冰将释，敦兮其若朴，旷兮其若谷，浑兮其若浊。孰能浊以澄（止），静之徐清。孰能安以久，动之徐生。保此道者不欲盈。夫惟不盈，故能敝不（而）新成。

第十六章

致虚极，守静笃，万物并作，吾以观复。夫物芸芸，各复归其根。归根曰静，静曰复命，复命曰常，知常曰明，不知常，妄作凶。知常容，容乃公，公乃王，王乃大，大乃道，道乃久。没身不殆。

第十七章

太上不知有之。其次亲之，誉之。其次畏之。其次侮之。信不足焉，有不信焉。犹兮其贵言，功成事遂，百姓皆曰我自然。

第十八章

大道废，有仁义；智慧出，有大伪；六亲不和，有孝慈；国家昏乱，有忠臣。

第十九章

绝圣弃智，民利百倍。绝仁弃义，民复孝慈。绝巧弃利，盗贼无有。此三者以为文不足，故令有所属。见素抱朴，少私寡欲。

第二十章

绝学无忧。唯之与阿，相去几何？善之与恶，相去何若？人之所畏，不可不畏，荒兮，其未央哉！众人熙熙，如享太牢，如春登台。我独泊兮其未兆，如婴儿之未孩。乘乘兮，若无所归。众人皆有馀，而我独若遗，我愚人之心也哉。沌沌兮，俗人昭昭，我独昏昏。俗人察察，我独闷闷。惚兮其若海，恍兮似无所止。众人皆有以，我独顽且鄙。我独异于人，而贵求食于母。

第二十一章

孔德之容，惟道是从。道之为物，惟恍惟惚。惚兮恍兮，其中有象。恍兮惚兮，其中有物。窈兮冥兮，其中有精。其精甚真，其中有信。自古及今，其名不去。以阅众甫，吾何以知众甫之然哉？以此。

第二十二章

曲则全，枉则直，洼则盈，敝则新，少则得，多则惑。是以圣人抱一为天下式。不自见故明，不自是故彰，不自伐故有功，不自矜故长。夫唯不争，故天下莫能与之争。

第二十三章

希言自然。飘风不终朝，骤雨不终日。孰为此者？天地。天地尚不能久，而况于人乎？故从事于道者，道者同于道，德者同于德，失者同于失。同于道者，道亦乐得之。同于德者，德亦乐得之。同于失者，失亦乐得之。信不足焉，有不信焉。

第二十四章

跂者不立，跨者不行，自见者不明，自是者不彰，自伐者无功，自矜者不长。其于道也，曰：馀食赘行（形）。物或恶之，故有道者不处。

第二十五章

有物混成，先天地生。寂兮寥兮，独立而不改，周行而不殆，可以为天下母。吾不知其名，字之曰道。强为之名曰大。大曰逝，逝曰远，远曰反。故道大，天大，地大，王亦大。域中有四大，而王居其一焉。人法地，地法天，天法道，道法自然。

第二十六章

重为轻根，静为躁君。是以君子终日行不离静（辎）重，虽有荣观，燕处超然。奈何万乘之主而以身轻天下？轻则失根，躁则失君。

第二十七章

善行无辙迹，善言无瑕谪，善计不用筹策，善闭无关键而不可开，善结无绳约而不可解。是以圣人常善救人，故无弃人。常善救物，故无弃物。是谓袭明。故善人者，不善人之师。不善人者，善人之资。不贵其师，不爱其资。虽智大迷，是谓要妙。

第二十八章
知其雄，守其雌，为天下溪；为天下溪，常德不离，复归于婴儿。知其白，守其黑，为天下式；为天下式，常德不忒，复归于无极。知其荣，守其辱，为天下谷；为天下谷，常德乃足，复归于朴。朴散则为器，圣人用之则为官长。故大制不割。

第二十九章
将欲取天下而为之，吾见其不得已。天下神器，不可为也。为者败之，执者失之。故物或行或随，或响（嘘）或吹，或强或羸，或载或隳。是以圣人去甚，去奢，去泰。

第三十章
以道作人主者，不以兵强天下，其事好还。师之所处，荆棘生焉。大军之后，必有凶年。善者果而已，不敢以取强。果而勿矜，果而勿伐，果而勿骄，果而不得已，果而勿强。物壮则老，是谓不道。不道早已。

第三十一章
夫唯兵者，不祥之器，物或恶之，故有道者不处。君子居则贵左，用兵则贵右。兵者不祥之器，非君子之器。不得已而用之，恬淡为上。胜而不美，而美之者，是乐杀人也。夫乐杀人者，不可以得志于天下矣。吉事尚左，凶事尚右。偏将军居左，上将军居右，言以丧礼处之。杀人众多，以悲哀泣之。战胜，以丧礼处之。

第三十二章
道常无名。朴虽小，天下不敢臣。侯王若能守，万物将自宾。天地相合以降甘露，民莫之令而自均。始制有名，名亦既有，夫亦将知止。知止，所以不殆。譬道之在天下，犹川谷之于江海。

第三十三章
知人者智，自知者明。胜人者有力，自胜者强。知足者富，强行者有志。不失其所者久，死而不亡者寿。

第三十四章
大道泛兮，其可左右。万物恃之以生而不辞，功成不名有，爱养万物而不为主，常无欲，可名于小。万物归焉而不为主，可名为大。是以圣人终不为大，故能成其大。

第三十五章
执大象，天下往。往而不害，安平泰。乐与饵，过客止。道之出口，淡乎其无味。视之不足见，听之不足闻，用之不可既。

第三十六章
将欲翕之，必固张之。将欲弱之，必固强之。将欲废之，必固兴之。将欲夺之，必固与之。是谓微明。柔弱胜刚强。鱼不可脱于渊。国之利器，不可以示人。

第三十七章
道常无为，而无不为。 侯王若能守，万物将自化。化而欲作，吾将镇之以无名之朴。 无名之朴，亦将不欲。不欲以静，天下将自定。

第三十八章
上德不德，是以有德。下德不失德，是以无德。上德无为，而无以为。下德无为，而有以为。上仁为之，而无以为。上义为之，而有以为。上礼为之，而莫之应，则攘臂而扔之。故失道而后德，失德而后仁，失仁而后义，失义而后礼。夫礼者：忠信之薄，而乱之首也。前识者，道之华而愚之始。是以大丈夫处其厚，不居其薄。处其实，不居其华。故去彼取此。

第三十九章
昔之得一者：天得一以清，地得一以宁，神得一以灵，谷得一以盈，万物得一以生，侯王得一以为天下正（贞）。其致之一也。天无以清将恐裂，地无以宁将恐废，神无以灵将恐歇，谷无以盈将恐竭，万物无以生将恐灭，侯王无以贞正而贵高将恐蹶。故贵以贱为本，高以下为基。是以侯王自谓孤寡不谷，此其以贱为本耶！非乎？ 故至誉无誉。不欲碌碌如玉、珞珞如石。

第四十章
反者道之用（动），弱者道之动（用）。天下万物生于有，有生于无。

第四十一章
上士闻道，勤而行之。中士闻道，若存若亡。下士闻道，大笑之。不笑，不足以为道。故建言有之：明道若昧，进道若退，夷道若纇，上德若谷，大白若辱（黑辱），广德若不足，建德若偷，质贞若渝，大方无隅，大器晚成，大音希声，大象无形，道隐无名。夫惟道、善贷且善成。

第四十二章
道生一，一生二，二生三，三生万物。万物负阴而抱阳，冲炁（气）以为和。人之所恶，唯孤寡不谷，而王公以为称。故物或损之而益，或益之而损。

第四十三章
天下之至柔，驰骋天下之至坚。无有入无间，吾是以知无为之有益。不言之教，无为之益，天下希及之。

第四十四章
名与身，孰亲？身与货，孰多？得与亡，孰病？是故甚爱必大费，多藏必厚亡。知足不辱，知止不殆，可以长久。

第四十五章
大成（盛）若缺，其用不弊。大盈若冲，其用不穷。大直若曲，大巧若拙，大辩若讷。躁胜寒，静生热。清静为天下正。

第四十六章
天下有道，却走马以粪。天下无道，戎马生于郊。罪莫大于可欲，祸莫大于不知足，咎莫大于欲得。故知足之足，常足矣。

第四十七章
不出户，知天下。不窥牖，见天道。其出弥远，其知弥少。是以圣人不行而知，不见而名，不为而成。

第四十八章
为学日益，闻道日损。损之又损，以至于无为，无为而无不为。故取天下常以无事，及其有事，不足以取天下。

第四十九章
圣人无心，以百姓心为心。善者，吾善之；不善者，吾亦善之，德善矣。信者，吾信之；不信者，吾亦信之，德信矣。圣人之在天下，惵惵为天下，浑其心。百姓皆注其耳目，圣人皆孩之。

第五十章
出生入死。生之徒十有三，死之徒十有三，人之生动之死地者，亦十有三。夫何故，以其生生之厚。盖闻善养摄生者：陆行不遇兕虎，入军不避甲兵。兕无所投其角，虎无所措其爪，兵无所容其刃。夫何故，以其无死地。

第五十一章

道生之，德畜之，物形之，势成之。是以万物莫不尊道而贵德。道之尊，德之贵，夫莫之命而常自然。故道生之、畜之、长之、育之、成之、熟之、养之、覆之。生而不有，为而不恃，长而不宰。是谓玄德。

第五十二章

天下有始，以为天下母，既得其母，以知其子，既知其子，复守其母，没身不殆。塞其兑，闭其门，终身不勤。开其兑，济其事，终身不救。见小曰明，守柔曰强，用其光，复归其明、无遗身殃，是谓袭常。

第五十三章

使吾介然有知。行于大道，唯迤（邪）是畏。大道甚夷，而民好径。朝甚除、田甚芜、仓甚虚、服文彩、带利剑、厌（餍）饮食、财货有馀。是为盗夸。非道哉。

第五十四章

善建者不拔，善抱者不脱，子孙祭祀不辍。修之于身，其德乃真；修之于家，其德乃馀；修之于乡，其德乃长；修之于国，其德乃丰；修之于天下，其德乃普。故以身观身，以家观家，以乡观乡，以国观国，以天下观天下。吾何以知天下然哉？以此。

第五十五章

含德之厚，比于赤子，毒虫不螫，猛兽不据，攫鸟不搏，骨弱筋柔而握固，未知牝牡之合而朘作，精之至也。终日号而不嗄，和之至也。知和曰常，知常曰明，益生曰祥，心使气曰强，物壮则老，是谓不道，不道早已。

第五十六章

知者不言，言者不知。塞其兑，闭其门，挫其锐，解其纷，和其光，同其尘，是谓玄同。故不可得而亲，不可得而疏，不可得而利，不可得而害，不可得而贵，不可得而贱，故为天下贵。

第五十七章

以正治国，以奇用兵，以无心取天下。吾何以知其然哉？以此。天下多忌讳，而民弥贫。民多利器，国家滋昏。人多技巧，邪事滋起。法令滋彰，盗贼多有。故圣人云：吾无为而民自化，吾好静而民自正，吾无事而民自富，吾无欲而民自朴。

第五十八章

其政闷闷，其民醇醇。其政察察，其民缺缺。祸兮福所倚，福兮祸所伏。孰知其极？其无定耶。正复为奇，善复为妖。人之迷，其日固久。是以：圣人方而不割，廉而不刿，直而不肆，光而不耀。

第五十九章

治人事天，莫若啬。夫惟啬，是谓早服。早服谓之重积德，重积德则无不克，无不克则莫知其极，莫知其极可以有国。有国之母，可以长久。是谓深根固蒂，长生久视之道。

第六十章

治大国若烹小鲜。以道莅天下，其鬼不神。非其鬼不神，其神不伤人。非其神不伤人，圣人亦不伤人。夫两不相伤，故德交归焉。

第六十一章

大国者下流，天下之交，天下之牝。牝常以静胜牡，以静为下。故大国以下小国，则取小国。小国以下大国，则取大国。故或下以取，或下而取。大国不过欲兼畜人，小国不过欲入事人。夫两者各得其所欲，故大者宜为下。

第六十二章

道者，奥也，万物之奥。善人之宝，不善人之所保。善言可以市尊，善行可以加人。人之不善，何弃之有？故立天子，置三公，虽有拱璧以先驷马，不如坐进此道。古之所以贵此道者何？不曰求以得，有罪以免耶。故为天下归。

第六十三章

为无为、事无事、味无味。大、小、多、少，报怨以德。图难于其易，为大于其细。天下难事，必作于易。天下大事，必作于细。是以圣人终不为大，故能成其大。夫轻诺必寡信，多易必多难。是以圣人犹难之，故终无难。

第六十四章

其安易持，其未兆易谋，其脆易破，其微易散。为之于未有，治之于未乱。合抱之木，生于毫末。九层之台，起于累土。千里之行，始于足下。为者败之，执者失之。是以圣人无为，故无败；无执，故无失。民之从事，常于几成而败之。慎终如始，则无败事。是以圣人欲不欲，不贵难得之货。学不学，复众人之所过。以辅万物之自然，而不敢为。

第六十五章

古之善为道者，非以明民，将以愚之。民之难治，以其智多。故以智治国，国之贼；不以智治国，国之福。知此两者，亦楷式。能知楷式，是谓玄德。玄德深矣，远矣！与物反矣！乃至于大顺。

第六十六章

江海所以能为百谷王者，以其善下之，故能为百谷王。是以圣人欲上民，必以言下之；欲先民，必以身后之。是以圣人处上而民不重，处前而民不害，天下乐推而不厌。以其不争，故天下莫能与之争。

第六十七章

天下皆谓吾道大似不有。夫惟大，故不有。若有，其小久矣。吾有三宝，持而宝之：一曰慈、二曰俭、三曰不敢为天下先。夫慈，故能勇；俭，故能广；不敢为天下先；故能成器长。今舍慈且勇、舍俭且广、舍后且先，死矣！夫慈，以战则胜，以守则固。天将救之，以慈卫之。

第六十八章

善为士者不武，善战者不怒，善胜敌者不与，善用人者为之下。是谓不争之德，是谓用人之力，是谓配天。古之极。

第六十九章

用兵有言：吾不敢为主而为客，不敢进寸而退尺。是谓行无行，攘无臂，扔无敌，执无兵。祸莫大于轻敌，轻敌几丧吾宝。故抗兵相加，哀者胜矣。

第七十章

吾言甚易知，甚易行。天下莫能知，莫能行。言有宗，事有君。夫惟无知，是以不我知。知我（吾）者希，则吾者贵。是以圣人被褐怀玉。

第七十一章

知不知，上。不知知，病。夫惟病病，是以不病。圣人不病，以其病病，是以不病。

第七十二章

民不畏威，大威至矣。无狭其所居，无厌其所生。夫惟不厌，是以不厌。是以圣人自知不自见，自爱不自贵。故去彼取此。

第七十三章

勇于敢则杀，勇于不敢则活。此两者，或利或害。天之所恶，孰知其故？是以圣人犹难之。天之道：不争而善胜，不言而善应，不召而自来，繟然而善谋。天网恢恢，疏而不失。

第七十四章

民不畏死，奈何以死惧之？若使民常畏死而为奇者，吾将执而杀之，孰敢？常有司杀者杀。夫代司杀者杀，是谓代大匠斲。夫代大匠斲者，稀有不伤手矣。

第七十五章

民之饥，以其上食税之多，是以饥。民之难治，以其上之有为，是以难治。民之轻死，以其求生之厚，是以轻死。夫惟能无以生为者，是曰贤于贵生。

第七十六章

人之生也柔弱，其死也坚（强）僵。万物草木之生也柔脆，其死也枯藁。故坚强者死之徒，柔弱者生之徒。是以兵强则灭，木强则折，齿坚于舌而先敝，强大处下，柔弱处上。人之所教，吾亦教之。故强梁者不得其死，吾将以为教父。

第七十七章

天之道，其犹张弓乎？高者抑之，下者举之，有馀者损之，不足者补之。天之道：损有馀而补不足。人之道：损不足以奉有馀。孰能有馀以奉天下？唯有道者。是以圣人为而不恃，功成而不处，其不欲见贤耶。

第七十八章

天下柔弱莫过于水，而攻坚强者莫之能胜，其无以易之。故柔之胜刚，弱之胜强，天下莫不知，莫能行。是以圣人云：受国之垢，是谓社稷主。受国之不祥，是谓天下王。正言若反。

第七十九章

和大怨，必有馀怨，安可以为善。是以圣人执左契而不责于人。有德司契，无德司彻。天道无亲，常与善人。

第八十章

小国寡民，使有什伯之器而不用。使民重死，而不远徙。虽有舟舆，无所乘之。虽有甲兵，无所陈之。使民複结绳而用之。甘其食、美其服、安其居、乐其俗。邻国相望，鸡狗之声相闻，民至老死，不相往来。

第八十一章

信言不美，美言不信。善者不辩，辩者不善。知者不博，博者不知。圣人不积，尽以为人己愈有，既以予人己愈多。天之道，利而不害。圣人之道，为而不争。

www.ingramcontent.com/pod-product-compliance
Lightning Source LLC
Chambersburg PA
CBHW052040220426
43663CB00012B/2390